THE CRAFT OF
BOOKBINDING

THE CRAFT OF BOOKBINDING

A Practical Handbook

with 8pp of colour plates

ERIC BURDETT

DAVID & CHARLES

NEWTON ABBOT   LONDON   NORTH POMFRET (VT)

British Library Cataloguing in Publication Data

Burdett, Eric
  The craft of bookbinding.
  1. Bookbinding
  I. Title
  686.3'02   Z271

  ISBN 0-7153-6656-4

First published 1975
Second impression 1978
Third impression 1983

Set in 11 on 13 pt Bembo and printed in Great Britain
by Butler & Tanner Ltd, Frome, for David & Charles
(Publishers) Limited, Brunel House, Newton
Abbot, Devon

Published in the United States of America
by David & Charles Inc
North Pomfret Vermont 05053 USA

Designed by Adrian Moore

To

GRACE

whose second name should have been Patience

and remembering

THOMAS CARLYON, ob 1937

and

THOMAS HARRISON, MBE, ob 1955

whose friendship
equalled their craftsmanship

CONTENTS

PREFACE

Few crafts can give as much satisfaction at all stages as bookbinding, from making a cloth cover for a paperback, or binding magazines for convenient storage, to the ultimate achievement of a fine binding in full leather, tooled and decorated. Those who practise the craft may have approached it from different angles and with different motives. The humblest of these, though one not to be despised, is the wish to tidy one's own small stock of books. The serious collector, or the bookseller, may begin with the desire to repair his books and so increase their value, and may find that only by practical experience of the craft can he fully understand and appreciate his subject. The professional bookbinder, even if he works with machines, may wish to deepen his knowledge of fine bookbinding. The artist-craftsman sees in bookbinding a satisfactory medium for both his craft and his artistry.

All these have been borne in mind in the writing of this book.

Since every volume is an individual, and must have individual treatment, the various operations, of which there are many, do not always follow the same order. The best styles involve most of them, but the simpler do not; all those that may be required have been dealt with in a logical sequence, but this sequence may not satisfy the requirements of a particular style. The beginner may therefore select for attention the operation, or part of an operation, which meets his immediate needs.

Before dealing with bookbinding processes, the workshop, equipment and tools are discussed. For the benefit of the beginner, improvisation of some equipment is suggested wherever this is reasonably possible. Although the results are seldom as good as with the professional article, excellent work has been produced using such equipment. Tools and smaller items are dealt with in the text, but an amplification of these references is contained in the section specifically devoted to the subject.

Bookbinding is divided into four main stages, and each forms a separate chapter. They are: *Preparatory Work*, which covers all the operations up to, and including, sewing; *Forwarding*, which concerns the actual building of the book; *Covering* in all its diversity; and *Finishing*, which deals with everything that concerns the decoration of the book cover, from lettering the title to gold tooling. Inlaying is part of cover decoration, but is dealt with separately, as are *Recessed and 'sculptured' boards*.

Because of its affinity with finishing, *Cover Design* follows it. While previously accepted basic principles cannot be ignored, they have, in the past, had an inhibiting effect upon cover design, and many of today's designer-craftsmen have discarded some of them and found a new freedom of expression. The bookbinder, however, is not only concerned with today's books but also with those of yesterday, and these demand separate thought and treatment. Because of this, he must be aware of design in earlier periods, not necessarily to copy but in order to design the covers of books of other days sympathetically. The purpose of the section is not only to bring the craftsmen up to date as regards cover design and trends, but to remind him of some of the changes that have taken place, especially during the twentieth century. The accent is on more recent work in the design field and includes photographs of bindings that, although exhibited, have not been illustrated before. As would be expected, these are the work of younger bookbinders, some of them without national reputations as yet, but worthy craftsmen.

Bookbinders' work is not always straightforward, and a bookbinder is often called upon to undertake what may be described as 'deviations from pure bookbinding'. Some of these receive attention under *Miscellaneous Items* where such things as single-section bindings, unsewn bindings, slip cases, pockets in books, and others, will be found.

Repairs to cloth- and leather-bound books should come within the purview of any book on bookbinding, and these follow. Dealing with such comparatively simple things as cleaning and reviving covers, renewing endpapers, and the rebacking of cloth-cased books, the section continues with similar, but more difficult work on leather bindings.

In *Materials*, adhesives, paper, boards, cloths and leathers are discussed. This is a subject of the greatest importance to the craftsman, who should know the cause and effect of their behaviour in use. A list of *Sources of Supply* is given, which in these days of so-called 'rationalisation' by manufacturers is of importance, although no list can ever be complete and any list must need revision from time to time.

Variations in bookbinding nomenclature demand a glossary of terms and one is included as an appendix.

Because of the complexity of the craft, the reader is urged to use the index frequently as cross-references are inevitable.

Although there are so many approaches to the subject, one thing should be constant in all: that the bookbinder's real purpose is to serve the book and not the reverse.

INTRODUCTION

*The workshop—equipment and tools—bookbinding styles and
sequence of operations in each*

INTRODUCTION

The Workshop

While it is possible for the amateur to work on the kitchen table, its use is so limited by size and strength, not to mention domestic requirements, that some kind of workshop is necessary if the craft is to be seriously pursued. As a fairly constant temperature is necessary, a 'workshop in the garden' is a hazard unless it can be kept slightly heated at all times. Good light is essential and the main workbench should be placed under a window. If possible, the bench should be about 30in wide, not less than 5–6ft long, and surfaced with linoleum or plastic laminate. Unless this bench can be extended, a second bench or table should be available. The main equipment must always be readily accessible. Lighter items can be lifted around when required, but this becomes tedious to the serious worker. Where space is limited, shelves may be fitted under the bench, but must leave comfortable foot-room at the front. If there is sufficient wall space, shelving is better, if not so wide that items on them tend to get mislaid.

The storage of paper can be a problem, for it should always be stacked flat and yet be accessible. A tall fitment built into a corner, with numerous shelves, can be a good solution for, if necessary, cloth and leather can be stacked above head level and so conserve floor space. Such a fitment must have a 3ft clearance in width and about 2ft in depth, with the projecting upper shelves about 30in deep.

Electric lighting must be adequate and should be adjustable to secure good lighting at specific points as required. Power points and a supply of clean water must always be available—paper-washing demands a sink with running water. Many bookbinding operations have to be done in a standing position, but the wise book-binder will have stools on hand and use them whenever possible.

Despite all that has been said, it is possible—if less convenient—to bind books in limited areas. Even a part of a room in use for other purposes can be successful if skeleton equipment only is used. Its limitations soon become apparent but it can be a good starting-point.

Equipment and Tools

Bookbinding requires a variety of specialised equipment and tools, the number depending entirely upon the approach to the subject. The professional hand bookbinder today must have labour-saving mechanical equipment that the amateur can dispense with, because the economics of commerce—and time is not the least important of them—do not concern him to the same extent.

The newcomer, especially if of an inventive turn of mind, can begin with a minimum of tools and equipment, acquiring more as he progresses. However, some items are essential fairly early, and some of these are not easy to improvise. I recall that my first sewing was done at thirteen years of age on tapes pinned and stretched on to the upright back of a chair donated by an amused parent. An old tennis racket press and also the fittings from a disused trouser press were used to improvise a press, while the wooden frame and adjusting bolts of a bed spring mattress of that early period provided the material for a small lying press. Now, years later, my workshop is well-equipped. I hope these experiences will encourage, not deter, the interested beginner.

THE LYING PRESS

The most essential item of equipment is the lying and cutting press combined with a plough. With it, for the time being, the newcomer can dispense with a standing or bench press, and it may be used for any operation that calls for pressure. It will not be long, however, before the other presses are somehow obtained.

The lying and cutting press (1) consists of two heavy blocks of hardwood connected by two screws, one at each end. These screws are traditionally of wood but metal ones are more satisfactory and durable, and occupy less space. The press rests upon a stand still often called a 'tub' on which the medieval binder rested his press. This must be quite rigid and well made. One side of the press is perfectly level, but the reverse, the cutting side, is usually fitted with two 'runners' between which the plough rests. The press is operated by iron bars called press pins, which, when in use, must be thrust right into the holes provided for them otherwise the wood

1 (opposite) *Lying and cutting press (showing book edge being ploughed 'in-boards')*

round them will soon be splintered. During backing, it is well to protect the wooden cheeks of the press from damage by placing over them two smaller pieces of angled metal—aluminium will do. If space permits, it is useful to have the lying press always ready for use, but the earlier idea of using it as a bench with a removable top will commend itself to the amateur with limited workshop space. A full-sized press measures about 40in overall giving 24in space between the screws, but smaller sizes of about 32in with 18in space are made. School suppliers stock smaller sizes and, within their limited scope, these are satisfactory, as long as only medium-sized books are being bound. For the professional workshop, a heavy model fitted with a central steel screw operated by a wheel and fitted with metal-backing cheeks is also available, but is expensive.

For lubrication, wooden screws require a light application of soap or candle wax from time to time, while graphite is used for steel screws. Avoid the use of oil at all times.

THE GUILLOTINE

While not essential to the amateur bookbinder, a small all-metal guillotine (2) is a desirable piece of equipment in any bindery.

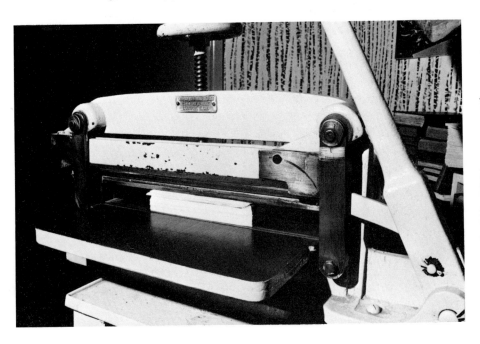

Commercial printing shops are, nowadays, usually equipped with advanced electric guillotines and, in consequence, the smaller hand lever models are more readily obtainable from specialised dealers in the trade. All guillotines are expensive but these models are much the cheapest. The smallest has a cut of about 15in but 18–20in is the more usual. It is important that the machine should be capable of cutting books up to about $2\frac{1}{2}$in thick, also that the gauge, against which the book rests when cutting, is absolutely parallel with the knife. This should be checked when a second-hand model is purchased.

Unless the atmosphere of the workshop is fairly dry, much care is necessary to guard against rust.

Further remarks on the use of the guillotine are contained in the section dealing with cutting book edges in Chapter 2, *Forwarding*.

STANDING AND NIPPING PRESSES

Upright presses, large ones being called 'standing' presses and the smaller ones 'nipping' presses, are normal requirements for a bindery, and satisfactory improvisation is not easy. The day of the 'copying' press is past, but from time to time these small presses are available—sometimes from scrap-metal merchants. They are useful but limited in use because of the small capacity, usually no more than $2-2\frac{1}{2}$in.

Iron nipping presses with platen measurements of about 18in $\times$ 12in and 22in $\times$ 14in, and 'daylight' (the greatest aperture between the platen and base) of 13in and 15in respectively, are available. They are made to stand on a bench or table which must be strong and rigid. The iron standing press is a larger, taller and heavier version with daylight of up to 3ft or more. A solid floor is necessary for this.

FRENCH STANDING PRESS (3)

This is the ideal press for the hand binder. It consists of a heavy wooden frame with a steel screw and an ingenious tightening device consisting of a free wheel at the base of the screw which hammers against two lugs on it. While it does not tighten to the same extent as the iron standing press, it is very satisfactory and has

2 (opposite) *Small hand guillotine, showing book packed ready for cutting*

the advantage of being considerably lighter, and can be used on wooden floors. It requires fastening by angle plates to the floor.

Unfortunately this type of press is not readily available, but they can be found.

As mentioned, it is possible to improvise by turning the lying press on to its side and using really heavy pressing boards. Once the item being pressed is in position and partially pressed, the lying press is returned to its normal position and the screws tightened with the press pins. This method is suggested for the newcomer, until such time as the correct press is available.

PRESSING BOARDS

A selection of pressing boards of different sizes will be required. They were originally of elm, but plywood boards are much in use today. These have the disadvantage of being easily damaged if heavily or carelessly used and the elm ones are much to be preferred if obtainable. They are stocked in many sizes from demy 12mo, 8in × 5in, upwards, but a selection of varying sizes is needed unless the work is specialised. It is not good policy to use large boards for small books for, apart from inconvenience in handling, the edges tend to become marked at the ends of the smaller books. Where pressing room is insufficient, $\frac{3}{8}$in-thick plywood boards may be used where the pile is of books all the same size; but thicker, stronger, boards should be interspersed in the pile where there is a change in the book size. At all times board surfaces must be kept perfectly smooth and level, for any imperfection will assuredly leave its mark on the book being pressed. Periodic sessions with sand- or glasspaper and a cork block should be a routine matter. The vibrating sanding attachment to the domestic electric drill is a great boon here.

Brass-edged pressing boards are available, but usually the thickness of the projecting metal edge is suitable only for the 'nipped' joints of cloth-cased bindings. This is discussed in Chapter 2, *Forwarding*.

PRESSING TINS AND PLATES

Pressing tins, which may be of tinplate or zinc, are necessary where

3 (opposite) *French standing press*

any pressing of the book which may result in marking the front and back leaves takes place. Their long edges must be quite smooth and they must be inserted into folds of paper in use. Their uses include placing between boards and book when 'setting' the back in the press. Placed either side of a folded plate or map they prevent the marking of the leaves on either side of them. Thanks to plastic-surfaced boards (obtainable as 'offcuts' and so quite cheap) pressing plates with nickel surfaces are less commonly in use than previously for 'crushing' leather grain or for 'plating' it to give a high polish on the completed book. Pressing plates are vulnerable to dampness and scratching and once the mirror-like surface is damaged they are of no use for their intended purpose.

FINISHING PRESSES

These are smaller horizontal presses for use on the bench when tooling the spines of books. They must be fairly heavy to be safe in use, for any unexpected movement when tooling can be disastrous. Smaller, lighter bench presses are useful for marking up books for sewing, for headbanding, and for lining up the spines of smaller books.

BOARD CUTTERS

These are essential for a well-equipped workshop. The professional will require nothing less than an all-metal lever model, capable of cutting heavy millboard accurately; it should have a 40in cut. Such machines are heavy and expensive. It is not difficult to obtain second-hand models through the trade. They should be thoroughly tested for cleanness and accuracy of cut, before purchase. Smaller, but efficient all-metal models are obtainable, but their use is limited because of the length of cut.

Many binders use 'bench knives' that consist of two steel blades bolted together at one end. The upper one is curved and fitted with a handle while the lower is drilled and countersunk for screwing to the end of a bench. They are made in various sizes, to cut from 16in to 42in. While not as heavy, and therefore not as effective, as the board cutting machine, they are very useful, and cheap by comparison. Their big disadvantage is that they have no clamping device to hold the board during cutting, but it is not impossible to devise one.

BOARD SHEARS

These seem to be no longer available except at second-hand, but are useful to split boards for trimming with the smaller board cutter or by ploughing. About 30in long, they are held at the end of the lying press—beyond the screw. The already roughly marked board is passed through them as the cutting is done, a little at a time.

SEWING FRAMES

These are the simplest item of equipment to improvise for sewing to tapes, not quite so simple for cord sewing, but still possible.

The traditional sewing frame consists of a base board, with an open channel cut at the front so that the sewing keys may be passed through and held in position. At either end is a hardwood pillar with a screw thread worked on it. Across these rests a crossbar capable of adjustment by, usually, oval wooden nuts on which it rests. The pillars are screwed into the base so that the complete frame can be easily dismantled for packing. The frames vary from about 20in to 30in between the pillars.

Improvised sewing frames of any convenient length are fairly simple to make, a tenon saw, a screwdriver and a drill being the only tools required.

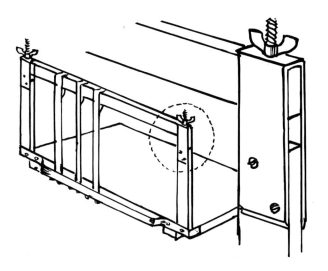

4 Improvised adjustable sewing frame

Tapes may be sewn loosely round the crossbar and pinned under the base board. It is possible, by fitting a piece of sturdy metal rod under the base board, and slightly away from it, at about 2in or 3in from the front edge, to use this in place of sewing keys for hempen cords which may be tightened round it and tied.

A superior improvisation is shown in illustration 4. Here the crossbar can be adjusted upwards by screwing down the butterfly nuts on the bolts fitted through the crossbar. The metal plates bolted to the tops of the uprights allow for sufficient play for this.

At the front of the base board is firmly screwed a piece of hoop metal angled at the ends so that the central part projects away from the base about $\frac{3}{4}$in, forming an aperture through which sewing keys can be passed for adjustable fitting.

FINISHING STOVES

These are essential for gold tooling and general finishing purposes. They are made for heating by gas or electricity.

The gas-heated model is cheaper and because the heat is more simply controlled, is preferred by many. A much improved electric model by Sydney Cockerell of Grantchester, England, is now available and is thoroughly recommended. One feature of it is a deep groove round the heating plate which allows the finishing tool to rest on the plate without damage to the edge of the engraved surface. The tool handles rest in the scalloped metal ring that surrounds the stove proper.

An improvised finishing stove is possible, provided a suitable gas ring raised on a central column, and a heavy circular heating plate, can be procured. Around the burner is fitted a circular metal 'tube', its diameter slightly smaller than that of the heating plate and its height rather more than that of the gas ring. Metal arms bolted to it support a circle of strip metal that has had V-shaped pieces cut from it with tinsmiths' snips; these support the handles of the finishing tools.

At least one binder used such a stove when no other was available and succeeded in winning a silver medal for 'Finishing' in the bookbinding examinations of the City and Guilds of London Institute. Even a small ring on a domestic cooking stove has been temporarily adapted for heating bookbinders' finishing tools.

GLUE-POTS

Despite the many types of adhesives now marketed, many bookbinders still use animal glue. This glue has to be heated in a water-jacketed metal container whose form has been more or less standard since gas was introduced for heating: a large, cast-iron water container into which fits a smaller cast-iron glue-pot, resting on its rim, both having wire handles. They are still available, the modern ones having a vitreous enamelled glue container which is cleaner in use. Some binders attach a strong piece of wire loosely across the top, fixing it to the lugs holding the handles; this permits the glue brush to be wiped and allows the surplus glue to drop directly into the pot and not on the sides.

This type of glue-pot is rapidly giving way to electrically heated ones with thermostatic controls which ensure a constant heat of 140°F (60°C)—the ideal, which prevents the glue overheating. They are obtainable with either single or multiple glue-pots. The latter provide for different types of glue for varying purposes while a third pot can be used to provide hot water for thinning glue as required. This will prevent water in the well becoming adulterated when glue brushes are dipped into it, as so often happens. Electrically heated glue-pots are fairly expensive, the multiple ones extremely so, and these are more suitable for the larger bindery.

An improvised glue-pot of the old type can be made from a water-tight tin can fitted into the lid of a domestic saucepan and soldered there. A wire handle will be necessary for the removal of the glue-pot from the water container. As with most improvisations, this is but a temporary substitute for the correct article but it serves its purpose.

(The subject of adhesives is dealt with in Chapter 8, *Materials*.)

Tools and Smaller Items of Equipment

Throughout the book, tools and their uses are described in connection with the operation being dealt with. This list amplifies these references.

AWLS

Not to be confused with carpenters' bradawls which have flat ends, whereas these are pointed. Two types are needed, a fairly fine one for making sewing holes when oversewing and for teasing out hempen cords when lacing boards to the book, and a larger,

5 Some tools used in forwarding
1 Strop and rap stick
2 Knives
3 Hemp keys
4 Metal straightedges
5 Bone folders
6 Tape keys
7 Paring knives and spokeshave
8 Square
9 Spring dividers and wing compasses

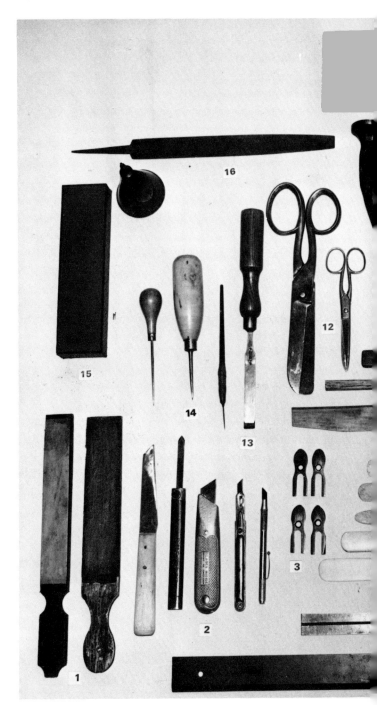

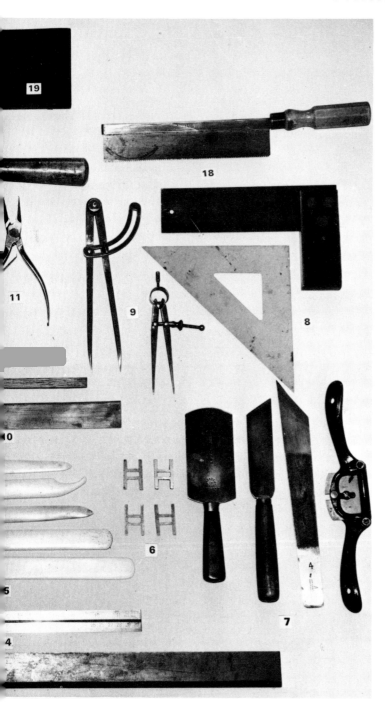

thicker one, usually known as a printers' bodkin for holing boards for lacing.

BAND NIPPERS

Used for drawing the leather on the spine of a banded book tightly against the band sides. The best types are either plated or chromed and are fitted with a spring to keep the jaws open when in use. It is vital that the edges of the jaws are kept free from damage, for the leather on which they are used is, in its damp state, extremely susceptible. Before use they should be checked to see that jaw surfaces are quite clean, and after use they should be wiped clean and dry. This is particularly important if they are plated or stainless steel.

BANDSTICKS

These are of two or three types and are dealt with in the chapter on *Covering* (p. 188).

BRUSHES

Bookbinders' brushes for adhesives are usually round and are measured by their diameters which range from $\frac{1}{2}$in to $2\frac{1}{2}$in according to their purpose.

Glue brushes These may be obtained with zinc, copper or iron ferrules, although the latter are much less used now. Those known as 'Glue tools, compressed, copper bound with wire bridles' are generally considered to be the best and usually range from 1in to $1\frac{3}{4}$in diameter. Larger ones, when needed, are neither compressed nor bridled and range from $1\frac{3}{4}$in to $2\frac{1}{2}$in diameters; 1–$1\frac{1}{2}$in are adequate for most work.

Glue-brush bristles soon lose their flexibility if allowed to remain in hot glue for long periods and should not be left permanently in the glue-pot. After use they should be wiped clean of as much glue as possible, using the glue stick or wire, dipped quickly into hot water (usually the well!) and twirled between the hands. They can then be moistened and set aside, resting on the metal ferrule, not the bristles. Once used, the bristles are always mildly stiffened and should be dipped into hot water to soften them before use.

As the bristles wear down, the wire bridling can be removed, so restoring their length. Often they have become too brittle by that time to allow the brush to be used for glueing large areas and it is used only for glueing up and back lining.

Paste brushes String-bound 'sash tools' are ideal for pasting but it is rare for bookbinders' suppliers to stock them nowadays. Being string-bound, there is no metal to rust and discolour the paste. Recourse must be made to metal-ferruled brushes with suitable bristles (those in glue brushes are often too harsh). It is possible to cover the ferrule completely with plastic, binding it in position with string bridling which prevents the metal rusting for a much longer period. Brushes used for polyvinyl acetate (PVA) adhesive must be thoroughly washed after use, or the bristles (only) left standing in cold water. If allowed to dry out after using PVA, strong domestic detergent is usually successful in softening the bristles again.

Sprinkling brushes Originally these had diameters from 2in to 3in, but with the advent of spray guns the manufacturing stationery and library bookbinders no longer use brushes. For single, or a few, volumes, a nail-brush with animal bristles, used with a sprinkling frame, is satisfactory. It must be thoroughly washed after use.

Burnishing brushes (edge gilding) The domestic blacklead brush has been replaced with the shoe brush. It must be quite new and unused and have firm, but not harsh bristles. On no account must it be used for any other purpose than for burnishing book edges prior to gilding them.

Glair brushes (edge gilding) Artists' 'ground' brushes, $\frac{3}{4}$–1in wide with soft bristles firmly set in rubber, serve admirably. Wash them in cold water after use, and check for loose bristles before using them.

COMPASSES AND SPRING DIVIDERS

Used for repetitive measuring. Spring dividers are made in a number of different sizes but, generally, a 5in or 6in length will serve most purposes. A second pair is useful if two different measurements must be repeated at one time.

Wing compasses provide for wider measurements and are locked in position by means of a screw. When not available, a strip of paper can be marked at a given width and this repeated. It takes longer and is about 1 per cent or 2 per cent less accurate!

FOLDERS

These should be made of bone; plastic has been tried and found wanting. While, in theory, one will suffice, most binders have a small selection for different purposes. If only one is on hand, it should be softly pointed and thinner at one end. Account-book binders use a heavy 'tusk' folder, and if a modified, thinner version is contrived by the letterpress binder it will be found useful for getting into awkward corners. Generally a 7in folder will serve, but longer ones are used where much paper folding is done by hand.

Some binders soak their folders in light oil for a night which softens their texture and lessens the need for lubrication in use by passing them across the hair.

HAMMERS

These are dealt with in Chapter 2 under *Rounding* and *Backing*, but the importance of their being kept clean and smooth on the pane is again emphasised.

KNIVES

These can be of almost infinite variety nowadays, but the basic knife for the bookbinder is that made primarily for the bootmaker; it is in general supply. Quality varies considerably and the new-comer is advised to buy a good one and, in this respect, price and quality go hand in hand.

One Scandinavian brand, 'Eric Borg', stands out above most others but is generally obtainable only from reputable leather factors. While such a knife can be used for most purposes there are specialised ones made with interchangeable blades, the extra ones often contained within the all-metal handle. The short, pointed blade is splendid for cutting bookbinders' board but less useful for general purposes. Penknives with fine blades are also useful for some purposes, including the cutting of leather inlays. A modern version of interchangeable blades within a thin cylindrical holder that can be turned within a small area is also excellent for inlaying purposes. The traditional fine-pointed double-edged adjustable mount-cutter's knife is another versatile tool, which because of its sturdy construction can be a lifelong asset to the bookbinder.

The best advice is to pay a good price for a knife and keep it in first-class condition, using as much of the blade as possible rather than just the point.

Sharpening is done on an oilstone of which there are two main types, 'India', a natural stone, and the man-made 'carborundum' stone. A small quantity of thin oil must be fed on to the stone when sharpening and good pressure placed on the blade; the sharpening is effected on the forward movement. The angle at which the blade is held should not be too great or a thick edge will result. As the edge wears so the steel behind it must be removed. The carborundum is a 'faster' stone than the India which gives a finer edge, so the one supplements the other. Oil should not be allowed to soak into the oilstone as this reduces its abrasiveness and it should be wiped clean after use. Boiling in water will assist in restoring abrasive qualities should this become necessary.

From time to time all edged tools will require grinding, and for this a hand rotary grinder is useful, but it must be at least 1in wide by about 5in diameter to be effective and should not be coarse.

Small independent grinding wheels driven by equally small electric motors are a boon in the larger workshop. Many still find it more convenient to take a number of edge tools at a time to the local grindery to have them re-ground and sharpened.

The 'rap stick', a piece of flat wood with medium and fine emery cloth affixed, can be of use, but it gives a rough, if quick, edge and the friction created could undermine the temper of the steel.

It is still a useful item when in a hurry but its use can become a bad habit.

KNOCKING-DOWN IRON

The bookbinder's anvil, it consists of a heavy flat piece of iron usually about $\frac{3}{4}$in thick and 10 in long, with a solid projecting bar across its width on the underside. The bar is screwed in the lying press at one end to serve as a hammering plate. The surface should be kept smooth, and if not quite perfect, should be well covered with clean paper. Its main uses are for hammering out the backing from sections of previously bound books, and hammering down the hemp slips and holed boards after lacing-on book boards. Minor uses are holding together sets of books for marking up for finishing and for holding in position the sides of book boxes that have been glued together. It is also useful as a weight. Weights, incidentally, are often needed, and a scrap-iron merchant can usually produce one or two which can be cleaned and enamelled.

The old-fashioned flat-iron, although far less satisfactory, can, at a pinch, be used as a substitute for the knocking-down iron.

SEWING KEYS

See under *Sewing* (p. 80).

SHEARS

These should be of good quality, large and strong enough for the heavy cutting often required of them. Full-sized, they measure about 10in overall with 4in blades. They should not be used for cutting any but thin board, and after being used for cutting glued materials should have the blades wiped clean and dry, after a quick dip into hot water to soften the glue on them. The use of the knife for this purpose does no good to either tool. Smaller shears may be the preference of lady bookbinders, but domestic scissors do not serve the purpose.

Left-handed workers must either learn to use the right hand with shears or obtain a left-handed pair. The reason for this is that the position of the cut cannot otherwise be seen.

STRAIGHTEDGES AND RULES

As implied, these two items of equipment have different purposes. The bookbinder's metal straightedge, if 18in or 24in in length, should be firm and fairly heavy to reduce the likelihood of slipping in use. This does not apply so much to a 12in straightedge because the fingers holding it can control proportionately more of its length.

Metal straightedges having a central projecting ridge offer protection to the fingers should a knife slip in use. Any straightedge must lie perfectly flat to be effective and safe. Where a long *rule* is needed, a brass-ended yardstick is satisfactory. Steel rules, when no longer new, are often illegible, and they have to be kept free of insidious rust.

TENON SAWS

A small saw, such as a tenon saw, is needed for cutting kerfs in the backs of books for recessing cords in sewing. The pitch of it should not be such as to cut unduly large kerfs, but the 'Dovetail' saw, which is much finer, usually cuts kerfs that are too fine. The saw is an integral part of a bindery and it is surprising how often its use is called for, if only for repairing wooden equipment.

TRINDLES

This delightful name refers to the flat pieces of forked metal that are placed between book back and boards when cutting the foredge 'in-boards'. Their purpose is to flatten the rounded spine so causing the curved foredge to assume a flat shape for cutting in the lying and cutting press.

Bookbinding Styles and Sequence of Operations in Each

CLOTH CASING

1 Collating. Check for completeness and correct sequence.
2 Pulling (to pieces). Turn out 'dog-eared' corners, remove all glue.
3 Remove backing by hammering sections on knocking-down iron.
4 Guarding. Repair and reinforce broken and damaged leaves. Press, but only when completely dry.
5 Endpapers. Affixing and reinforcing if single folded type.
6 Sewing. To tapes. Three or four according to width used and size of book.
7 Reducing backswell where necessary.
8 Glueing the back.
9 Cutting edges in guillotine or by ploughing.
10 Rounding (with hammer, on bench).
11 Edge decoration, solid or sprinkled colour.
12 Backing, in lying press with backing boards.
13 Boarding. Cut boards with correct 'square' and fitting comfortably in the joint.
14 Back linings, either simple or 'Oxford' hollow.
15 Covering. Use thin glue, rub well down with folder, fit round book and leave to dry under a weight.

16 Pasting into cover and pressing. Leave to dry in press.

17 Finishing. Lettering etc. on spine using gold foil or leaf. Unless waterproof cloth has been used for the cover, an 'aerosol' spray wax can be used to resist subsequent marking.

QUARTER-LEATHER LIBRARY STYLE (FRENCH JOINT)

1 Collating.

2 Pulling.

3 Hammering out sections to remove backing.

4 Guarding and repairing, map mounting, plates guarded.

5 Making cloth-jointed or linen-reinforced 'made and insetted' types.

6 Sewing to tapes. If 'tight-back' these must be accurately placed to appear as raised bands on the spine. Kettle-stitches recessed by making a small saw kerf before adding endpapers.

7 Reducing backswell.

8 'Tipping' first and last sections and endpapers with paste.

9 Cutting edges, guillotine or plough.

10 Rounding.

11 Edge decoration. Top edge gilt or coloured and burnished.

12 Prepare 'split' boards.

13 Backing and back setting.

14 Cutting boards to size for a 'French' joint and moulded head-cap.

15 Back linings, mull and 'Oxford' hollow, reinforced if needed. Make flanges. (Omit Oxford hollow if tight-back.)

16 Attach boards, leave adequate space in joint and press between paper-covered tins.

17 Cut and pare leather for spine, also vellum for French corners if required.

18 Cover spine, and fit French corners. Leave to dry under weight.

19 Trim leather, and side with cloth.

20 Finishing, letter spine, tool as required.

21 Trim out boards, fill in if necessary.

22 Paste down board papers (no trimming required). Use rods of correct size in French joints or metal-edged pressing boards if suitable.
   Leave to dry in press.

HALF-LEATHER, WITH 'DRAWN-ON' (LACED) BOARDS

1 Collating.
2 Pulling.
3 Hammering out backing.
4 Cleaning soiled leaves, washing and sizing if necessary.
5 Guarding and reinforcing sections as necessary.
6 Press book when completely dry but remove folded maps.
7 Endpapers, making up style required, usually 'made and insetted'.
8 Marking up back of book for sewing on five (or more, if need be) cords. Cut saw kerfs for recessing cords and kettle-stitches. If the book is sewn on tapes, only marking up is necessary.
9 Add endpapers.
10 Sewing. Do not sew 'two-sections on' unless absolutely unavoidable. Leave 2in cord length each side when cutting down.
11 Reducing backswell.
12 'Tipping' first and last sections and endpapers.
13 Preparing boards. Cut joint edge before lining, and leave to dry out.
14 Cutting book edges, unless to be ploughed 'in-boards'.
15 Rounding.
16 Edge gilding, may be done at this stage or after boards have been attached.
17 Backing.
18 Cutting (or ploughing) boards to size.
19 Boarding. Holing and preparing boards for lacing.
20 Lacing.
21 Setting the back, while book is pressed between tins. Leave to dry.
22 Ploughing book edges if cut in-boards.
23 Edge gilding, if not done at stage 16.
24 Headbanding and setting. Lining if binding is to be tight-back.
25 Back linings, unless tight-back.
26 Banding, if required.
27 Preparing book for covering. Back cornering, slightly filing board edges and removing extreme corner tips.

28 Capping up, to protect all edges when covering. If only top edge gilt, cover head of book only.

29 Fitting corners or foredge strip (allow to dry) and covering spine. Corners may be mitred when dry.

30 Siding. Trimming edges of leather and paring or filling in-boards if preferred.

31 Trimming out and filling insides of boards.

32 Finishing.

33 Trimming out paste-down leaves, and putting down (the boards open).

34 Pressing.

FULL LEATHER

Operations are as for half-leather except for the following:

5a The book edges may be trimmed and gilded before sewing.

7 Zig-zag or leather-jointed endpapers may be used.

10 Sewing may be done on raised cords (double, if the book is large) for a 'flexible' (tight-back) binding.

13 Boards will require full linings and a counter-lining on the inside to counteract leather contraction.

24 Headbanding. If the book is large, double headbands may be warranted.

28 Capping up of all edges is necessary.

29 Covering. If a heavy or 'flexible' binding, the bands will probably need tying down between boards.

31 Corners to be mitred before trimming out.

33 Trimming out. If the inside borders are to be tooled, or a leather doublure is fitted, this must be done *before* finishing (no. 32).

I

PREPARATORY WORK

*Folding paper—pulling—paper washing—guarding and repairing—
plates, maps and diagrams—treatment of single leaves—
endpapers—different methods of sewing*

PREPARATORY WORK

Folding and Pulling

When learning a technique it is desirable to study its origin, and essential to know its purpose. This knowledge not only forms a good background, but assists in a greater appreciation and understanding of good craftsmanship. Bookbinding is not the result of invention but rather of evolution: it has taken centuries, and many craftsmen, to produce the refinements known to us today.

When books took the form of scrolls written by scribes, evolution began. First the way in which they were read was changed from vertical to horizontal, with tabulated lettering, the pages appearing side by side along the scroll. The next step was to fold the scroll concertinawise; in this way it could be stored flat and read with greater ease. If stitched through the side near the back it looked not unlike check-books of today and it is interesting to note that books made in this manner were being produced in Japan and Korea as late as the 1930s. By cutting through the foredge fold of this 'concertina' book, it was possible to write on both sides of the leaves. When vellum and parchment were used by the scribes it was an obvious step to sew folded sheets to leather thongs, which permitted the leaves to open flat. The insertion of one fold inside another made further improvement and so the 'section' was born. With the more general use of paper smaller books were possible, and insetting gave way to folding. Today gigantic machines print sheets large enough to make four or even eight such sections and with the many different folding machines now in use there is a variety of ways in which these large sheets may be folded into book sections. The printer must know which particular machine will be used by the binder in order to impose the pages correctly. Because with machine-made paper the main fibres tend to run in one direction, known as 'grain direction', and because paper folds more readily *with* the grain, it is better that the book be made with the grain direction running from head to tail. Stock sheets of paper are said to have either a 'long grain' or a 'short grain' indicating that the grain is either along the length of the sheet or along the width, and this is invariably marked on the wrappings of unbroken reams.

In order to ensure that grain direction is correct, folio and octavo sizes must be made from sheets with a short grain and quarto and 16mo from long-grained.

However, because most stock sizes are 'double' (and often quadruple or 'quad') readjustment is necessary in these cases, the grain direction being the same with 'quad' sheets and reversed with 'double' ones.

There is still an accepted order for *hand folding* which is as follows.

FOLDING

At the foot of the first page of each section will usually be found a 'signature' which takes the form of a letter or arabic numeral and is used to indicate the position of the section in the book. Sheets for folding are placed flat on the bench with the 'inner' side uppermost and the first page—with the signature—in the bottom left-hand corner facing the bench. A bone folder is taken in the right hand and placed centrally on the sheet. With the left hand the right-hand edge is brought over the folder to the left where a careful check is made to ensure that the printed pages fall exactly into position one over the other before creasing with the folder. If margins are to be uniform in the finished book it is essential that sections are 'folded to print' and not just folded to paper (6).

6 Regular folds

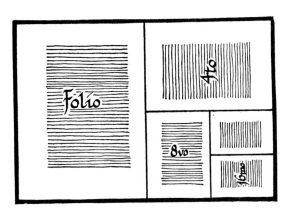

This first fold produces—on a blank sheet—two leaves and four pages and is known as 'folio'. For the next fold, which is 'quarto' (4to), the top half of the folded sheet is brought over to the bottom and creased along the fold: this results in four leaves and eight pages. Before making the next—'octavo' (8vo)—and subsequent folds, it will be necessary to slit the previous fold to just beyond half-way to avoid buckling the paper. The fold is then made as for folio, right over left. A fourth fold made from top to bottom will produce a 'sextodecimo', usually known as 'sixteenmo' (16mo), having sixteen leaves and thirty-two pages. Such sections should be of thin paper to be satisfactory.

These are the 'regular' folds. When the sheet is printed for 'duodecimo' or 'twelvemo' (12mo), the four pages forming the upper portion of the sheet may form an offcut, the remaining eight pages being folded as a normal octavo. The four-page portion is folded separately and wrapped round the octavo section.

PULLING TO PIECES

Before pulling a book for rebinding it is wise to check it carefully page by page for completeness; unless omissions are reported before the book is taken down, legal responsibility lies with the binder. Collating, as this check is termed, is done most thoroughly by turning each leaf separately and checking pagination and plates. Each plate should be marked on the reverse side (verso) with the number of the page it faces, to ensure that the plates are replaced correctly.

7 *Collating*

An easier method, although less thorough, is to take a number of leaves firmly by the bottom corner between finger and thumb. A sharp twist of the wrist will cause them to splay out at the top corners, and by flicking the leaves over with the left hand the pagination can be quickly checked (7).

Sometimes it may be wiser not to resew the book, particularly when it has already been rebound and the existing sewing is in good order. Very occasionally, especially when recasing only is called for, even machine sewing may be adequate if reinforced (see p. 334).

Pulling should be done with care, as unnecessary damage is easily caused when cutting the original sewing. With cased books the covers should be removed by cutting through the endpapers, mull and tapes, at the front and back joints (8). It is sometimes

8 Cutting the book from its case

possible by gently pulling the front cover, first lifting the endpaper fly-leaf and pulling it away with it, to cut the sewing between the linings and the backs of the sections, thus completely releasing them from the original binding and sewing. This requires not only care but experience, if the backs of the sections are not to be cut, and should be done only with books of little value, until competence is attained.

The safer but slower method is to open each section at the centre and cut the threads before easing the section away from the book linings (9). The thumb, which receives harsh usage in bookbinding, may here be used to press away the linings before opening up each section (10). After cutting the threads, grasp the section firmly in the left hand, holding the rest of the book down with the right, so that it comes away *en bloc*. This will help to prevent the outside

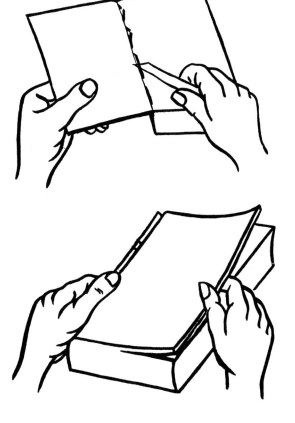

9 *Cutting the threads before removing a section*

10 *Easing off the back linings when removing a section*

fold from being damaged. Where an excessive amount of glue on the back of the book makes pulling difficult without undue tearing, it is often effective to hammer the back gently after the covers have been removed. This tends to break up the glue and assists the removal of sections. In extreme cases it may be necessary, after cleaning away as much of the back linings as possible with a knife, to soak the back by coating it with paste. After a while it will be found that the paste has imparted moisture to the linings and they may be removed with a sharpened piece of flat wood or a blunt knife. This requires care. Afterwards the back should be cleaned off with a damp sponge—not a wet one—and the book pulled before the sections dry out. In laying the sections down they should be alternated so that the back of one overlaps the foredge of the previous one. This prevents the damp parts coming into contact with each other and permits quicker drying. It is not a method to be used if there is a possibility of damage or soiling, or weakening of the paper fibre by overdamping. Rather than subject a book to this treatment it may be wiser to leave the original sewing, particularly where original boards have to be used again.

During pulling, all 'dog-eared' corners must be turned out and torn portions of folds straightened. Glue still adhering to the backs and sides of sections must be removed: it is wiser to insert the knife edge under the glue to prise it off, rather than try to cut it away. If the original sewing holes have allowed glue to percolate through to the centre of the section it should be carefully removed; a matchstick cut to a point can be useful for this purpose.

After pulling it is necessary to flatten the 'joint' made when the book was originally backed. The usual method is to fix a knocking-down iron at the end of a lying press and gently but firmly hammer out the groove, a few sections at a time. The normal bookbinder's hammer, which is similar to that used by cobblers, having a slightly spherical pane, or head, must be kept clean and smooth. All too often the head is pitted, or has glue adhering to it; this must be removed and the surface cleaned with emery cloth. Best results are achieved if the hammer is held fairly close to the head, with the sections laid on the iron, the bent fold of the joint facing downwards rather than upwards. Each hammer stroke must be true, or dents and cuts in the section can result. Uneven, heavy blows will cause the paper to cockle. This treatment is harsh for old or soft paper, and it will be found better to unbend the original joints by passing them between finger and thumb, or by pressing them downwards over the edge of a pressing board.

Very occasionally the craft binder has to deal with books that have been wire-stitched through the side. Such wires must be removed with care if unsightly markings are to be avoided. One method is to open the clenched-over ends carefully with a very blunt knife. The book is turned over and a screwdriver or similar blunt-ended instrument is inserted under the wire, the end resting on a flat piece of metal placed on the book (a coin may be used). In this way leverage sufficient to ease the stitch out may be applied without damage to the paper (11). Pliers may then be used to remove the wire stitch. Where the thickness of the book makes this difficult, sections may first be eased off from the back.

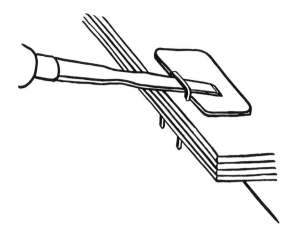

Paper Washing

Only in very special work is the bookbinder called upon to wash, tone and size the leaves of books. The process demands a knowledge of the behaviour of the chemicals used, and unless the bookbinder has a broad knowledge of chemistry he is dependent upon those who have made a study of the subject. It is possible to remove most stains from paper. The problem is to leave both paper and print unharmed, and the best advice is not to use dubious methods.

Paper should be subjected to washing only as a last resort after other methods have had to be discarded. Surface dirt on paper can be removed by the judicious use of a very soft rubber; day-old bread can be even kinder to the paper surface, although a clean, soft brush should be on hand to remove the soiled crumbs frequently. Cuttlefish is a mild and clean abrasive which actually removes the surface of the paper and so should not be used if this is not of really good quality. Even the mildest abrasive can be disastrous if used on poor quality or thin paper.

Oil stains can be persistent and while immersion in a bath of petroleum will usually dissolve the stain, it cannot be said to be the safest method and demands that great care be exercised when using it. The petrol may be generously applied to the stain and will dissolve and spread it, but the solvent must be blotted off before it dries. Mild discoloration will be removed or lessened by re-sizing. Gelatine or isinglass can be used for sizing, the proportions being one ounce in a quart of water. This should be maintained at a heat of 120°F (49°C). The gelatine should first be dissolved in a small quantity of cold water before adding the hot. The sheets are passed through the bath, allowed to drain a little, and blotted before hanging on string lines that have been covered with folded strips of paper.

CHLORAMINE-T

When bleaching has to be resorted to, Chloramine-T, which is a mild bleaching agent, is about the safest and simplest method. It is sold commercially in powder form and because it is unstable should be stored in a well-stoppered bottle. One ounce should be dissolved in 2½pt of water, being mixed only as required. The important thing about Chloramine-T is that it leaves no corrosive residue. Local application is possible, using a paint brush. After use, the leaf should be placed between blotting paper and under boards, being examined within the hour when it can be treated again if necessary. The sheet may be immersed in a bath of the solution.

SODIUM HYPOCHLORITE

One part of commercial sodium hypochlorite (marked '10% w/v available chlorine'), diluted with twenty parts of water, is a good paper bleach. The mixture must not on any account be used beyond a 6 to 20 strength. Chlorine generated by this will remove the colour from many stains and even varnish; during the process most writing inks will be removed. Should it be necessary to retain them this can be done by painting them over with a 5 per cent solution of nitrocellulose in a solvent consisting of equal parts of acetone and amyl acetate, before washing. This can be removed after the operation when the sheet is dry, by a wash of acetone. Bleaching continues until stains are faint, the sheet then being passed through a bath consisting of 2 per cent sodium theosulphate (photographic hypo) which removes any chlorine left behind. It is then washed thoroughly for about fifteen minutes, in a bath (or tray) into which running water is conveyed by a length of cloth tied to the tap, to prevent splashing and possible damage to the very soft paper (12). For safety, it is always wiser to use a supporting sheet of paper under that being washed; with very weak paper it will be necessary to insert it between a fold of paper during the process. Re-sizing will be necessary.

12 *Paper washing*

Guarding

Books that have previously been bound may require both repairing and reinforcing at the folds. Occasionally new sections must be reinforced before binding—especially those which come at the beginning and end of the book. Contrary to general belief, this work demands experience, great care, and discretion. Guards must not cause the back of the book to swell to such a degree that a well-formed binding is impossible; they must therefore be thin and tough. They may be of good-quality bank paper or, if the work justifies it, hand-made bank-note paper. Record paper which is usually toned and rather heavier may be used where suitable. The substance selected depends upon the nature of the work—from 15lb large post for heavy guards to 7lb for the lighter work. Rag tissue may be used for guarding books printed on very thin paper.

The width of the back margin must be the controlling factor for the maximum width of guards; half an inch is a useful average, but guards from one-quarter to three-quarters of an inch wide may sometimes be necessary. For general work they are cut in bulk and

13 *Cutting repairing guards*

stored; for special work they are marked out with a pair of dividers and cut individually with a knife against a steel straightedge (13).

The use of knife and straightedge, whether it be for cutting guards or other purposes, requires care, for it can be hazardous to the newcomer. The knife edge should be sharp, a blunt knife being far more dangerous in use. The metal straightedge must be placed accurately in position and held there firmly by the left hand. The knife is placed with its side against the edge of the straightedge, its point barely reaching the edge of the paper being cut. The first movement is slightly forward, which cuts into the paper there without fear of drawing it backwards under the straightedge; the cut is then continued, drawing the knife towards the worker. Important points are that, first, greater pressure is needed on the straightedge than on the knife, and second, that the knife should be held at a fairly flat angle so that not only the point of the blade is used for cutting, and, most important, so that its side is firmly against the straightedge. Never allow careless speed to endanger the thumb and fingers holding down the straightedge. For the finest work, particularly on old volumes, guards are often torn against a steel rule, giving a feathered edge. This is less noticeable than a cut edge. Furthermore, where there is overmuch guarding, a cut edge, falling at a uniform distance from the back, may cause the leaves to bend at that point rather than at the fold, and with use the paper will tend to fracture there.

It is important that machine-made papers for guards should be cut with the paper grain or 'machine direction' along the length. When pasted, expansion will then be kept to a minimum. If the grain runs in the other direction the guards will contract when dry and the sections will arc so that the book will not open freely or lie flat. If the machine direction cannot be detected at a glance, damp a sample on one side. The paper will curl and tend to form a tube: the grain runs along the tube, not round it. While repairs to folds must be adequate, to go beyond this can result in the additional paper causing 'backswell' to an extent that a well-formed binding becomes impossible. If there is doubt, it is better to use guards where absolutely essential and check backswell before adding to them. Alternatives are to use thinner bank paper or to oversew badly damaged sections where necessary, rather than guard them.

Guards are lightly pasted, using a not-too-thin paste, and are placed carefully in position. They should be tapped with the ball of the hand, rather than rubbed, to avoid undue stretching. Stretch may also be prevented by pasting the surface of plate glass and laying the guards on to the paste.

As a general rule pairs of leaves are guarded on the inside of the fold, with the exception of the pair at the centre of the section, which, when guarding is necessary, should be guarded on the outside. If this rule is not followed the inside guard may be disturbed by the sewing needle while the surface of the guard is often too hard to allow knots in the sewing thread to become comfortably embedded. This can result in 'starts' (or sturts) appearing at the foredge during the subsequent process of rounding. Guards placed on the outside of sections usually result in a less satisfactory glueing-up, although under certain circumstances this method may be desirable to prevent possible discoloration of valuable manuscripts. In such cases guards are usually cut from jaconet or fine linen.

In dealing with valuable manuscripts, however, it may be desirable to use a continuous guard. This must be accurately marked and folded, otherwise it will tend to become out of square. A piece of guarding paper is cut, the width being the length of the book sections, the grain direction being along the width. Its length must be enough to form sufficient folds to take all the sections, one in each fold. For example, if a guard width of $\frac{3}{8}$in is required each section will require $\frac{3}{4}$in of paper, so that if there are twenty sections a minimum of 15in length of paper is necessary.

Using spring dividers set at $\frac{3}{8}$in, carefully and accurately mark along both long edges of the paper. First work on one side of the paper, folding it upwards at every alternate mark, and then repeat the process on the reverse side, folding at the other markings and so making a 'concertina' of the sheet.

It will be found easier and quicker if a fine-pointed folder is used and run lightly along the straightedge before folding the paper.

While this method effectively prevents glue from penetrating between the sections it requires great accuracy in making the concertina. Sewing is more difficult and the whole process takes considerably longer. It does not repair broken folds and consequently adds thickness to the book at the back. It should be used with discretion.

METHODICAL WORKING

To avoid errors it is quite important that guarding be done

methodically. Only one section should be dealt with at a time. If it is necessary to open it up, do so as shown in illustration 14, which

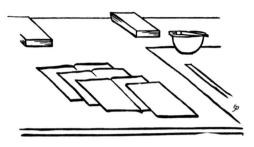

14 Methodical working when guarding

permits every fold to be treated without disturbing the page sequence. The operation will be carried out more speedily if guards are pre-cut slightly shorter than the book. Where a pair of leaves are completely separated the pasted guard should be laid on the bench and each leaf laid accurately in position on it.

DRYING

Where heavy guards are used it is normally better to stack the sections unfolded, and to refold when dry. Lightly guarded sections are folded, placed between pressing boards, and left under a light weight to dry thoroughly, before being subjected to heavy pressure (15). If this is not done the edges of the guards may stick to each other and the back of the book becomes a solid mass.

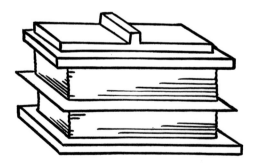

15 Guarded books drying out

TONING GUARDS

Guards must sometimes be toned so that they do not clash with the colour of the book paper. Several homely agents such as permanganate of potash in a weak solution, coffee, and, very occasionally, strong tea may be used for this purpose. It is easier to tone the paper before cutting into guards, by either brushing or wiping the stain on with cotton wool.

A small selection of pre-stained sheets of different tones should be kept on hand so that the most suitable may be used. Normally it is necessary to stain only one side of the paper, as the reverse is pasted down to the book.

Repairing Tears

When a page tears, the fibres happily tend to overlap one another at front and back. A satisfactory repair can be carried out by pasting these edges with rice or cornflour paste, brushed on with a fine camel-hair brush. The pasted tear is laid on to a piece of rag tissue

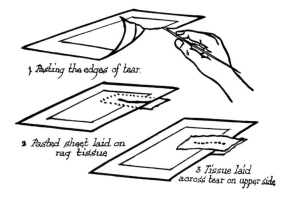

1 Pasting the edges of tear.

2 Pasted sheet laid on rag tissue

3 Tissue laid across tear on upper side

16 Repairing a torn leaf

(Japanese or lens tissue is ideal) and a second piece is laid over the tear on the other side (16). The page is allowed to dry under light pressure. When the surplus tissue is gently removed, some fibres will be left behind to secure the fracture. The lightest rub with flour-paper will remove surplus fibres which may obscure the print. Corn or rice flour is used in preference to wheaten paste because it is less likely to discolour the paper.

Where the corner of a leaf is missing, a piece of paper similar in texture and colour is placed in position under the torn sheet, and the shape of the tear is lightly marked on it (17). This shape is very carefully torn away and joined to the damaged leaf by the fore-going method. If it is found necessary to carry out frequent paper

17 *Marking a piece of paper that will replace a missing corner*

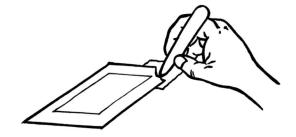

17 *Marking a piece of paper that will replace a missing corner*

repairs, the bookbinder should collect an assortment of papers of all kinds and periods. Original endpapers from antiquarian work are a good source of supply. Much time will be saved if the collection is classified into colour, weight and texture.

Worm or other holes are filled with unsized paper (blottings) made into a pulp with gelatine size, stained to the paper colour, and worked into the holes with a small folder. When dry, flour-paper is used to smooth the surface.

Plates

The insertion of plates into books has always presented a problem to publishers' binders, and of the three methods generally used, none is completely satisfactory. Obviously it is more convenient to the reader to have a plate facing the text dealing with its subject, and in edition binding this is usually effected by 'tipping' it in the book with a narrow strip of adhesive. Plates dealt with in this way cannot be satisfactory, because, unless creased beforehand, they will not lie flat when the book is used. Furthermore, they impose a strain on the leaves to which they are attached, and this often causes both to come apart from the book.

Books are sometimes made up with plates in printed pairs, folded and inserted in the sections to fall at the nearest appropriate point in the text. While this is a more satisfactory method of book production, it is very rarely possible for both plates to face their appropriate pages. For this reason, and also because it is more economic, plates are often made up into complete sections and bound at intervals in the body of the book, or together at the end.

When the position of plates is shown in the list of illustrations, the binder has nothing more to do in either of the last two methods except normal preparation for rebinding. If the position of plates is not given, the binder may be required to insert them facing certain pages of text. The method of tipping-in plates is not to be tolerated in craft bookbinding, and where this method has been used the plates should be carefully detached, the strips of adhesive pared away, and the plates mounted on to suitable guards. These should be of best quality machine-made bank paper (if hand-made bank-note is not warranted), the guards cut with the grain of the paper running along the length. The weight of the guard paper used will depend upon the plate and the number to be inserted. When a stronger guard is needed, fine linen or jaconet can be used.

The quickest method of guarding is to remove all plates from the book, first making certain that there is a list of illustrations, or alternatively marking each lightly with a pencil on the back with the number of the facing page. Guards must be cut to the length of the book, the width being governed by the size of the plate and varying between $\frac{1}{2}$in and 1in. When the plates have been cleaned of their original adhesive they are laid out as shown in

18 *Plates fanned out for pasting before guarding*

illustration 18, face downwards. The amount projecting is approximately half the width of the guard to be used, and this is pasted evenly. A minimum of adhesive must be used, and this may be attained more effectively by the use of the finger in conjunction with the brush.

After pasting, the plates are slightly separated by fanning out, using the thumbnail, stroking the sheets lightly away from the pasted margin. The guards are laid over the pasted strips, covering the paste completely. The plates are then knocked up to the head and foredge, and allowed to dry under light pressure. Heavy pressure should not be used, or paste may be forced out from the guards and damage adjacent plates.

When dry the plates are inserted into the book, the guards being hooked round the fold of the section and sewn in with it. Where a plate falls in the centre of a section, the hook of the guard must be folded to the back so that it does not project on to the face side when sewn; the guard may be attached to the page of text facing the reverse side of the plate. This facilitates sewing and does no harm, provided the guard is not of heavy paper. The grain direction must, of course, run along the length of the guard.

Where many plates have to be included in the book, excessive swelling must be prevented by judicious paring of the plate when the original adhesive is removed, and by using thinner guards. If the plates are printed on heavy paper or thin card, and are inflexible, hingeing is necessary. This is done by cutting away a strip from the back margin, and guarding the plate with linen. The width of strip will depend upon the size of the plate. The hinge itself must be rather wider than the thickness of the stock upon which the plate is printed. If the hinge is too narrow it will not function properly; if too wide the plate will tend to sag. Where the size and weight of plates are exceptional a double strip hinge may be necessary. If fine jaconet is available, both sides of heavier plates should be lined.

These methods of guarding are shown in illustration 19.

19 *Four methods of guarding plates* .

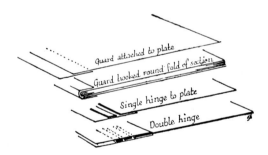

Guard attached to plate
Guard hooked round fold of section
Single hinge to plate
Double hinge

INLAYING PLATES

Occasionally additional illustrated matter has to be bound into the book. This is known as 'grangerising', after James Granger, an eighteenth-century author and print collector, a copy of whose *Biographical History of England* contained over 3,000 portraits. Fortunately it is rarely necessary for the binder to add plates in such profusion.

Additional illustrations are often unmounted and of varying sizes. Mounts must therefore be selected to harmonise with the book. When mounting illustrations printed on very thin paper, pasting must be as light as possible to reduce stretch to a minimum. This is best done by laying the print on to a piece of glass which has been pasted.

Illustrations on thicker paper must be mounted in the following way. Cut the illustration $\frac{1}{8}$in larger on all four edges than is required to show. Lay the illustration in position on the mount, and at the four corners, $\frac{1}{8}$in in, mark the mount with a minute pin-prick. Cut the centre of the mount away at these points, using a very sharp knife. With care, the underside of the mount and the upper side of the illustration can be pared away on all four edges for a distance of $\frac{1}{8}$in, special attention being given to the corners of the mount. Using the cut-out portion of the mount as a pasting template, paste the pared edges of the illustration with a minimum of cornflour paste, using the fingers rather than a brush. Lay the mount in position and rub down carefully through paper (20). An excess of paste is fatal to the success of this work.

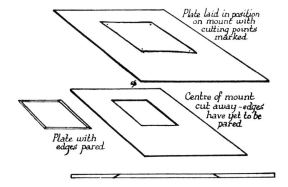

Plate laid in position on mount with cutting points marked

Centre of mount cut away - edges have yet to be pared

Plate with edges pared

20 *Inlaying a plate*

The outline of irregularly shaped illustrations may be marked through lightly on to the mount with a finely pointed folder, and the mount cut away $\frac{1}{8}$in within this outline. Thereafter the procedure is similar.

Maps and Diagrams

From many points of view it is better for maps and diagrams which are more than three times the size of the book page to be housed in a special pocket constructed on the inside of the back board (see under *Miscellaneous Items*, p. 325). However, this method is not always acceptable, and it may be necessary to guard them into the body of the book.

Maps and diagrams will often require repairing or strengthening, and this is best done by mounting them on jaconet, thin cambric or white linen. Tracing linen, as used by draughtsmen, if washed, lightly starched and ironed, makes an excellent substitute. If the map or diagram is printed on fairly thin paper, mounting is a straightforward job, but must be done with care. Because of the expansion of paper when pasted, and contraction when the paste dries, 'pull' must be offset by lightly damping the mounting material with a cloth or sponge and pinning it tightly out on a clean smooth surface. A bench covered with linoleum is excellent for this work.

21 *Map mounting*

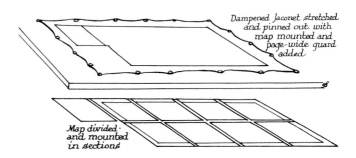

Dampened Jaconet stretched and pinned out with map mounted and page-wide guard added

Map divided and mounted in sections

The material must be cut larger than the map to allow for working and trimming (21).

The back of the map is pasted thoroughly with a paste of creamy consistency, care being taken to ensure that there are no lumps or 'holidays'—unpasted portions. For paste, a string-bound brush is preferable to a metal-ferruled one, as the latter tends to rust and can cause discoloration of the paste, as can copper-ferruled brushes. String-bound 'sash tools' as used by house decorators are splendid for paste but are rapidly being replaced and so are difficult to obtain.

The paper to be pasted is laid upon a sheet of waste paper that is considerably larger, to avoid paste getting on to the bench. Unless it is too large the paper is easier to paste if its length lies across the bench. It is held at the near end by the outspread fingers of the left hand. Taking a brushful of paste with the right hand, all the fingers being clasped firmly round the brush handle, proceed to brush firmly but not too vigorously, from the centre of the paper, distributing the paste evenly all round and going well beyond the edges to ensure complete coverage there. More paste will possibly have to be taken up from time to time. Experienced bookbinders develop the ability to twist the brush in the hand between strokes which assists in equal distribution of the paste. When the major part of the sheet has been covered transfer the left hand to the pasted portion and complete the pasting by brushing towards the body. It is important that the paste be quite evenly spread.

The longer side of the map is laid down first, the remainder being lowered carefully to prevent creasing and undue stretching of the paper. Assistance should be obtained for this operation when the work is large. The surface of the map is lightly rubbed over with the hands, and a rubber roller ('squeegee') is then used to ensure perfect adhesion with a minimum of expansion. When rubbing down it will be found helpful if the hands are rubbed lightly on the hair from time to time. This imparts to them a very slight amount of grease and acts as a lubricant. The work may be rubbed down through clean paper with a folder if difficulty is experienced in getting satisfactory adhesion. When a considerable amount of map-mounting has to be done the domestic rubber-rollered wringer can be used to great advantage, although the width is limited to about 15in.

A map folded once only, and measuring when folded $\frac{3}{8}$–$\frac{1}{2}$in less than the page width, may be attached at the fold to a strong guard, wide enough to allow the fold to be set well away from the back of the book. This will allow the map to open freely to be perfectly legible.

For ease of reference, folded maps inserted in the body of the book should be 'thrown out', ie, mounted to guards equal to the

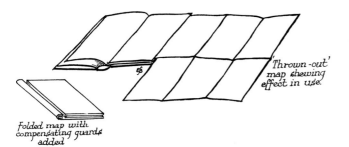

22 Map 'thrown out'

'Thrown-out' map shewing effect in use.

folded map with compensating guards added

full width of the page. This allows maps to be opened out clear of the book (22). The concertina fold is usually considered to be the most satisfactory, and is made as follows. The top of the opened map is placed level with the head of the book, and the lower portion folded up towards the head at a point allowing sufficient margin for the trimming of the book at the tail. If a second fold is necessary, the extra portion is folded down towards the tail, at a point which allows for edge-trimming at the head. The first vertical fold is made at the foredge in towards the back at a point which allows for foredge trimming. The second is made in the back, allowing room for the insertion of compensating guards of sufficient width to allow the free unfolding of the map when the book is bound. This amount may vary from $\frac{3}{8}$in to $\frac{3}{4}$in, according to the size of the book. These folds are repeated until the map is contained within the size of the book. Guards, equal in thickness to the folded map, and the full length of the book, are placed in the fold of the page-wide guard to which the map is attached, and the whole is sewn as a section.

This method is the usual one employed, but as the map unfolds towards the reader the book must be held further away if it is to be read while the book is open. The alternative method is to fold the map from the head of the book. This makes edge-gilding difficult and spoils the appearance of the book, but effectively prevents dust getting into the map.

A heavy map, when mounted in one piece, will tend with use to become illegible at the folds. To avoid this the map may be cut into divisions slightly shorter than the trimmed depth, and $\frac{1}{2}$–$\frac{3}{4}$in narrower than the page width. These divisions are mounted, leaving space for folding between the portions. If folds other than the concertina are used, extra width must be allowed where folds become bulky.

ENDPAPER MAPS

These should be removed and mounted to be incorporated into the book proper at the end. If, as is not unusual, they are repeated at front and back, it will be sufficient to join both fly-sheets carefully together, matching the leaves for exact continuity of the map (or diagram). Should the maps be different it will be necessary to soak off the board papers, first removing all bookcloth on the board and inside border to avoid the possibility of the dye staining the paper. On no account should such maps or diagrams be used again as end-papers.

Single Leaves

The problem of binding books consisting of single leaves has not yet been solved satisfactorily. In the second half of the nineteenth century a method known as 'caoutchouc' (which is French for rubber) was introduced with the object of eliminating sewing and at the same time giving greater flexibility. It seemed that both aims had been achieved, for the rubber solution, together with the canvas used for reinforcing the spine, held the leaves together and was extremely flexible. The economic advantages of this method resulted in a spate of plate-laden books bound by 'unsewn' binding. Unfortunately the rubber perished after a comparatively short period and many lavishly produced books disintegrated!

Attempts to eliminate sewing from bookbinding have been made from time to time without any great success, although the enormous output of 'paperbacks', nearly all of which are unsewn, might seem to disprove this. The use of vinyl acetates and improved methods of production have greatly improved unsewn binding, but books must stand the test of time before the success or failure of these methods can be judged. It is certainly too early for unsewn methods to receive the serious consideration of craft binders.

Sometimes it may be found that the condition of a book to be rebound does not lend itself to the normal method of guarding. In such cases it may be simpler and better to reduce the sections to single leaves by cutting away the backs. Before deciding on this course of action, the width of the back margins, the suitability of the paper, and the grain direction must all be considered. The grain direction of machine-made papers must run from head to tail if the book is to open satisfactorily. It must be remembered, however, that under the most favourable conditions single leaves bound by the oversewn method will never open really flat.

If plates are included in the book it is necessary to crease them along the back, $\frac{3}{16}$–$\frac{1}{2}$in from the edge according to the size of the book and the width of the back margin. If plates are printed on paper too thick to be folded in use, they must be hinged.

When the book has been prepared for oversewing it is knocked up squarely at the head and back and placed in a lying press or on the bench with waste boards back and front. The back is thinly glued, either all over or for a short distance at the head and tail. This holds the leaves together until they are oversewn, and for this reason the latter method of glueing is to be preferred, as there is less chance of thread fracture, and the final glueing-up will be more satisfactory. If the book is ultimately to be sewn on recessed cords the saw kerfs must be made at this stage. When dry the book is divided into sections of a thickness suitable for the paper and the size of the book.

To ensure that leaves open uniformly and as far back as possible, further preparation is desirable before oversewing. Place each 'section' in turn on a piece of thick strawboard, foredge to the front. Lay over the section a piece of thin millboard, level with the head and parallel to the back, at a distance from the edge equal to the amount of oversewing required. On the millboard mark the position of kettle-stitches at head and tail, and make a series of sewing

23 *Making sewing holes for oversewing single leaves as a section*

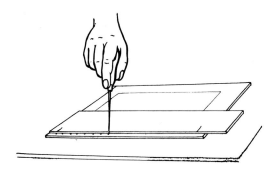

holes with a fine awl, commencing and finishing at the positions of the kettle-stitches (23). Sewing holes should not be much more than $\frac{1}{4}$in apart, or $\frac{3}{8}$in on larger volumes, and from $\frac{1}{8}$in to $\frac{1}{4}$in from the back edge according to the size of the book and the type of paper. When all sections have been prepared, they are oversewn in turn. Each section is laid on a bench slightly overlapping the edge, and sewn with thin thread, nos 50 to 35 (24). A knot is made at the end of the thread, and sewing commences by passing the needle and thread through the first hole until the knot is embedded. The

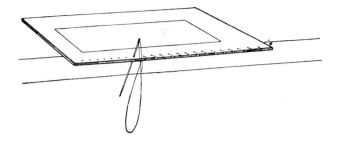

needle is passed through the same hole again and the thread is drawn tight. Thereafter the back is oversewn, drawing the thread tight at the second or third holes only. A double stitch is made at the last hole, passing the needle through the loop of the first stitch to secure the sewing. When all sections have been oversewn separately the stitches are embedded in the paper by carefully tapping with a hammer on a paper-covered knocking-down iron.

The sections are now ready for book sewing by any 'hollow-back' method—flexible sewing on raised cords is unsuitable for oversewn sections. Kettle-stitches should be made just beyond the commencing and finishing points of the oversewing. Confusion is often caused by the use of the terms 'whipstitching' and 'overcasting' referring to oversewing. They are not synonymous, as reference to any textbook on needlework will show.

The industrial sewing-machine can be used for sewing single leaves into sections. It is difficult, however, to begin and finish sewing at uniform distances from the head and tail of each section, and the threads must be tied off at each end by hand. If the sections are sewn from end to end, the threads will be cut when the book edges are trimmed, thus weakening the sewing. The longest stitch made by the normal domestic sewing-machine is of insufficient length for sewing sections; its use will result in near-perforation of the paper and a consequent weakening of the binding.

The older method of oversewing as the book is being sewn is more difficult for the inexperienced. It has the advantage of being quicker, and as the thread used for oversewing is also that used for the actual sewing, it does not have the disadvantage of the separately oversewn sections where the sewing thread must needs lie some distance from the back inside the section, causing some swelling at that point. On the other hand, the thread used is rather

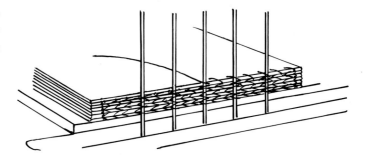

heavy for oversewing. Its best use is for the larger, heavier book (25).

Unsewn binding is dealt with in Chapter 6, *Miscellaneous Items*.

Endpapers

Key to endpaper diagrams: A *Waste sheet*; B *Board paper*; C *Joint*; D '*Made*' *fly-leaf*; E *White fly-leaf*; S *Sewing point*.

Between a single fold of paper which comprises the simplest form of endpaper and the involved type that may include a leather joint with silk fly-leaves and doublure, there are a surprising number of varieties.

Endpapers probably originated in improvements on the primitive method of binding manuscripts. When these were sewn on thongs, attached to boards covered with leather, the resulting book was satisfactory in use; but its appearance when the covers were opened, showing the thongs and board edges, was unattractive. If plain leaves were sewn at the beginning and end of the book, and the outside leaf was pasted to the board, the joints were both stronger and neater. If a quarto fold was used an additional fly-leaf was provided, and also an outer leaf that served as a protection to the board leaf during the forwarding processes. The one disadvantage was that the sewing actually took place in the joint with the result that the spine adhesive found its way through the needle-holes, causing disfigurement.

This method has so much to commend it that the late Thomas Harrison, the eminent bookbinder, by adapting it and improving it, produced the 'Cresset' endpaper which will be dealt with later.

Endpapers, being part of the binding, as distinct from the book, should be considered in relation to the colour scheme of the binding. The use of plain white endpapers, no matter how good in quality, is desirable only in exceptional cases as their whiteness will not enhance the beauty of the cover colour as a carefully chosen tint will. Coloured ends can also tie up a colour scheme into which book-edge treatment enters. It is not suggested that colour should be used indiscriminately or that any one shade should be used for all bindings—even though the incomparable Roger Payne exercised his penchant for puce-coloured ends in so many of his bindings! The choice of paper is important: it should be firm and strong but flexible. Where machine-made paper is used, it is vital that the grain should run from head to tail. This ensures greatest flexibility at the joint and eliminates the possibility of the board warping there.

'TIPPED' ENDPAPERS (26–1)

In their simplest form endpapers consist of single folds of suitable paper which are 'tipped' to the first and last sections at the beginning and end of the book. Where feasible, the strip of adhesive should not greatly exceed the width of the backing, while it is important that the fold, which will form the joint, is placed level with that of the section to which it is attached. There is no margin for error here; let it be short of the back and the endpaper will split at the joint when the cover is opened; let it project beyond the back, and if it does not break during the backing process, creases in the joint must result, or, even worse, the backing will consist of a folded end-paper only! Where a number of single-fold endpapers are to be pasted they are fanned out as when dealing with plate guarding. Paste should be of medium consistency; on no account must it be allowed to seep underneath, causing wider and uneven paste margins.

This method, if it gives any strength to the joint at all, does so at the expense of the book, as it is inevitable that a strain is thrown upon the first and last leaves. With publishers' binding in which this form of endpaper is applied, too often it will be found that, after use, the first and last leaves have become detached from the book, although still adhering to the endpapers. Where the paper of the book is inferior to the endpapers—and this is almost invariably the case—this can be avoided only by reinforcing the outer folds of

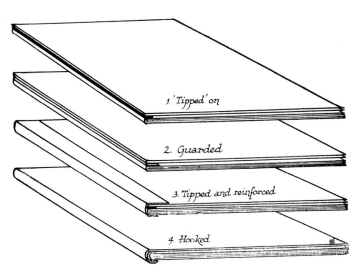

26 Four types of single-fold endpaper

1. 'Tipped' on

2. Guarded

3. Tipped and reinforced

4. Hooked

the first and last sections. With India-paper editions it is usual to machine together all the leaves forming the outer half of these sections at a point slightly away from the fold. This provides the necessary resistance to the 'pull' of the tipped-on endpaper.

GUARDED ENDPAPERS (26–2)

A better method of attaching the single-fold endpaper is by the use of a guard of tough bank paper or fine linen. This allows greater freedom in opening and largely removes any strain from the section.

'TIPPED' AND REINFORCED ENDPAPERS (26–3)

With heavier work the fold may be 'tipped' or guarded in position before sewing and a linen guard about $\frac{3}{4}$–1in wide pasted round both with but $\frac{1}{8}$in of it on the inner side of the section. This reinforcement is sewn with the book but it is important that it adheres firmly, especially to the endpapers, as any looseness will manifest itself in the joint after the book is completed.

HOOKED ENDPAPERS (26–4)

A single folded endpaper may also be hooked round the section and sewn with it. This eliminates tipping with paste and consequent strain on the section. While the endpaper is very secure, the hooking results in a double fold of paper between the first and last two sections. This does not matter if the paper is not unduly thick and the hook does not greatly exceed the width of the backing.

Usually, with the single-fold endpaper—which should generally be confined to cased work—a shade of paper not dissimilar to that of the book is used. A coloured paper, such as a suitable cover paper, may, however, add to the attractiveness of the bound volume. With coloured endpapers it is customary to line the fly-leaf with white paper which, in addition to making it firmer, gives the endpapers the appearance of being part of the book proper rather than of the binding. Whether this is necessary or desirable is a matter of personal opinion, but there is certainly no functional reason why endpapers should not be coloured in their entirety. Probably the introduction of Cobb's endpaper, which was much used during the last century for less-expensive bindings, and which was usually light in quality and too often dark in colour, caused the custom of lining to become firmly established.

'MADE' ENDPAPERS (27–1)

The 'made' endpaper, as it is known, requires a minimum of materials and labour, and it is simple in construction. The method of making consists of pasting the outside page of a fold of white paper and mounting a fold of coloured paper to it. It is important that the two folded edges meet exactly. After a light rub with the hands and a quick 'nip' between boards in the press the endpapers are allowed to dry either by hanging on a line or under very light pressure. The pasting of the white lining paper rather than the

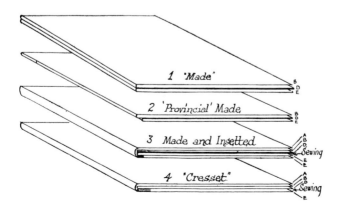

1 'Made'

2 'Provincial' Made

3 Made and Insetted

4 'Cresset'

27 *Four types of*
'made' endpaper
(*see key to letters*
on p. 62)

coloured causes any 'pull' that might result to be towards the book, preventing the unsightly appearance of a fly-leaf that curls away from it. Made ends are 'tipped' to the book in the same way as single-fold ends, and are merely a refinement giving an additional fly-leaf. While less strain is imposed upon the first and last leaves of the book, strain is partly transferred to the fold of the white lining.

'PROVINCIAL' MADE ENDPAPERS (27–2)

The 'Provincial' made endpaper is an alternative method of making, the only difference being that the white lining is set away from the fold of the coloured end by a distance approximately equal to the height of the backing, ie $\frac{1}{8}-\frac{1}{4}$in according to the thickness of the boards to be used for the cover. This allows the coloured fold to be tipped directly to the book and so puts less strain on the fold of white paper. The fact that the fly-leaf no longer opens right to the back is largely offset by the backing.

'MADE AND INSETTED' ENDPAPERS (27–3)

The 'made and insetted' endpaper, although using extra paper, is an improvement on both these styles because it has the advantage of being sewn on with the book and provides an outside 'waste' sheet which serves to protect the endpapers during forwarding. As its name implies, it consists of a made end tipped into a fold of white paper, the sewing taking place in the fold immediately behind the first fly-leaf.

Where a quantity is being made it is quicker to paste the folded white leaves in bulk (as with plates) and mount them accurately to the white leaves of the 'made' endpaper, stacking them and leaving them to dry under a weight. The outer white leaf can now be quickly and tightly folded back over the coloured board paper to form the waste, protective leaf. This should be clearly marked to prevent the complete endpaper being sewn the wrong way round, which is disastrous if unnoticed.

'CRESSET' ENDPAPERS (27–4)

The 'Cresset' endpaper, the modern improved version of the original quarto-fold sewn front and back of the medieval bindings, is typical in its simplicity and effectiveness of the improvements in book construction given to us by Thomas Harrison. It consists of a

quarto fold of paper the last two leaves of which have been reinforced with a narrow strip of linen. This is done simply by cutting
the 'bolt' connecting them at the head, opening the leaves flat and
fixing the pasted linen at the fold. The endpaper is sewn through this
to the book in the normal course of sewing. Nothing could be more
simple or effective, providing, as it does, a waste protective sheet
and two fly-leaves with the sewing behind the joint and not through
it as happened in our forefathers' time.

Its one disadvantage is that it is limited to white paper because of
the linen reinforcement which, being almost inevitably white,
would contrast unpleasantly against coloured papers.

ZIG–ZAG ENDPAPERS

The boards of a bound book should open perfectly flat without
strain upon the endpaper at the joint. In theory this is reasonably
simple if care is taken, but because with pasting paper the fibres
expand, contracting again later, it is not so simple of accomplish-
ment. The zig-zag or concertina fold endpaper was invented to
provide for this technical dilemma and while not very popular with
the trade binder, who considers it fussy and uneconomical, has
something to commend it. As with other operations in bookbinding,
description is a poor substitute for demonstration and what appears
involved is not actually so. Each endpaper requires three folds of
paper slightly larger than the book size. One of them may be
decorative, while one of the others, when folded, must be $\frac{1}{4}-\frac{3}{8}$in
wider than the book. The quickest method of making is as follows.

The decorative fold is tipped into the wider fold of white paper,
the margin of paste varying from $\frac{1}{8}$in to $\frac{3}{8}$in according to the size of
the book (28–1). When dry the endpaper is turned over and what
was the lower sheet is folded back level with the edge of the pasted
portion (28–2). It is now folded back on to itself, level with the fold
of the endpaper which produces the zig-zag (28–3). Into this is
inserted the remaining fold of white and it is through this fold that
the sewing takes place (28–4). The single white sheet on the opposite
side of the colour fold is the protective waste sheet which is ultimately removed. It is a wise precaution to mark this to ensure that
it is on the outside when the endpaper is sewn with the book. As
will be seen, the actual end sheets are now mounted to the zig-zag
which is between them and the sewing and so allows considerably

*28 Making a
zig-zag endpaper*

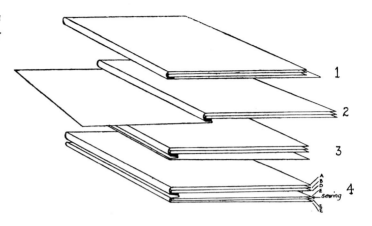

more freedom in the joint when the book is opened—provided
precautions are taken when glueing-up the back.

If it is necessary to line the fly-leaf, this can be done beforehand,
or the fly-leaf may be mounted on to the wider white fold (as with
the 'made' end) and a zig-zag made afterwards, in which case there
will be no waste sheet unless one is added. This may be done by
tipping one into the zig-zag, and it has the added advantage of
preventing glue entering there during glueing-up (29).

*29 Zig-zag
endpapers—an
alternative
method*

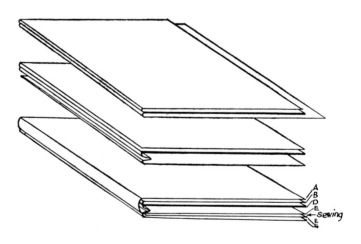

Description of the zig-zag, or concertina fold, endpaper would be
incomplete without reference to the ingenious form suggested by
Thomas Harrison (30). Where the coloured fly-leaf needs to be

30 *Zig-zag
endpapers—the
Harrison method*

lined this is done by pasting the upper page of the white fold, but
before mounting the waste sheet is laid down so that its edge overlaps the fold of the pasted sheet by a distance equal to the width of
the zig-zag. The coloured fold is now laid down with the fold
exactly level with that of the white. After a light rubbing and a
quick press the endpaper is left to dry. The waste sheet is then
folded back over the coloured. An additional white fold inserted in
the original one permits the endpaper to be sewn with the book;
alternatively, it may be 'tipped' in position with paste. The ingenuity of the method, together with the saving of time, commends
it, but whether it is better for the zig-zag fold to open away from
the fly-leaf instead of with it, as with the other method, is a matter
for individual judgement.

LEATHER-JOINTED ENDPAPERS (31)

Although the merits of the zig-zag fold may be disputed as regards
easing the opening at the joint, none will deny its usefulness in
connection with leather-jointed endpapers. Here its purpose is not
one of easement but rather of concealment. The use of good-quality
paper is important, as the zig-zag may have the edges of the leather
joint and coloured fly-leaf tipped on to its upper side and the waste
sheet on the lower. If the white fold is opened out fully and its
upper side pasted out to the centre of the zig-zag, the coloured sheet
may be completely mounted on it and into the zig-zag at one time.

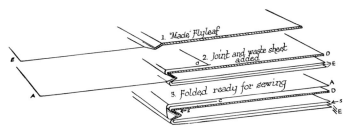

31 *Leather-jointed
endpaper*

When dry, the sheet is re-folded round the zig-zag as before. The leather joint, pared to its exact thickness ('thinness' might be a better word), is now tipped into the zig-zag fold on to the turn-in of the mounted coloured sheet. On the lower side of the zig-zag the waste sheet is tipped; when dry it is folded over the leather joint and the 'made' fly-leaf. An additional fold of white paper is inserted into the single fold of white, the sewing taking place both through this and through the other fold of the zig-zag, so that all papers and the leather joints are sewn with the book. With small books a leather joint can be incorporated in place of the cloth in a cloth-jointed endpaper (described later), but in this case it will not be sewn through, the sewing taking place *behind* the fly-leaf behind which has been inserted an extra fold of paper. As the board paper will not be added at this juncture, a sheet of paper should be placed over the fly-leaf and under the leather joint to keep the former clean and the latter from being impressed into it.

To prevent the fly-leaf becoming marked by the leather during subsequent operations, a sheet of stout cartridge or thin manilla card should be inserted between them, remaining there until the binding is completed. It is very important that the leather joint be pared to a thickness uniform with that of the turn-ins of the covering leather.

More frequently, leather joints are added after the book is covered, in which case the coloured fly-leaf is mounted afterwards, the edges slightly overlapping those of the leather joint. In such cases the purpose of the joint is one of elegance only and the method should be confined to smaller and lighter volumes.

SILK ENDPAPERS

Silk is not the best choice for endpapers, and unless used with leather joints it should be confined to books with all edges gilt. The gilding of the cut edges helps to seal them and prevents the fraying which is otherwise bound to take place.

Before mounting, the material must be dampened and ironed on the reverse side to give a firm surface devoid of creases. Using a thin glue or PVA, the paper surface is lightly and evenly glued out; the silk is carefully laid on to it and rubbed down through paper. Alternatively, the material may be firmly pinned out face downwards on a board and the glued paper mounted to it. If there is an excess of glue and it is too thin it will penetrate the silk, leaving an ugly stain. There must be absolute adhesion over the whole surface if the endpapers are to endure: any looseness in the joint will be fatal. Another method is to paste the material, which has been cut an inch longer each way than the mounting paper, with a starch paste, mounting it to the lining on a clean board. Assistance will be required to effect this evenly and without creases. After rubbing down through paper, the board may be stood to edge, the overlap of pasted material holding the endpaper to the board until dry. When mounting any fabric it is wise to have the warping threads running in the opposite direction to the paper grain.

'DRUMMED' SILK ENDPAPERS

Where a leather joint is used, the silk is usually 'drummed' to paper to form pads, which are then glued in position on the fly-leaf and board, slightly overlapping the leather joint which has been fitted after the book has been covered.

When sewing such a book, in addition to the white folds, which are sewn as endleaves, single folds of paper are loosely inserted and remain in position during the forwarding processes. By removing and taking a fractional trim off the edges to allow for the turning over of the silk, pads may be made from them which will exactly fit the book even though there be some slight inaccuracy in the cutting of it. When making up, the edges of the paper are glued to a distance equal to the turn-in of the silk. This is laid centrally on to the material, the edges of which are neatly and firmly turned over on to the glued margin, the fabric having been pulled quite taut. Particular care will have to be exercised at the corners if they are to be both neat and secure from fraying. A piece of strawboard cut to the size of the unglued portion of the cartridge paper and laid in position there will do much to prevent movement of the silk when working. It is also advisable to work on a board which may be turned round without causing movement of the work and so facilitates the turning-in of the silk.

VELLUM ENDPAPERS

Vellum may be used for ends but its 'mulish' behaviour makes doubtful the wisdom of its choice. Owing to its limited flexibility, it should be used with a zig-zag fold and a leather joint inserted and sewn. Unless the book in which it is used is large it is better to make the zig-zag of Japanese vellum into which the vellum fly-leaf, its long edge well scraped and pared, is stuck. The semi-transparency of vellum makes it desirable to line it with paper, which also helps to control its almost unpredictable behaviour. If paste is used for this, the paper must be expanded by damping to offset 'pull'. A thin glue, well whipped, provides a good adhesive which reduces 'pull' to a minimum but is not as flexible as paste. Alternatively PVA may be used. After mounting, both sides should be well rubbed down through paper with a folder and the vellum left to dry between clean boards under medium pressure.

With the advent of polyvinyl acetate the binder has an adhesive which not only reduces 'stretch' but is white and remains flexible, and which, mixed to a suitable consistency, is ideal for this type of work.

CLOTH-JOINTED ENDPAPERS (32)

Where utility is the keynote, a strong, sewn-in, cloth-jointed endpaper provides maximum strength in the joint. The best-known is that used in account bookbinding, which has little pretension to beauty but does a really good job of work. When adapted to letterpress binding it performs equally good service where strength is of prime importance, as in the case of heavy reference volumes bound in quarter- or half-leather.

Strips of cloth are cut $\frac{3}{4}$–$1\frac{1}{2}$in wide, according to the size of the book and nature of the binding. Each endpaper will require a cloth strip, a fold of white paper, one of fair quality waste and two single coloured sheets, all equal to or slightly larger than the book area. The cloth strip is lightly glued on the back and laid lengthwise on

32 *Cloth-jointed endpaper*

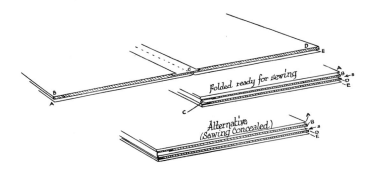

the bench, and the folded edge of the waste sheet is laid down on it, covering two-thirds of the width. On the remaining one-third is laid the fold of white, almost touching that of the waste; both are lightly rubbed with the hands. The endpaper is now turned over and accurately folded, with the cloth on the inside. The coloured leaves are now pasted out (or a mixture of glue and paste can be used) and the waste and white leaves are lined with them, their long edges slightly overlapping the edge of the cloth joint. After they have been firmly rubbed down they may be given a light but quick 'nip' in the press and hung on lines to dry. If they are to have a neat appearance, the width of the cloth joint must be nicely gauged. This is determined by the backing height, which it must slightly exceed on the fly-leaf side. Although it is not possible to generalise, the margin of cloth showing on the paste-down side needs to be approximately twice this width. The sewing takes place through the cloth joint.

To conceal the sewing, the cloth joint may be inserted into a zig-zag fold as with leather joints, but it is seldom that the work on which it is used justifies the trouble entailed by this method. Where tinted ends are used, the edge of the joint may be inserted between the two papers forming the fly-leaf in a 'made' endpaper. In this case the cloth joint will appear on the board side only, the sewing taking place in the fold of tinted paper and so making two coloured fly-leaves. The simplest method of construction is to make in the usual manner, substituting a fold of tinted paper for the single sheet on the 'made' fly-leaf and laying right up to the fold of the cloth joint.

RETURNED CLOTH JOINTS (33)

A 'returned' cloth joint is made by machine-sewing the fly-leaves and the cloth joint to the outside half of the first and last sections. These have their edges flush with the fold of the section, the face side of the cloth being towards the section. This is then 'returned' from the sewing point to the back edge of the section, where it is glued and finally folded back over the section. This method is best used with heavy books printed on thin paper, when the machine sewing of the outside half of the first and last sections is desirable. Even greater strength results if a linen strip is incorporated, which may be hooked round the next section and sewn with it.

33 *Returned*
cloth joint

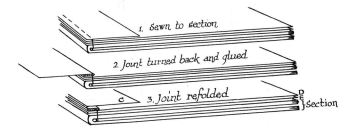

1. Sewn to section

2. Joint turned back and glued

3. Joint refolded

} Section

Other methods or variations in the making of endpapers are
possible but, whatever the method used, a nice balance between the
book and its binding must be maintained. In all but simple cased
work, a waste sheet should be incorporated in the endpapers. This
effectively protects the end sheets during forwarding and provides a
casing for the making of flanges in split-board bindings.

Sewing

If it is decided to trim the book edges before sewing the book, this
should now be done. Purist collectors disapprove of even the trimming of book edges, but it may be desirable to remove worn or
very uneven ones for the benefit of the book. It is most important
that only the minimum amount of paper be cut away to achieve
this. Trimming may be done by knife and straightedge, using a
template to ensure uniformity, or a bench knife may be used, each
section being cut separately. The gauge should be set so that the
shortest leaves are left uncut, and the tail cuts are dealt with first
followed by the foredge cuts. The head should not be trimmed before sewing. Even if the guillotine is used for the purpose, the whole
book being cut at one time, many consider the final effect preferable
to the clean-cut edge resulting from cutting being done after the
book has been sewn and the back glued. Whichever method is used,
it is in the interest of the book that the head be cut later so that it
can be either gilded or coloured and burnished and so prevent dust
and dirt penetrating the book. Even where deckled edges of hand-
made paper have to be left, it is a matter of common sense to
lightly trim any badly projecting edges to avoid soiling by dust.

The purpose of book sewing is to connect the leaves in such a way
that they will be firm and yet open easily when bound, and also to
provide the best means of attaching the book to its cover. In

choosing the most suitable method of sewing a particular book, the binder must consider the style of the binding as determined by the nature of the book, the quality of the paper, the make-up of the sections, the kind of use the book will receive, and the amount to be spent on the work.

The craft binder is tempted to keep to traditional methods, even when they are no longer suitable. When today's materials, for instance book papers, are different from or inferior to yesterday's, then yesterday's techniques must be modified in the light of the binder's experience and judgement.

Briefly, the various sewing methods are as follows.

'FLEXIBLE' SEWING ON CORDS (34)

This is the traditional method of book sewing, hempen cords having replaced the leathern thongs originally used.

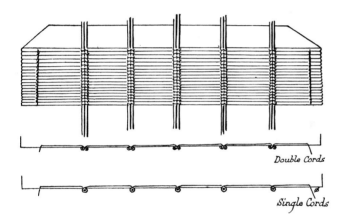

34 *'Flexible' sewing on cords*

Double Cords

Single Cords

Except by comparison with a 'fixed back' binding where the spine is glued and lined to an extent that makes it solid and quite inflexible, the term 'flexible back' is a misnomer and had far better be replaced with the expression 'tight back'.

There is no doubt that if sewing only is being considered there is no method to compare, especially when double cords are used. Not only does the thread extend the complete length on the inside fold of the section, but by encircling every cord, which in turn is tightly covered by the spine leather, it is virtually locked at every stitch.

This fixing of the leather tightly to the spine has certain disadvantages that offset the strength given by it. One is that when the book is opened the spine leather must crease to the detriment of any gold tooling on it. Another is that when rebacking becomes necessary—as it must at some time—the removal of the spine covering may easily result in damage to the sewing. Where the preservation of the original spine is important, repairs may even have to be limited to the insertion of new hinges only.

The method does not in any case lend itself to books printed on coarse or heavy paper, or where the sections are thick. If used on small or light volumes the hempen cord—and consequently the bands—must be proportionately thinner, or flexibility will be reduced or almost eliminated.

RECESSED OR 'SAWN-IN' CORDS (35)

This method is attributed to Nicholas Derome who is said to have introduced it so that his bindings might have 'hollow' backs in order that the tooling on the spines might not be damaged by the opening of the books. It has, in the past, received more criticism than it fairly deserves. If used with discretion and executed carefully it has a good deal to commend it, especially with books composed of poorer-quality paper. It is unfortunate that it lends itself to scamped workmanship and deception; that is not the fault of the method but of the binder.

35 Sewing on recessed or 'sawn-in' cords

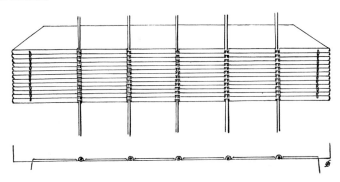

Because the thread merely passes over the cords and does not encircle them as with the previous method, sewing cannot be as strong, but it can often be quite suitable and adequate. Recessed cords should not be used in books which demand sewing on thick cords, as the saw 'kerf' or cut has to be of such a depth that near-mutilation of the paper at the back results.

The addition of false bands to the hollow lining has led to the practice of sewing on too few cords. The addition of false bands on the spine which exceed in number the cords to which the book is sewn and by which the boards are attached is a form of deception which amounts to dishonesty and cannot be tolerated.

TAPE SEWING (36)

Because it gives a back that is nearly level and also provides great flexibility, the use of tapes in book sewing has rapidly overtaken that of cords. Provided tapes of a width proportionate to the size of the volume, or, better still, a greater number of narrower ones, are used, the method is very satisfactory. Any reduction in strength that may be occasioned by the loss of thread in the centre fold of sections, where it passes round the tapes on the outside, is balanced by the flexibility of the sewing. The use of narrower tapes reduces the possibility of looseness at these points. Linen tapes should be used in preference to cotton, which should be reserved for cheap casings.

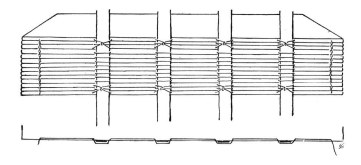

36 Sewing on tapes

The use of tapes has in the past required a method of attaching boards alternative to that of lacing usually used with cords. Because of this, until the introduction of the 'supported French groove', tape-sewn books could not receive the same support in the joint as bindings with laced boards. Whereas with laced boards the back edge fits snugly into the shoulder formed by the backing, those of the tape-sewn volume cannot because the tapes must pass between the two for at least half the board thickness. An additional space is required to make the 'French joint' and so there cannot be the same 'snugness' and firmness. The use of a laminated board, the lower portion of which fits tightly into the joint, largely offsets this drawback. When it is remembered that the fibres of the covering material are no longer folded back at right angles but roll gently in a semi-circle, even without the supported French groove one loss is balanced by this considerable gain. With it, there is a quite substantial improvement in technique.

FRENCH SEWING (37)

Neither cord nor tape is used with this method, the sections being sewn together by thread only. It should be used only with small and light bindings where the thinness of the cover boards does not permit normal methods of attachment. Its main purpose should be to produce a light and neat-looking binding with no pretence of great strength.

37 French sewing

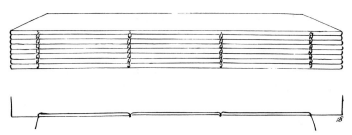

SEWING MATERIALS AND EQUIPMENT

The purpose of sewing books by hand is to provide the greatest possible strength, so it is common sense that only good-quality materials should be used.

Thread As the fibre in ordinary cotton is only about an inch in length whereas that of flax may be many inches—even up to a foot—linen thread only should be used, and as bleaching tends to destroy wearing qualities it should be unbleached. Its thickness, and therefore strength, is classified by the gauge of the cords used in making, together with their number. Linen thread is usually stocked as fine as no 50/2 cord and up to no 12/3 cord, which is very thick. As a general practice no 16 in either 3, 4 or 5 cord is used for very heavy work. A 2 cord thread is seldom as strong as a 3 cord of the same thickness; because of this it is better to use a higher-gauge 3 cord when thinner thread is required. Generally, about four or five thicknesses will cover every requirement, nos 36, 25, 20 and 16/3 cord with a 16/4 cord for very heavy work providing sufficient variation of thicknesses and strength for practically all work. Thread is sold by the pound in skeins or cops. Most craft binders prefer the skeins, which, after untying and cutting, give convenient lengths and may be looped round the uprights of the sewing frame. Unless it is being used continuously, it is convenient if each skein is very loosely plaited. This prevents intermixing and tangling of the various thicknesses. It in no way interferes with the removal of single lengths which are taken at the loop, not at the ends. The waxing of thread by drawing it over a piece of beeswax reduces friction as it passes through the paper, and by making it damp-resistant lengthens its life.

Needles Needles for book-sewing need to be strong, with open eyes that will not cut into the thread and will yet allow it to pass freely through the hole made by the needle. Firms such as Messrs Abel Morrel and Messrs Kirby make needles especially for book-binders, and nos 20 (for finer work) to 16 will be found to cover most requirements. Where there is a tendency for them to rust they may be kept in asbestos powder which may also be used on the fingers of those book sewers whose hands tend to be damp. If rusted they can be cleaned by rubbing between very fine emery paper, and the age-old method of rubbing them on the floor with the sole of the shoe is still used.

Hemp cord Hemp cord used in bookbinding falls into two main categories, each of which can be obtained in numerous thicknesses. They are 'seaming' and 'netting' twine and each is obtainable in two finishes, 'soft' and 'laid', the latter being firmer in texture. Thickness is known by the number of cords twisted together to make the twine but is not similar in each. Hemp seaming twine is made in varying thicknesses from 3 cord to 8 cord and is very much finer than hemp netting twine which is usually stocked in no $2\frac{1}{2}$/3 to 10 cord. A 'soft' finish is usual for recessed cords while a 'laid' makes up well for banded work. It is difficult to convey cord thicknesses by measurement, but as near as this is possible no $2\frac{1}{2}$/3 cord 'laid' netting twine is about 2mm in diameter, 5 cord about 2·5mm and 10 cord 3·5mm, the 'soft' finish being slightly less. 'Soft' seaming twine 3 cord approximates to 1mm and 6 cord to 1·5mm.

As these twines were not originally designed for use in the book-binding trade it is necessary to be conversant with them to order correctly. Tape and webbing used in book sewing (the latter usually confined to very heavy work such as ledgers) is slightly stiffened and is obtainable in widths from $\frac{1}{4}$in to 1in made either of cotton or linen. It should always be selvedged and not have cut edges, the latter being very much weaker. Soft or unstiffened tape tends to crease when it is pulled through the sewing when the book is cut down from the sewing frame; if stiffened overmuch, it becomes harsh and much of its flexibility and strength are lost.

THE SEWING FRAME

The sewing frame, or press as it is often called, has changed little over the centuries. Consisting of a battened base with a slot cut about an inch from the front edge for most of its length, it has two uprights on which a screw thread has been turned. Across these is a bar adjustable by wooden nuts upon which it rests. Sometimes this is fashioned in a slightly barrelled shape which results in uneven tension when the tapes or cords fitted to it have to be moved. A new-style single-pillar sewing frame invented by Philip Smith is now available.

The difficulty and annoyance of having to sit with the left arm round an upright, or between it and the book being sewn, is removed by the frame being completely open at that point. Whether it is as rigid as its predecessor is something upon which a personal pronouncement cannot be made; but the idea is good (see also p. 86).

Sewing cords or tapes are held firmly in position by the use of special 'keys'. These are flat pieces of metal formerly of brass but now often of duralumin. Those for use with cord are forked—not unlike miniature tuning forks—while those for tape resemble a sans-serif H but with two crossbars.

Because of the variety of cord thickness as compared with width of tapes, and because with raised-banded work it is not possible to draw them through the sewing, cords are attached as required to loops of string or cord called lay cords which remain on the crossbar of the frame. They permit the use of shorter lengths of cord and yet allow the crossbar to be sufficiently high for convenient working. With tape sewing it is usual to cut fairly long lengths—maybe two yards each—sewing them loosely round the bar so that they may be adjusted as required. To eliminate wastage of tape and time, a special frame with fitments to hold complete spools of tape on the crossbar was produced. The fitments could be moved sideways and the tape clipped to prevent slipping. Although these seem to be no longer available, some bookbinders have improvised along these lines.

By threading the keys on the tape beforehand and working alternately from crossbar to key and key to crossbar, it is possible to set up any number of tapes using one length only. It is debatable whether the saving of tape effected is not more than offset by the time taken to set and reset tapes by this method.

Setting up the sewing frame For sewing on cords the crossbar is adjusted so that the distance between the lay cords and the base of the frame is equal to the thickness of the book plus two inches and the thickness of a pressing board which will be placed between book and sewing frame. The use of a sewing board simplifies the sewing of the first few sections.

The first cord is attached to the lay cord as shown in illustration 38 and is drawn firmly downwards to the base. Here it is brought

38 *Attaching the cord to the lay cord*

round the neck of the sewing key which is held with the forks resting under the base board (39–1). The cord is wrapped round the key (39–2) which is now turned over, allowing the cord to come between the forks (39–3). By holding the key upright with the cord held with it, it may be inserted through the slot and turned sideways underneath, thus holding the cord firmly and yet permitting adjustment sideways (39–4).

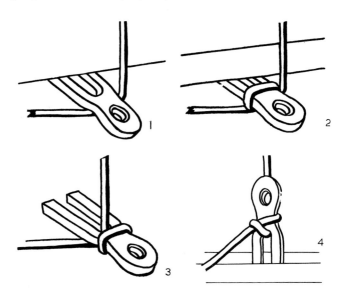

To obtain the correct tension the key may have to be held at a slight angle—up or down—according to the distance of the slot from the edge of the base board. Once this is known all the cords can be given uniform tension, which is important. The cord is not cut from the ball until the key is set, when it may be done quite close to the frame.

With tapes the method is very similar except that all the tapes are cut and attached to the crossbar beforehand. To set them the tape is passed between the two crossbars of the tape key (40–1) and the key is turned over *in a forward direction* which secures the tape in it

40 *Use of key when sewing on tapes*

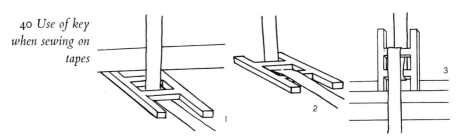

(40–2). By turning it away from the binder again to an upright position it may be inserted into the slot and secured by placing the prongs underneath the base (40–3). It may be necessary to re-adjust the position of the key when turning it to ensure uniform tension of the tapes.

When all cords or tapes are adjusted to their correct positions for sewing, the crossbar is raised and tension increased to a point where they are quite taut. This is necessary if books are to be sewn both quickly and well. Because of the damage done to tapes and frame, and the looser tension obtained, the use of drawing pins in place of sewing keys is bad practice.

Assuming that there is no possibility of 'set-off', books should be subjected to pressure before sewing, using metal plates interspersed between every few sections throughout the book. Pressing boards and plates must have surfaces that are quite level, as any unevenness will be transferred to the paper of the book. Care is also required to ensure that sections lie uniformly over one another in the pile. It is unwise to sew a book immediately it has been removed from the press, especially if the paper is of an open texture. During pressing all air will have been forced out of the paper and there will be a gradual intake later. If the book has been sewn before this, the sewing may be too tight and the back thinner than the remainder of the book. Rounding will be difficult as will backing, which may result in broken kettle-stitches.

SEWING ON CORDS

Upon removal from the standing press, the book is placed between boards which may be of wood or millboard but should not be pressing boards. After knocking up squarely at the head and at the back, book and boards are lowered into a lying or finishing press until only about $\frac{1}{2}$–1in is left projecting, and the press is tightened. Endpapers should have been removed beforehand. Unless the book edges have already been trimmed or are to remain uncut, the points at which they are to be trimmed are marked on the back. This decision demands careful thought and examination of the book. Obviously the smaller the trim the better, and the practice of leaving some of the shorter leaves untrimmed as 'witness' is one to be commended. Where, however, there are a considerable number of these it must be realised that the pressure on the remainder at the cutting point is reduced accordingly, and it may be that it is insufficient to ensure a well-cut edge. In such cases trimming should be done beforehand.

Between the cutting points the back is now divided according to the number of bands required. These are usually five but variations either way may be according to necessity or fancy.

The division of the spine into panels is not one to be lightly dismissed. Consideration should be given to the lettering or any decoration to be placed there later. An essay upon the importance of mathematical precision in the designing of book spines was written by Lewis Carroll, who was an eminent mathematician as well as an author. In it he discussed not only the number and size of spine panels but the placing of lettering in them. Assuming five bands are required, the back is divided into six panels between the cutting points, that at the tail being about one-third larger than the remainder in order to give a balanced effect to the finished spine. Spring dividers are used for marking out, and it is not long before the eye can accurately assess the panel size. Using a small carpenter's square against the side of one of the boards (41), the band positions are clearly marked across the back with a soft pencil. Only *after* this

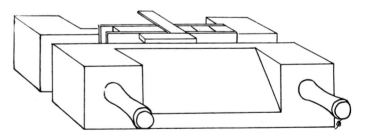

41 *Marking up for sewing on cords*

has been done should the positions of the kettle-stitches be marked. Their position at head and tail will vary according to circumstances, but there is no valid reason why the stitch length should be shortened by placing them unnecessarily far from the edges. A margin of $\frac{1}{4}-\frac{3}{8}$in at the head and very slightly more at the tail left after the book edges have been trimmed is satisfactory.

The kettle-stitch positions must next be lightly cut with a small, not-too-sharp tenon saw, to a depth sufficient only to accommodate the knot formed in the making of the kettle-stitch. Again, accuracy is necessary: if the kettle-stitch is not level with the back it will show either as a ridge or as a hollow on the spine of the finished book. Where sewing is on recessed cords the remaining band marks have to be sawn to a depth and width which will exactly accommodate the cord used. This presents a problem; the book must be sewn on cords thick enough to give maximum strength and yet not damage the book by sawing in too deeply. The golden rule is that the saw kerf should not penetrate beyond the centre fold of the section. Where this does not permit the use of cord sufficiently strong there are the alternatives of sewing on a greater number of cords or using them in pairs, side by side, with a saw kerf wide enough for them to fit in. Yet a third method is the use of three fine cords arranged triangularly, the saw kerfs being cut at an angle to receive them. With books to be sewn on single cords that are wider than a normal saw kerf it is a good plan to undercut the kerfs slightly, as shown in

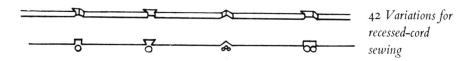

42 *Variations for recessed-cord sewing*

illustration 42. This not only results in firmer sewing but assists in glueing-up the back by reducing the chances of glue entering the sections at these points.

TAPE SEWING

With tape-sewn work there is not the same necessity for meticulous placing, unless the tapes are to show as bands on the spine, but there is need for care. An adequate number of tapes should be used, it being better to use narrower ones and more of them. This not only allows more points of attachment to the boards but also gives shorter stitches with consequent firmer sewing. To give stronger attachment at the head and tail there is a natural tendency to place tapes too close to these points. It is very easy to weaken the book by having too short a stitch between tape and kettle-stitch, which can result in the fold of the section tearing away there. This applies particularly at the tail as leaves are usually turned over from the bottom. There must also be sufficient paper resistance to the cutting action of the thread, especially when this is fine.

The position of the tapes at either end having been decided upon, the remainder should be set out equidistantly. If tapes are to appear as bands on the spine—whether this be tight or hollow—they should be set out as for cords. Generally if the position of the first tape is clearly marked on the back of the book (and this is a great help in accurate sewing), there is no need of other markings except kettle-stitches. These should be quite clearly defined and may be very lightly sawn in even for hollow work. With tight backs, sawing-in is a necessity. In extreme cases very light saw kerfs may be made each side of the tapes to assist the book-sewer, but the method should be restricted to books on very hard paper with exceptionally thick sections.

When sewing, the book-sewer should adopt a comfortable position which permits the work to be done with minimum effort. The frame should be placed along the edge of the bench while the sewer takes up a position at the left-hand end of it and at right-angles to the bench. A stool, being higher, is preferable to a chair, and where much work has to be done its height should be adjustable. Usually tapes or cords are positioned on the sewing frame so that the sewer's left arm passes between the upright and the book. If the book is at all large this constricts the arm movement and has a cramping effect. It will be found to be more comfortable if the book is sewn two or three inches away from the left-hand upright, the arm going round this during sewing (43).

43 Position when sewing

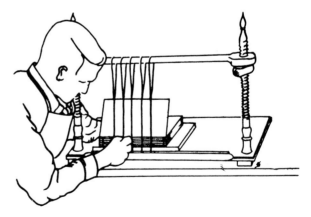

Before sewing, a check should be made to ensure that sections are in their correct sequence.

SEWING ON RAISED CORDS

The cords having been positioned to agree with the markings on the book, and the crossbar raised to tighten them, the cord and kettle-stitch positions are marked on the front endpaper, which was removed before marking up. After a quick check that the sections are in the correct sequence, the unsewn book is placed on the bench at the back of the sewing frame in a position that makes it readily accessible. Its position may be either with the backs of the sections facing the worker, in which case each section must be turned over from head to tail before sewing, or with the foredge facing forward, when the section is turned over towards the sewer. In either case the front of the book is uppermost.

A pressing board is placed on the frame against the cords and the first section (or endpaper) is opened to the centre—the sewing point—and placed face downwards on the board with the head at the right hand. It is accurately positioned against the cords, the left hand being in the centre of the section. During sewing, sections are held in position with the ball of the hand, leaving the fingers free to operate the needle. Left-handed workers are inclined to rebel at this at first, but as both hands are used almost equally nothing is gained by trying to sew in the reverse way. With the section partially open the threaded needle is passed into it from the outside at the kettle-stitch mark—this should be done with the needle held at an upward angle which assists its passage centrally through the fold (44).

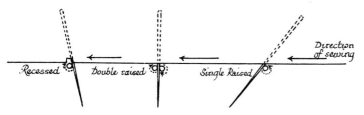

44 Needle angles when sewing on cords

With single cords it must come out at an angle on the far side of the cord (in this case the side nearer the worker) and, encircling it, be returned into the section by the same needle-hole. This is repeated at every cord, each stitch being tightened from the outside as it is made, until the end of the section is reached when the exit is through the kettle-stitch mark. The thread *must* be drawn *along* the book and not at right-angles to it to avoid tearing the paper of the section.

The second section is laid over the first, level at head and at back, and sewn in the same way. The thread having been brought out of the kettle-stitch mark at the head it is now tied in a reef knot to the loose end where about $1\frac{1}{2}$in should have been left for the purpose. This knot, which must be quite secure, is simply made by tying a half-hitch from the left to the right hand and a second from the right to the left hand.

Kettle-stitches The third section is now sewn and from this point it will be necessary to secure each section to the previous ones by means of the kettle-stitch (45). This apparently ridiculous name

45 *Making the kettle-stitch*

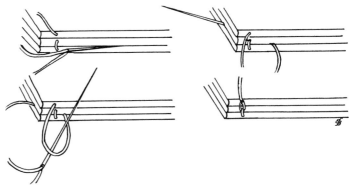

comes from the German *Kettelstich* which in turn is derived from *Kettel*, a small chain, plus *stich*. It is a form of button-hole stitch and is made by passing the needle—at an angle to prevent the point from fouling the paper—between the second and third sections down, bringing it out at the end and passing it through the loop thus formed and tightening. Actually it is usual to take the needle through the loop, saving an extra movement. The sewing is continued to the end of the book when the thread is secured by making a double kettle-stitch between sections 3 and 4 as well as between 2 and 3. There are two points to be observed here. During sewing, sections should occasionally be pressed together with the thumb or gently hammered with a smooth piece of hardwood about $\frac{3}{4}$in square and about 8in long. This is to prevent their becoming slightly bow-shaped at the centre and to keep the sewing firm and so control undue backswell. The other point is that when making the kettle-stitch too much pressure should not be exerted on the book at that point, for this could result in the sections being drawn too tightly together which, in turn, could cause the fracture of the sewing thread during backing.

Tying threads To tie a fresh length of thread a weaver's knot is used. It is made as follows. The end of the original thread is brought to the outside of the book, leaving an inch or so. The new thread is looped (46–1), A being the short end. The longer end B is brought up through the loop (46–2) and placed over the short end of the original thread D (46–3). The encircling loop C must not be tightened. The new thread is tightened at B (46–4) drawing the short end D through the encircling loop which tightens behind it (46–5). Both short ends are cut quite close to the knot which is carefully taken through to the inside of the section as the sewing is continued.

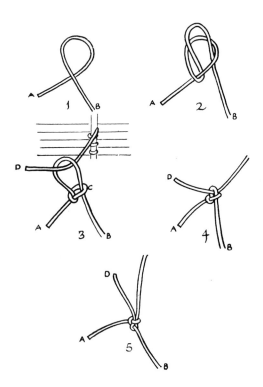

46 *Tying threads
(the weaver's knot)*

Sewing on double cords Sewing on double cords differs only in that the thread passes between them through the original needle-hole. The thread should be first taken round the cord on the far side, otherwise there is a risk of tearing the section when the stitch is tightened. If very solid bands are required it may be necessary to encircle the cords more than once with the thread to ensure uniformity of thickness throughout.

Recessed cords With recessed cords the thread merely passes through the kerf and over the cord, returning through the kerf again. It is a very much quicker method, but it is important that the cords be drawn firmly into the recesses. Whereas with raised cords only one volume can be sewn at a time, with recessed cords or with tapes it is possible to sew several in one pile, separating them when removing from the sewing frame.

Sewing on tapes Except that sewing holes are not usually already made, as with recessed cords, sewing on tapes is similar inasmuch as the thread merely passes over the tapes. While sewing holes should be fairly close to the tapes they should not be so close as to cause the tapes to crease when these are pulled through when cutting down.

47 *Tying down end sections when sewing on tapes*

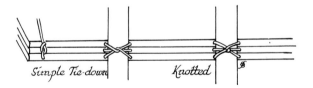

The first and last few sections should be tied together as shown in illustration 47, which has the effect of consolidating the beginning and end of the book. Whether this should be carried out through the whole of the book is an arbitrary point. Much depends upon the tension of the sewing. Where this is tight, to tie down throughout will not only make backing difficult but may cause an undue strain on the thread.

French sewing With so-called French sewing a frame is not used, the sections being sewn at the edge of the bench. When sewing the first section the needle enters at the kettle-stitch point and is brought out once or twice along the back, loops being left through which the needle passes when the second section is sewn. The thread is drawn tight at the end of this section, when it is tied, and from then on the sewing is connected to the previous section at these points. The method is not noted for the strength it gives a binding and this is reduced even further when sewing 'two-sections-on'.

Sewing 'two-on' Sewing 'two-on' (48), as it is usually known, may be used with any type of book sewing but should be reserved for those volumes where to sew 'all-along' would result in the back swelling so much as to become unmanageable. The alternative in

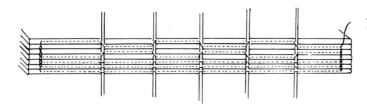

48 *Sewing 'two-sections-on'*

such cases is the use of very thin thread, which lacks strength and tends to cut the paper.

After the first few sections have been sewn normally, each thread sews two sections instead of one. The needle and thread are brought to the outside at the first tape or cord and the centre of that section is marked by placing a small slip of card or a very light folder in it. The next section is placed in position and the sewing continued in it. At the second tape or cord the marker is transferred to the centre of the upper section, the hand taking its place, and the sewing continued. Each section is thus stitched alternately in this manner. A more useful marker is one made of thin card about 6in long and cut rather in the form of a pair of trousers. In use a 'leg' is placed in the centre of each of the two sections being sewn and is removed only when their sewing is completed. It will be necessary to make a double kettle-stitch commencing at a lower point than usual. The last few sections are sewn 'all-along', as were the first. As with recessed cords, it is the abuse or misuse of the method that has condemned it with the craftsman. It should be used, where possible, with not less than five cords or tapes, which give three stitches in each section.

Sewing on thongs For heavy bindings that must endure, the sewing may be done on thongs cut from alum-dressed (tawed) or natural goatskin, PIRA-treated. By assessing the ultimate thickness of the sewn book, thongs may be slit centrally for that distance and the book sewn as with double cords. To give even greater strength, vellum slips covered with goatskin may be used, in which case laminated boards should be used.

SEWING POINTS

Points requiring careful attention in sewing are: passing the needle centrally through the fold of the section, and maintaining uniform thread tension. With raised bands this latter can be done only by tightening each stitch as it is made. Keep the sewing needle slightly greased by passing it over the hair from time to time. The amount of swelling required in the back will depend upon whether a fully rounded or flat shape is wanted, and on the height of the backing, which in turn will also decide the kettle-stitch tension. The width of the back must be kept uniform and this is best done by pressing the sections together at each cord or tape during sewing. A very small mallet or smooth piece of wood can be used for the purpose. Kettle-stitches should be drawn tight with an upward and outward movement to prevent tearing of the section or their being pulled away from their correct position.

In cutting down books from the sewing frame the crossbar is lowered, permitting the sewing keys to be eased away and brought out through the slots in the frame. Books sewn on recessed cords or tapes and in a pile are removed singly by inserting the fingers between the books and gently easing them away, the cord or tape passing under the stitches. It is very easy to pull the book completely from them, and while it is possible to re-insert cords or tapes with the aid of a bodkin (sempstresses' not printers'!) and re-thread, the sewing usually suffers during the operation. Where cords are to be laced into boards a minimum of 2in should be left when cutting down, although with laminated boards the amount may be considerably more. With tapes the amount will vary from 1in upwards according to the method of the board attachment and the book size.

2

FORWARDING

*Control of backswell—glueing the back—cutting book
edges by guillotine and plough—rounding—edge
gilding and colouring—backing—book boards,
preparation and attachment—
headbands—back linings*

FORWARDING

Control of 'Backswell'

After sewing, any undue swelling in the back of the book must be removed. The amount necessary to produce a well-shaped book will depend upon the binding style, whether it is to be only lightly or fully rounded, and the height of the backing, as determined by the thickness of the boards.

It is largely a matter of taste just how rounded in shape the back of a book should be, but there are certain functional considerations to be borne in mind. The almost flat back beloved by Cobden-Sanderson must be very well contrived if it is to retain its shape in use and not become slightly concave. It has, however, the merit of allowing the spine lettering and decoration to be seen at a glance. This cannot be said of the very fully rounded book which, although it will keep a good shape on the shelves, is more liable to break down at the spine in use.

It will be seen that there cannot be a hard and fast rule, but as a rough guide swelling should be somewhere between a quarter and one-third of the book thickness for boarded work.

One method of reducing backswell is to knock up the book squarely at the back and lower it into the lying press until about an inch is left projecting, the slips (tapes or cords) being left outside.

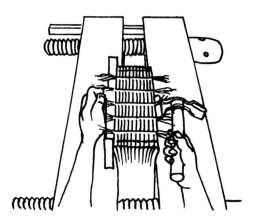

49 *Hammering out backswell in the lying press*

The knocking-down iron is placed on the edge against the side of the book and the back is hammered against it with horizontal blows from the opposite side. The method is safe, as any heavy blows from the hammer are offset by meeting only hand-resistance (49).

A quicker method is to extend permanently the base of a small iron nipping press (a copying press serves admirably) by building a solid wooden platform 2–3in wide and level with it. If a press for this purpose only is justified, the platen may be cut away equally each side, leaving it in the form of a clamp.

The book is placed in the press with its back left projecting, and this is carefully hammered until the necessary reduction in thickness

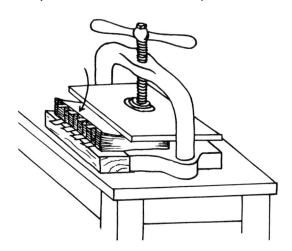

50 Hammering out backswell in the nipping press; the arrow shows the direction of the hammer strokes

is achieved (50). Because of the uneven thickness of the book the hammer strokes must be outwards. To prevent the possibility of sections slipping inwards under the blows, the thumb or a finger should be firmly pressed on to the book slightly away from the back and near to the point of hammering. Unless care is taken it is possible to damage the book during the process.

Control of the swelling during the sewing of the book is the real solution to the problem as, although hammering will reduce it, it is inevitable that a slight loosening of the sewing must result and there may be damage to the fibre of the paper.

Attaching and Pasting up Endpapers

Endpapers are now fixed or, if sewn with the book, pasted up (51).

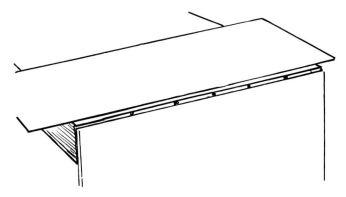

Where possible the margin of the paste for the purpose should be related to the backing height, while the amount used should be sufficient only to provide adequate adhesion.

It is very important that the fold of the endpaper should be exactly level with that of the section to which it is pasted. There is no margin for error. Cords or tapes must be turned back away from the book before 'tipped' endpapers are added.

The 'pasting up' of sections at the beginning and end of the book has much to commend it as it is here that the greatest strain occurs and here that, too often, the glueing-up is weakest. Again, the margin of paste should be quite narrow or the free opening of the book will be impeded. After pasting up, the book should be allowed to dry under a weight, when the back can be glued.

Glueing up

The book is knocked up between boards kept for the purpose and placed either on the edge of a bench or in a lying press with the back projecting, the latter method being usually reserved for books sewn upon raised cords (52). A piece of galvanised metal with its edge turned over at 90° will be found useful to prevent the accumulation of glue at the bench edge. The knocking-up of the book to the back must be quite carefully and accurately done. It must be level at the head, which must be at right-angles to the sides, while all sections must be flush at the back. If for any reason a section will not knock up, a metal plate placed in its centre will have the desired effect.

The glue should be of medium consistency; if too thin it will flow too far in between the sections, if too thick it will form a hard film—or even crust—on the back where flexibility is essential.

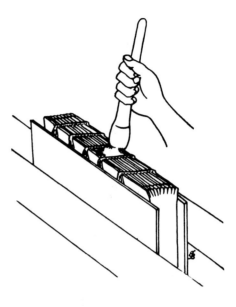

*52 Glueing up
in the lying press*

'Flexible' glue, which contains a hygroscopic additive preventing it from drying out completely, has partly offset this danger, but its use will not compensate for inadequate workmanship.

A fairly short-bristled glue brush is charged with really hot liquid glue which is rapidly worked over the back and in between the sections, the book being firmly held in position by the free hand (53). The brush strokes should be always outwards from the centre, or an accumulation of glue on the edges or sides will result.

*53 Glueing up
on the bench*

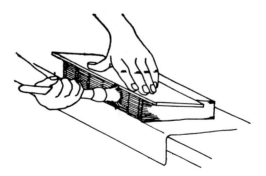

The brush-bristles should be used to work the glue into the interstices between the sections. A piece of newspaper screwed into a ball and rubbed quickly over the surface will work glue between the sections and remove surplus.

After removing the boards, the endpapers and slips must be wiped clean of glue with a piece of rag. Zig-zag endpapers must be opened up and any glue wiped away; unless this is done the zig-zag may be quite ineffective.

If by any chance a section has slipped it must at once be returned to its correct position. To do this the book must be gripped firmly, back uppermost, by one person, while another, very slightly separating the sections at the point to be corrected, holds the offending section together with all the sections on one side. The remaining block of sections is pulled down level with the low section, which is now held with them while the remaining portion is brought level (54). It may be necessary to repeat the process at the

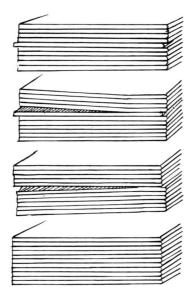

54 *Lifting slipped sections for glueing up*

opposite end, while the glue will require rubbing in each side of the straightened section.

With banded work glue must be prevented from accumulating at the sides of the bands, and some binders limit glueing-up to the spaces between them. This leaves the already tight sewing round the cords freer when movement is necessary during backing.

Cord slips should be untwined (not completely unravelled) before glueing up, thus preventing possible damage by pressure against the sides of the book. Books sewn on tapes or recessed cords need not be glued singly but the number should be limited to the back area that can be conveniently handled with thoroughness.

It should always be borne in mind that the whole purpose of glueing up is to connect section to section by sealing the spaces between them with glue. Glue on the backs of the sections reduces flexibility, and where there is overmuch can result in damage to them during subsequent operations.

Cutting Book Edges

The sequence of forwarding operations varies slightly according to the bookbinding method. The main differences occur between binding 'in-boards' and 'out-of-boards', while individual techniques account for others. The traditional method of binding 'in-boards' is being used less and less, but this does not alter the fact that there is no better way of binding a book that must endure. Because the book is rounded, backed and 'set' before the edges are cut with the plough, these have a smoothness that can be obtained in no other way. Because ploughing 'in-boards' is done at a later stage it is dealt with at the appropriate place rather than here.

However, the demand for this class of work is almost negligible, and to keep in line with the economics of his calling the hand bookbinder must accept quicker methods.

THE GUILLOTINE

In the past the guillotine has provided the line of demarcation between the trade and craft binder, but today most hand binders are equipped with some alternative to the plough for the cutting of book edges.

It is not fair to judge the guillotine by the rough, scored book edges sometimes seen compared with the beautifully smooth ones produced by the plough in the hands of a skilled operative. Where the guillotine is used for every kind of cutting—including, too often, millboards—it cannot be expected to produce work comparable with the well-ploughed edge. The bookbinder's guillotine should be used for book edges only and the knife should be kept in the peak of condition. It is only by such care that book edges can be cut cleanly and smoothly with no fear of the paper fibre being fractured at a point slightly away from the cut, as happens when the knife is dull. It is also important that the knife should run flush with the edge of the clamp, or there will be a risk of fibre fracture although the knife edge is good.

Resistance to the cut can be far more easily gauged with a hand-lever guillotine than with a hand-rotary model, and this is an advantage that should not be overlooked by the hand binder.

With hand work, guillotining book edges usually takes place after glueing up the back. The glue should be firmly set, and it may sometimes be desirable to round the back before this, flattening it again before the edges are cut. This helps to keep 'starts' or 'steps' on the foredge to a minimum where the paper is coarse or the sections thick.

Except where the book is being cut to a given size, the trim should be restricted to the smallest possible margin. Where a book edge is uneven, it will be necessary to cut to the shortest leaf, otherwise it cannot be clamped sufficiently solid to make a clean cut. Where for any reason this is not possible, pieces of thin pasteboard interspersed between the leaves will help to prevent the breaking-down of the paper. Where only a very few leaves are to remain untrimmed, this precaution is unnecessary.

The foredge is usually cut first and, with the cutting point marked, the clamp is raised sufficiently to allow the book to be placed against the back gauge. This is now adjusted so that when the clamp is lightly touching, its front edge is level with the cutting mark. Here a geometrical point arises, inasmuch as the back of the book is usually thicker than the foredge; when placed on the bed of the

55 *Guillotining
the foredge*

guillotine, with the book against the gauge, the book assumes the shape of a portion of an elongated right-angled triangle (55). If cut in this shape, the over-all width will tend to narrow at the base.

Where the swelling is only moderate, the difference may be almost negligible, but with a heavily swollen back it will be necessary to equalise the angles by placing a wad of paper of suitable thickness under the book at the foredge. This is cut with the book, and, to prevent any possible marking of the book, has its long edges fanned outwards. A piece of card wider than the clamp, placed on the upper side of the book, will prevent marking by clamp pressure. It must be flush with the front edge of the clamp, as the knife edge is liable to damage should it cut through it.

The book is held firmly against the gauge by finger pressure on the foredge, whilst the clamp is brought down, securing the book firmly for cutting.

The tail is next cut, the back swelling being offset by a cutting pad of paper fanned out sideways and inserted between book and clamp as shown in illustration 56. Nice judgement is required in the

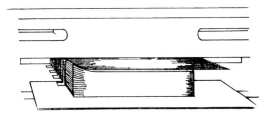

56 Use of the cutting pad when guillotining head and tail

positioning of the cutting pad if pressure is to be uniform over the whole edge. Cutting pads can be made by glueing together strips of strawboard, each overlapping the other at the ends at an angle, and finally shaping them with a knife. Because a variation of the angle is often necessary and there is risk of damage to the knife edge by cutting through the pad, a wad of paper fanned out as required will be found more satisfactory, even though it takes slightly longer to adjust. The placing of the back of the book to the left-hand side permits the positioning of the cutting pad by the right hand and so is more usual. If this is reversed the guillotine knife, which invariably runs diagonally from left to right, no longer has first to cut through the glued back, which tends to damage the fineness of the cutting edge much more than if reversed. Left-handed operators find this method simpler than do right-handed operators, but results justify its use by both.

When using the guillotine it is unnecessary to bring the knife into contact with the book at great speed—unless the knife edge is in bad trim, in which case it must not be used for cutting book edges.

While all guillotines are fitted with cutting sticks, some hand bookbinders prefer to set the knife to cut upon a piece of soft cardboard, since there is less chance of damage to either book or knife in this way. With plastic cutting sticks which permit the cutting of the book without damage to the stick, no cutting board is necessary provided the adjustment of the knife is accurate. An occasional wiping of the blade with a specially prepared rolled and oiled rag helps to keep the edge clean and 'sweeter' in use.

USING THE PLOUGH

The lying and cutting press is a most important part of the craft bookbinder's equipment, and while it is possible to improvise a lying press it is extremely difficult to make a plough for cutting. One side of the press is used for general purposes such as backing, the gilding and burnishing of edges, holding the knocking-down iron when hammering, and holding millboard shears if they are used. The reverse side is used exclusively for the cutting of book edges and, where necessary, for trimming the edges of book boards; it should not be subjected to misuse of any kind.

The plough comprises two blocks of hardwood, usually beech, connected by a wooden screw with a projecting handle and two guides. The right-hand block is fitted with a metal bolt and plate with a dove-tailed slot into which the plough knife is fitted. At each side of the cheek is a metal plate and between these the bolt passes to the upper side where a wing nut tightens and firmly secures the plough knife in position for cutting. The knife is sharpened from the upper side only. The knife edge must be kept really sharp at all times or it will tear the book edges. It must also be checked to ensure that it runs horizontally and is level with the base of the plough. If it is not level the side plates will have to be re-positioned or replaced. If the knife does not run horizontally the book edge will be cut at an angle. To check, open the press, place the plough between the two wooden guides (there may be only one, in which case the base of the plough will be grooved so that it slides over it), and turn the screw handle to bring the knife across the opened press until it meets the opposite side. If true, the point of the knife will be level with the surface. Should it be below, it will need packing at the back on the upper side; if above, on the lower (57). The thickness of the packing (which may be a small piece of millboard)

57 *Adjusting the plough knife*

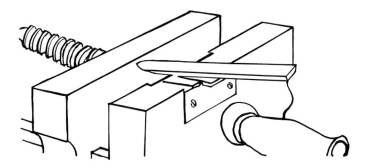

will depend upon how far out of true the knife runs, and only checking will show this.

Cutting and backing boards are similar except that those for cutting have their top edges level, whereas those for backing are at an angle. They are slightly wedge-shaped on their width and are available in various lengths to accommodate different sizes of books.

CUTTING OUT-OF-BOARDS

To cut the foredge, first mark the cutting points at each end of the book using either a pair of wing compasses or a piece of paper or thin pasteboard on which has been marked the distance of the cutting point from the back of the book. If this is marked at both ends of the book it will ensure that the cut is parallel with the back. Laying a cutting board across the slightly opened press, place on it a piece of strawboard (the 'cut-against') level with its top edge. On this, lay the book with the foredge level with the top of the board, and place the second board (called the 'runner') with its top edge level with the cutting marks. Holding boards and book quite firmly between the fingers and thumb of the right hand—and this requires very firm pressure to prevent slipping—lower them between the press cheeks, which have been approximately adjusted, and press downwards until book and boards are held by the press. Placing thumbs and forefingers, which should be crooked, on the edges of the cutting boards, continue to press evenly until the front cutting board is level with the cheek of the press. It will be necessary to adjust the press from time to time.

If the placing of the book between the cutting boards has been accurately done, the back board should project above the press cheek to an amount equal to that being cut from the book. If it does not, then the book has slipped sideways and must be reset, otherwise the book margins and width will be unequal at front and back. When the book is accurately in position the press may be tightened with the iron press pin. It is important to tighten both screws uniformly.

The plough, with its knife projecting a distance that is rather more than the thickness of the book and its cutting point clear of the book, is placed with its left-hand side between the guides (or on the single guide). With the left hand gripping the wooden screw, and the right its handle, the plough is propelled forward smoothly but with some downward pressure. The knife is brought into contact with the book by turning the screw *very slightly* with the right hand. Until experience has been gained it is wise to restrict the advance so that only a few leaves are cut at one time. Ultimately, how many can be cut with one forward movement will depend upon the sharpness of the knife and the quality of the paper. The experienced book-binder will cut on both forward and backward movements of the plough, but newcomers are advised to restrict cutting to the forward one. To cut effectively the knife edges must be really sharp, the press uniformly tight and cutting controlled to only a few leaves at a time. Do not cut through the 'cut-against', or the cutting boards will be damaged.

To cut the head and tail of the book before rounding, mark the cutting point, using a carpenter's square to ensure accuracy. It will be necessary to place a cutting pad (as used in guillotining) on the 'cut-against' to allow for backswell. Without it the book must become misshapen under pressure, with calamitous results. If the book paper is of good quality it is probably better to round it before cutting head and tail, but even then it may be necessary to offset some of the remaining backswell by a cutting pad. When the book is rounded the projecting leaves at front and back are under only slight pressure, so unless the paper is of very good quality there can be some damage there. When cutting head and tail, the cut is toward the foredge with the back of the book facing the worker.

The main causes of failure to produce a smooth cut edge are:

1 The plough knife insufficiently sharp or the angle of the cutting
   edges too acute.
2 The base of the knife not flush with the cheek of the cutting
   press, in which case the book must be adjusted in the press so
   that the top edge of the front cutting board is level with the
   base of the knife and not the cheek of the press.
3 The cutting press insufficiently tightened.
4 The knife being advanced too rapidly so that too much paper
   is being cut away at one time.

CUTTING IN-BOARDS

This is done at a later stage after the book has been rounded and
backed and the boards attached. It is still considered to be the best
time at which to cut edges because the book has taken its final shape
so that any further movement of the leaves is unlikely. As the book
has already been rounded the foredge is concave and must be forced
into its original flat shape before cutting. All this is difficult, and
most craft binders prefer to cut the foredge before the book is
rounded, which at least ensures that the curves at foredge and back
are uniform which is seldom the case when cut in-boards.

Using trindles To flatten the foredge for cutting in-boards,
'trindles', two pieces of flat steel with apertures cut away centrally,

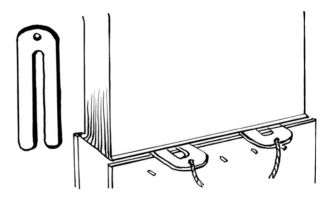

*58 The use of
trindles*

are used. Cutting positions having been measured and marked, the
book is held firmly in both hands with the boards open, and the

back is knocked flat upon the bench. The book, held firmly in this position, is raised and the boards are allowed to drop downwards. This allows the trindles to be inserted round the end hemp slips and between book and boards, thus keeping the book flat (58).

If the book is large or 'obstinate' it may be tied in the flattened position by passing tape several times round it near the joint. To prevent damage the tape must be tied at the book edges with care.

The cutting board, with the 'cut-against' on it and level with its top edge, is placed across the slightly opened press (this is to simplify picking up the book later). The book, face uppermost, is laid on it with its foredge also level with the edge of the cutting board. The runner is placed level with the cutting marks on the book. Book and boards, held firmly, are now taken up, and the trindles are removed and lowered into position in the press. If cutting is to be square, the amount that the rear cutting board projects above the press must be equal to the distance that the book projects *above* the runner at the front.

The edge cut, the book is removed from the press and returned to its original shape.

The extent of the 'round' and the quality of the book paper both have a bearing upon the successful cutting of the book edges at head and tail. Because the foredge is concave the leaves at the beginning and end of the book are not under pressure when it is in position for cutting. The greater the concaveness of the foredge the more leaves there are not under pressure and the risk of tearing when ploughing them is increased. Should the paper not be of good quality, tearing becomes almost inevitable. At this late stage the only hope is to intersperse a number of strips of thin card (not strawboard) at the beginning and end of the book. When actually ploughing, the cutting at those points should be done on the backward movement of the plough rather than the forward. This will minimise tearing at the corners. The only answer to this problem is to cut the book out-of-boards if the paper is not of good quality, and not to over-round the book at any time.

The accuracy of edge cutting will largely depend upon the square-ness of the boards.

When cutting head and tail edges a 'cut-against' is inserted be-tween the book and the back board, making sure that it is tight against the backing shoulder. The front board is eased away from the hemp slips and lowered until its top edge is level with the cutting point. With its back towards the worker, the book is put into the press with the lowered front board level with the cheek so that the plough knife glides over it (1, 59).

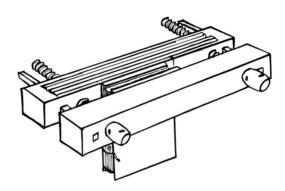

Always check that the book has not twisted while being placed in the press, for this will result in a badly misshapen volume.

Rounding

Rounding is an essential operation if books are to retain their shape. It is a process which in the course of time has evolved to offset the swelling which previous operations produce.

The thickness at the back of a book after sewing must necessarily be greater than at the foredge because of the concentration of thread there. If much guarding has been necessary, the thickness is correspondingly increased. If books are left in this wedge-shaped state, one of two things must happen to them. When placed upon shelves they will, under pressure, tend to go sideways with the spines at an angle to the shelf edge, or the backs will become concave or otherwise misshapen. By making the back convex at this stage, followed by 'backing', both these faults are virtually eliminated.

The 'round' will vary according to the amount of swelling. Where sections are thick and few and sewing too tight, it may be difficult to produce any sort of round. Conversely, if there are many thin sections sewn with too-thick thread the shape will tend to be excessively round and possibly difficult to control. As with most problems, the middle course provides the best solution, and to this end backswell should be controlled from the early stages in binding, by considered choice of guarding paper, sewing thread, and sewing tension.

A book with a flattish spine looks well upon the shelves but it is

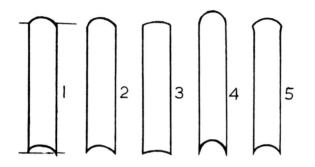

60 *Rounding forms*
1 *Uneven*
2 *Asymmetric*
3 *Insufficiently rounded—will eventually become concave*
4 *Over-rounded—may break down in use*
5 *A good shape, with enough backswell left for backing*

almost inevitable that in use it will become concave, unless heavily lined, which in turn greatly reduces flexibility and throws a greater strain on the paper of the book. On the other hand, the fully rounded book popular in the Victorian era has much to condemn it. Not only does the over-rounded spine tend to make for difficulty in reading the title lettered on it, but, what is more important, the book too frequently dies not of old age but of a broken back (60).

Rounding may take place before or after the cutting of the book edges, depending upon whether the book is bound in- or out-of-boards. With the former the glue should still be in a flexible state after glueing up. Where the book edges have been cut the glue should be softened either by going over the back once or twice with a sponge moistened by dipping into the hot water in the well of the glue-pot or by holding the back of the book in the steam from the well. The glue must be soft enough to 'give' to the rounding but not tacky so that it sticks to the hammer.

Lay the book flat upon the bench—some binders use the lying press—with the foredge forward. Pull the top half of the book forward, leaving the back at an angle. Hold the book firmly down to the bench with the fingertips placed along the back edge. The thumb placed along the foredge helps considerably in producing a good shape, but can leave a mark on a cut edge. The back is gently hammered at a point above half-way while the fingers draw the sections forward, keeping the book still flat on the bench (61). Hammer blows should not be too heavy: the fingers do the major part of the shaping. After a while the book is turned over and the

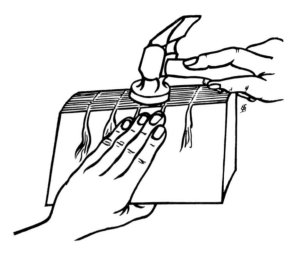

61 *Rounding the back, using the hammer*

process is repeated. With care the back will begin to take a good shape and the book should be examined away from the bench to check this. Reversing the book from time to time, the hammering and pulling forward of the sections must be continued until the best possible shape is produced. A certain amount of swelling will still be required for 'backing', the amount being determined by the height of the 'shoulder' which is related to the thickness of the boards to be used.

With books of moderate thickness there is a tendency to concentrate the hammer blows along the upper edge, often to the detriment of the shape and particularly to the endpapers. This can be avoided if the handle of the hammer is held parallel to the back of the book rather than at right-angles. Imperfect workmanship during earlier processes may be revealed during rounding, usually by the appearance of 'starts' or 'steps' at the foredge instead of a gentle curve. These are usually caused by faulty glueing up, but may be due to sections not having been knocked tightly into the folds, to inadequate tension at the kettle-stitches, or to a knot in the thread being too large or not embedded in the paper.

The rounding of bibles and similar books printed on India paper with edges gilded before rounding is usually effected without the use of the hammer. Laying the book flat upon the bench with the left hand placed firmly on it at the back, take about two-thirds of the leaves at the foredge by the right hand and bend them slightly

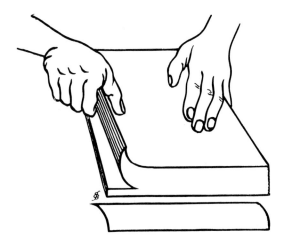

62 *Rounding the back, using only the hands*

upwards and backwards. By holding these firmly, releasing the hold on the back, and bringing the leaves back to their otherwise original position, the book is given a semi-elliptical shape (62). It is turned over and the process is repeated until by careful finger movement a rounded shape is produced with no disturbance of the gilt edges.

Edge Gilding and Colouring

SPRINKLING

When the titling of books was transferred from the book edge to the spine the bookbinder lost no time in using the edges to beautify the book. This has at times been overdone, for the real function of edge decoration is not embellishment but protection from dirt, dust and handling. That gilding offers the best protection there is no doubt, but where cost prohibits this, 'sprinkling' or solid colour—especially if burnished—provide a degree of protection and can add to the appearance of the book.

With the exception of some library rebinding, sprinkled edges are seldom found on letterpress work, being generally confined to cheaper stationery work. The sprinkled edge has few pretensions to beauty, but does prevent finger-marks showing when books are carelessly used.

In the past it was effected by grinding powdered pigment (usually 'Venetian' red) with paste and a few drops of oil and mixing with water. This was kept in a covered receptacle such as a bucket, in the top of which was a hole large enough to allow the entry of a fairly large brush. A pile of books was placed foredge uppermost on waste paper on the bench and tied together, the brush was placed in the colour and, with the bristles still under the cover, revolved between the hands until only a minimum amount of colour was left in the brush. By dint of careful beating of the bristles against an iron bar (usually a press pin) held slightly away from the books their edges were quickly covered with a fine sprinkle of colour. This was repeated on all three edges.

Today a 'sprinkling frame' made of interlaced copper and having a long handle which rests under the arm of the hand holding it has replaced the iron bar. The colour is taken up on a small, short-bristled brush—similar to a nail-brush—which is shaken as dry as possible and lightly rubbed across the mesh, producing similar results with far less effort. In workshops where there is much sprinkling done the air-compressed spray gun is used. Ingenious effects are possible by the use of a second colour and even stencils, but these are seldom used. The newcomer can obtain a sprinkled effect on book edges by diluting water poster colours. Taking up a very small amount on a tooth- or similar brush and rubbing the bristles against a folder or the edge of a wooden ruler sheds a spray of colour over the area. The book is tied up between waste boards and stood upright so that the colour falls downward on to the book edges. The bench should be covered with a sheet of newspaper. Two-colour effects can be obtained by the use of a second colour or by sprinkling over an already solid-coloured edge.

SOLID COLOURING

Solid colouring is usually restricted to the top edge and is done by piling books at the edge of a covered bench, holding them firmly under hand pressure and sponging the colour on to the edge, working always from the back to the foredge and commencing from the top of the pile.

Aniline stains in water are usually used, but fade when exposed to the light. Spirit stains are unsuitable, as they penetrate the book paper to an alarming extent. If pigment colour (such as showcard colour) is used it should be of the finest quality, and only sufficient in quantity to cover the edge applied. Stains require considerably more pressure on the pile than pigment colour, and where only a few books are being coloured the use of the lying press is recommended.

BURNISHING

Burnishing in bulk is done with stained edges by briskly brushing the edges with a short-bristled brush. For individual or a few volumes a better result is obtained by using a burnisher. The book or books are placed in the lying press with a cutting or gilding board on each side and tightly secured. The coloured edge is first lightly rubbed over with a piece of soft leather that has been beeswaxed. Burnishing may be done by means of an agate or other burnisher—even a well-polished folder gives good results. The burnisher is worked firmly but lightly at first along the edge, the pressure increasing until a good, even polish is produced. Care must be exercised that the edge is not indented at any point by too heavy or uneven pressure. If the foredge is burnished a 'dog's tooth' agate or other curved burnisher will be necessary. The professional binder keeps a supply of beeswax on hand by rubbing the block of it liberally on the side of the lying press and using the pad of a clean finger to apply it. On no account should the block of beeswax be rubbed directly on to the coloured edge which results in a surfeit of it there.

EDGE GILDING EQUIPMENT

Edge gilding is a very specialised operation. The equipment required is as follows.

Lying or gilding press, the latter being used for gilding in bulk.

Gilding boards, similar to cutting boards but thicker at the wide edge—they should be of a fine, close, even grain such as beech.

Gilders' scrapes, as used by cabinet makers, to produce an absolutely smooth book edge. For solid gilt foredges to be gilded in the round those made in the form of a French curve will be found admirable as some part of them can usually be found to fit the curve of the particular foredge being gilded.

Scrapes should be maintained in good cutting condition and are sharpened by holding them vertically and rubbing the edge on a suitable oilstone. The rubbing is quite vigorous, the 'burr' produced at the edge being removed by judicious rubbing with the scrape flat on the stone. The edges are then slightly turned over by being rubbed either on or with a piece of hard steel such as the side of a chisel. To prevent damage to the surface of the oilstone, turn it on edge for the sharpening.

Fine glasspaper to get a finish to the edge.

Size, either vellum or gum tragacanth, to prevent the absorption of the glair on books composed of coarse-fibred paper. Vellum size is made by cutting vellum pieces very small and boiling them in water until the gelatine is extracted; when cool the substance should be that of jelly. It is used warm and in liquid state; it does not, however, keep long and must be made as required. Pure gelatine may be used. Only on coarse wood-pulp paper is it necessary to use gum tragacanth in a fairly thick solution. Alternatively a thick solution of alum made from crystals dissolved in water may be used. On India or other bible paper a 10 per cent alum solution can be used. On all books it is a wise precaution to separate the leaves slightly by twisting the book and, with a pad of cloth, dusting French chalk between them. With art paper it is essential if the leaves are to be prevented from sticking at the edges.

Surfacing paste of either Armenian bole (sometimes called red chalk) or blacklead or a mixture of both is used to prepare the edge immediately before laying on the gold leaf. It is made by grinding with the addition of a little water and a few drops of glair on plate glass. It should be kept in a shallow, wide-mouthed receptacle fitted with a screw top. The blacklead should not be in the form of prepared grate polish which may have additives.

Water glair, used as the gold size, is made by thoroughly beating the white of an egg and mixing with water. The amount varies with individual gilders from a cupful to a pint. Much depends upon the paper of the book and the preparation given to the edge. The glair should be allowed to stand for twenty-four hours before straining through fine material. Straining is necessary as the finest impurity is likely to cause a break in the surface of the gold.

Where the book is composed of 'art' paper, glair should be very weak indeed—even water may serve. If glair is allowed to get on to the outside of the neck of the receptacle containing it, it will effectively stick the screw cap to it: immersion in hot water will release it.

Gilding tip or gilding frames. For transferring gold leaf from the gilding cushion to the book edge three methods present themselves:

1 Strips of bank paper rubbed lightly across the hair or forehead.
2 A 'gilder's tip' which consists of long, springy hairs set in a frame, often of cardboard, usually about $3\frac{1}{2}$in wide.
3 Gilding frames made quite simply in plywood or hardboard with georgette or other fine-meshed material glued tightly in position over the aperture.

While all three methods are satisfactory, gilding frames have the advantages that the cut gold may be mounted ready for use beforehand and that if for any reason the gold leaf adheres too firmly it may be released by gently blowing through the mesh. Many binders prefer the paper strip method, as with it sufficient gold leaf can be taken up to cover the whole edge being gilded, thus preventing a time-lag during which the glair may tend to dry out.

Camel-hair brush about 1in in width for 'floating' the glair on the edge. The bristles should be 'set' in rubber to preclude the possibility of their becoming detached and so leaving ungilded 'hairlines' on the edge.

A burnishing brush is required for the surfacing paste; the bristles should be quite short and firm but not harsh as with some nylon nail-brushes which are otherwise quite suitable. When obtainable, the old-fashioned 'grate brush' used for blackleading of grates is most suitable, being fitted with a handle.

Burnishers in both curved and flat forms will be necessary. Bloodstone makes one of the finest burnishers of gold, while agate follows close behind. The latter is obtainable in flat and 'dog-tooth' forms—the tooth agate, being curved, is suitable for foredge burnishing. Whichever stone is used, it is wise to protect its highly polished surface by enclosing it in a soft leather sheath when not in use. Being brittle, burnishers should always be kept in a safe place— spring clips are useful for this purpose.

Beeswax is used for 'setting' the gilt edge and for assisting actual burnishing.

Bookbinders' *gilding cushions* consist of a piece of wood usually about 15in × 6in × ¾in, its surface padded and firmly covered with rough calf which is tacked at the board edges. In use it must be completely free from any form of greasiness and quite firm; should dampness cause the surface to loosen it should be restored to firmness by warming before use.

The gilders' knife used in conjunction with the cushion has a long, perfectly straight cutting edge so that the fingers holding it need never be in close proximity to the gold leaf when cutting. It should have a sharp, slightly roughened edge in order that the gold may be divided by it without cutting the surface of the cushion. The roughness can be obtained by gently rubbing it at an angle on smooth emery cloth or even a smooth cement surface.

Cutting is done by laying the whole length of the knife on the gold leaf, holding it down firmly but gently, and moving the blade backwards and forwards across the leaf. The slightly roughened edge of the blade, combined with the padding of the cushion leather, prevents this from being cut.

EDGE-GILDING TECHNIQUE

The room in which edge gilding is to be done should be dry and free from draughts. Precautions should be taken against air disturbance caused by the sudden opening of a door. Apart from disturbing the gold leaf a draught may cause dust to settle on the glaired edge prior to the application of the gold and so ruin the work.

Book edges to be gilded must be cut in the best possible manner; any score marks or indentations will almost certainly ruin the work. An edge skilfully cut by means of the plough forms the best surface for gilding, but, provided the knife edge is both sharp and free from blemish, a guillotined book edge is satisfactory.

When the quality of the book paper is such that there is no 'suction', sizing can be dispensed with. If the book is composed of or contains art paper it will be necessary to French chalk the edges to prevent the leaves from sticking together. This is done by fanning them sideways and liberally dusting with the powdered chalk.

While book edges may be gilded in bulk, only the gilding of individual volumes will be considered here.

The book is placed on the lying press with the edge to be gilded lying across the slightly opened cheeks. A gilding board is placed with its thick edge level with that of the book, which is now turned over, and a second board is placed similarly on the reverse side.

Two points should be noted here. If the grain of the wood does not run parallel with the edge of the board, ensure that it runs downwards, from the back of the book. As scraping is done from the back towards the foredge, this will result in the edge of the gilding board remaining smooth if the scrape comes into contact with it. In reverse, the edge can become very roughened. The second point concerns the ends of the boards, which must be at right-angles to the top edge. Where the book has been cut 'in-boards' it will have been necessary to turn these back and set the gilding boards flush into the shoulder of the backing, and if the angle of the end exceeds 90° it will not be possible to do this; consequently there will be no board pressure at that point, which in turn will endanger the gilding there.

The book with boards in position is now taken firmly by the hand, an operation requiring care but simplified by the book being across the open press, and lowered into the press with the back of the book towards the worker. Because of the wedge shape of the gilding boards it is possible to place the book securely in the press and yet be able to adjust its position afterwards. This is done by opening the press very, very slightly and pressing on the boards until they are flush with the press cheeks.

If more than one book is to be gilded at the same time and they vary slightly in size, gilding boards may be placed between them. By the use of pieces of thin tinplate, about 3in wide and folded into a V shape, interspersed between the boards, the angle between them will be offset and the books can be held without slipping. Where the total width is too great for them to be held firmly, the lying press can be turned on edge, a sufficiently wide pressing board used to lay the 'pile' of books upon, and the whole rested in position on the inside of the lower cheek of the press, which is then tightened.

The edges are now scraped. The worker stands at one end of the press with the back of the book nearest him. The scrape is held in both hands between fingers and thumb with its top edge inclining away. Using firm pressure, it is passed over the book edge, cutting away the smallest amount of paper as it does so. It is important that the edge is uniform and quite smooth, care being taken that the scrape is not allowed to score the book edge at any point.

After scraping, the edge may be lightly glasspapered with a fine-gauge paper. On no account should the hands be allowed to come into contact with the edge after this, as they would impart grease to it, the smallest amount of which is fatal to the success of the gilding operation.

If there is porosity the edge should be sponged over with a coat of size and left to dry.

Where a finely burnished gilt edge is required it may again be lightly scraped, preferably before the size has quite dried out; otherwise glasspapering will suffice to bring a good surface to the edge.

The surfacing paste of Armenian bole and/or blacklead is now sponged on and allowed to dry for a while. Vigorous brushing with a stiff brush serves to remove surplus paste and also gives the surface a good burnish. At this stage the edge may be burnished by working an agate or bloodstone lightly but firmly across it. Beeswax must not be used.

Gold Leaf. Loose leaf of the best English quality only should be used. Unalloyed beaten gold sold as Pure Fine Gold (24 carat) is the finest, and none less pure than 23 carat should be used. Gold leaf is sold by the 1,000 leaves $3\frac{1}{4}$in square and packed in booklets of 25 leaves.

A leaf of gold—preferably double thickness because of possible flaws—is now removed from its book and cut on the gilder's cushion into strips rather wider than the book thickness.

The cushion must be quite dry and free from any grease—a little powdered Bath brick poured on and worked into the leather with the gilder's knife will ensure this. The cushion must be thoroughly cleaned of loose brick dust by the use of the knife with the cushion on edge.

The knife, which has a long, narrow blade, should be sharp but with its edge slightly roughened. It, too, must be without trace of grease on the blade; a rub on the cushion will ensure this.

The book of gold is laid at the left-hand end of the gilder's cushion and opened at the first leaf of gold. This is removed on the knife edge from book to cushion either by very carefully easing the blade under it or by creating the slightest air disturbance at the leaf edge by the use of the knife blade, which has the effect of causing the gold leaf to fold gently back into halves (63–1). The knife is now laid on the cushion with its blade edge close to the fold and with a very gentle breath of air the leaf is lightly blown back to its original position but with the knife blade under it (63–2). By turning the blade on edge (63–3) the leaf may now be carefully removed to the other end of the cushion (63–4). By laying it down on one side of the fold, the leaf may be laid out flat by gently turning the knife in the hand so that the gold leaf unrolls (63–5). If a slight breath of air

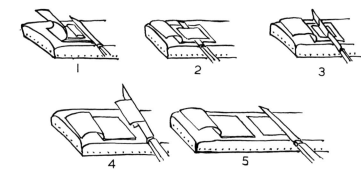

63 Edge gilding— taking a leaf of gold from the book to the cushion

is directed on it centrally the leaf will be flattened on the cushion ready for cutting. If there is any fear of uncontrolled draughts it is advisable to enclose the cushion on three sides with a screen made of folded strawboard. The leaf is then cut to size.

To transfer the gold leaf to the edge, the grease required for the purpose is obtained by passing the paper, tip or frame either across the forehead or over the hair.

If frames are being used they may now be 'loaded' each with a strip of gold leaf, by pressing the greased gauze lightly on to it. The edge glair, already strained, is placed on one side of the press with gilding frames on the other. A generous layer of the glair is floated on to the edge with the camel-hair brush, working from back to foredge. If the edge has been properly prepared the glair will remain on the surface; if it should be absorbed then the indications are that the preparation is inadequate and re-sizing necessary. The gilding frame with the gold leaf attached is lowered in position over the book (64). As soon as contact is made the leaf will transfer itself with lightning rapidity to the edge and care must be taken that there is no movement of the frame or the gold will split. Further pieces of gold are added, each very slightly overlapping its predecessor until the edge is covered. The 'gilder's tip' or strip of paper is used in much the same way. To remove any doubt regarding the distribution of glair under the gold leaf the press may be tilted, first from end to end and then sideways, which will cause the glair to re-circulate under the leaf. Finally, the surplus glair may be released by standing the press on edge, when the fluid will flow from under the leaf. Should it bind at the edge of the gold, a touch with the finger-nail will release it. It should not be allowed to soak into the gilding boards but be carefully wiped away.

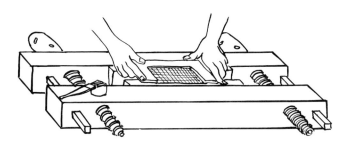

64 Edge gilding—using a frame to lay down the leaf

The press is returned to its normal position and the edge is allowed to dry. After a little while, say five minutes under normal conditions, a piece of bank paper twice as wide and slightly longer than the book edge, and lightly beeswaxed on the upper side, is placed across the edge, being held taut by the fingers and thumb of the left hand at the edges. The pad of the forefinger of the right hand is gently rubbed along the paper so that the gold is pressed on to the book edge without any movement. This has been found to be efficacious in ensuring that all parts, especially the edges, are adhering to the book edge.

Complete drying may take twenty minutes or more, according to the air conditions prevailing. Only experience can guide here, but if the edge is still very damp the cloudiness caused when it is breathed upon will remain some while; when dry it will disperse immediately.

Before becoming absolutely dry the edge may be 'set' by using the burnisher through the firmly held bank paper, waxed side uppermost. The burnisher is moved lightly across the surface covering the edge, particular attention being paid at points where the gold leaf overlaps and at the back. The edge is now left to dry completely.

It is then lightly rubbed over with a piece of soft leather that has been beeswaxed. This will assist the burnishing.

Burnishing is done across the edge except when the foredge is gilded in the round, when the tooth burnisher is used along it. The burnisher is worked firmly but very lightly at first, the pressure gradually increasing until a brilliance is achieved. It must be held squarely on the edge as this can be easily damaged by excess pressure at one point.

Should there be one or two places where the gold has failed to adhere these may be lightly touched with ethyl alcohol (spirits of wine) and fresh gold very quickly laid on. Being spirit, the alcohol quickly evaporates, allowing the repaired portions to be re-set and burnished until uniform with the remainder.

Before the final burnish the press should be slightly loosened; this results in a greater brilliance and also serves to 'cut' the gold and so loosen the leaves. If this is not done the edges must be 'broken' when the book is removed, by mildly knocking the book against the surface of the lying press.

To gild a foredge in the round the press should be slightly tilted sideways and the edge dealt with in two halves, the press being tilted to the opposite side for the second half. As mentioned, a tooth agate worked along the edge is used for burnishing.

VARIATIONS IN GILT EDGE FINISHES

Rough gilt The edges are gilded before the book is sewn. If they are trimmed to a uniform size the work is straightforward, but if not, the leaves must be carefully knocked up flush with the edge being gilded. Rough gilt edges are generally considered by the connoisseur to be the most acceptable, but while very attractive they do not offer the same protection as solid gilt.

Antique or dull gilt This probably takes second place with the purist and has a pleasant dignity. The gold is burnished through paper only.

Gauffered This consists of tooling the edges after gilding, using warm, brightly polished finishing tools. Open, lace-like patterns are the most effective; but the method has lost the popularity it gained in the second half of the nineteenth century.

Colour under gilt　　Used extensively on bible and prayerbook work, it consists of staining all edges, usually in red or blue, gilding taking place over the top of the stains. Pigment colours are unsuitable.

Marble under gilt　　This is seldom seen nowadays; it consists of marbling all edges before gilding them so that, as with the foregoing method, the effect is seen when the book edge is at an angle.

Painted foredges　　This is an extension of the two previous methods, whereby a watercolour drawing is executed on the foredge, which has been clamped with the edge at an angle. The drawing should be done quite lightly with the minimum of watercolour. Double foredges are effected by fanning the edge from the opposite side on which a second watercolour is painted. When the book is opened from the front, one painting is seen, and another is seen when it is opened from the back. Foredge paintings give delight to most collectors, but the true bibliophile should be forgiven if he regards them as the ultimate in the art of 'one-up-manship'!

Backing

If a book is to stand up to hard usage it must retain its shape, and in this respect backing is a vital operation. Although the primary purpose of backing is that of providing suitable accommodation for the boards of the cover, it does very much more.

By taking up inevitable backswell it uses it to shape the book so that, when covered, the boards lie level with the back and do not stand above it. This is done by hammering the back outwards over the angled edges of 'backing boards' to form a projecting 'shoulder' running the length of the book at front and back. The backs of the sections are made to bend outwards and overlap each other at angles which slightly increase from the centre of the book. This causes them to become interlocked so that while the free opening of the book is in no way impaired it returns to its original shape after use. Into the 'shoulders' formed by the backing fit the joint edges of the cover boards and it is the support given by them at these points, combined with the interlocking of the sections, that enables a well-bound book to stand on the bookshelves without losing its shape at the spine.

From early days backing has been done by the craftsman in the lying press, using a backing hammer and a pair of backing boards. Much experience and care are required to produce a well-shaped back with shoulders exactly the height demanded by boards of a particular thickness related to the method of binding. Moreover, there must be no creasing of the leaves of the book.

Backing boards are usually of oak or beech, the former being harder while the latter is close-grained and does not tend to splinter. In section they are wedge-shaped with the bottom edge—the narrower edge—rounded to prevent damage to the side of the book. The top edge is planed at an angle of approximately 60° which makes it possible to form the 'shoulder' at right-angles to the book. This is difficult if the angle of the backing board is more than 60°; if it is much less the edge tends to break down under the hammering. Board edges require planing from time to time to maintain them. Brass-lined backing boards are obtainable, and will last almost indefinitely. When new the edges are often sharp and endanger the end sheets of the book. They should have any harshness removed with fine emery cloth. They should also be checked to see that the brass lining lies flush with the inside surface of the board, or the book may be marked under pressure.

Backing hammers are almost identical with bootmakers' and can be obtained in two styles. The 'London' pattern has a wedge-shaped pane at one end and a rounded one at the other, while the double-ended pattern consists of two different-sized rounded panes. In the hands of an experienced worker the 'wedge' of the London pattern, provided its edges are smooth, effectively brings the outside sections of the book down to the board, ensuring a right-angled shoulder.

Hammers are obtainable in varying sizes and weights, but most bookbinders prefer them heavier rather than lighter as, when controlled, they produce results quicker and better because fewer strokes are needed.

For flexibly sewn books the normal backing hammer may be found to be too wide for hammering between the raised cords; in such cases an ordinary carpenter's hammer will be found suitable. To prevent any possible damage to the sewing the hammer face (or pane) must be kept clean and smooth.

The thickness of the board to be used for the cover is the main factor in determining the height of the backing, and until the crafts-man's eye has become completely dependable this should be strictly checked for accuracy. The tendency is generally to back too high, the result being an unpleasant and unsightly joint in the finished binding, which ultimately causes the book to twist sideways when under pressure on the bookshelf.

There is some loss in height in backing by hand, and the distance gauged should be fractionally greater than the board thickness—but it is very slight. With hollow-back work, the back linings must be taken into consideration and the backing reduced to a point where *with the linings* the total shoulder height does not exceed the thickness of the board.

The rounded book, its shape checked for symmetry, is laid flat across the slightly opened lying press with the back facing right. A backing board is placed on it with the angled edge the height of the backing away from the back and parallel to it.

Except with cased work, tapes or cords should remain outside the backing boards.

Book and board are now turned over with care to avoid any movement of the latter. With smaller books this is done by inserting the fingers into the open press and gripping the book and board firmly between fingers and thumb and reversing them. With larger volumes it will be found necessary to use both hands, placing the book centrally across one press cheek and gripping it at each end. The second backing board is positioned on the other side and the book and boards are again gripped firmly and held vertically with the back uppermost.

They are now gently lowered into the press, which should have been opened wide enough to receive them but not so much as to allow them to pass right through. By gentle, uniform pressure on both boards they are pressed downwards until the outsides of the top edges are level with the surface of the press. A check must be made that the book has not slipped out of position and that its rounded shape is as it should be before the press is tightened. Tightening must be done evenly, changing the press pin from one screw to the other as necessary; it should also be as great as reasonably possible.

With very large and heavy books it is sometimes impossible for one person to adjust them in the press. In such cases the method outlined in the previous section on edge gilding can be used.

The worker stands at the end of the press for the backing operation, and complete control of the hammer is necessary if it is to
be successfully accomplished. The placing of the index finger along

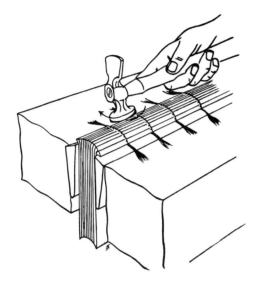

65 *Backing in the
lying press*

the handle when gripping it will be found to prevent the hammer
slipping sideways (65).

Unless the book is very thick, backing should commence slightly
away from the centre of the back with the hammer moving at
right-angles to it in a concave arc. The blows must always be
sideways or a misshapen back and badly creased back margins of
leaves will result. To make the glancing blow necessary it will be
found that the wrist must be used if the hammer is to be effectively
turned. The earlier blows should be firm but light and made along
the length of one section working from head to tail and having
the effect of turning it very slightly outwards. This is repeated,
gradually working over the back until the whole of one half has
been covered and the outside section is lying firmly on the edge of
the backing board. The other side is dealt with similarly. The
hammering is done with the hammer at an angle to the book of
approximately 30°. This relation is to the book and in consequence
of its rounded shape gives the impression of changing. When—and
only when—the outside book edge is lying flat on the backing

board, the shoulder may be consolidated by gentle tapping with the opposite end, the wedge end, of the hammer, used sideways.

There are many pitfalls in backing (66). If hammering takes place at the centre of the back instead of slightly away from it, a 'valley' is formed there. Conversely, if it does not commence high enough a 'rabbit' back usually results. Creasing of the back margins of the book will result from direct hammer blows and those that are not at right-angles to the back. The greatest pressure occurs across the book's width at the point where the edges of the backing boards rest; all above that is free of direct pressure and offers less resistance to ill-placed hammer blows. This is why the higher up on the back hammering is done the lighter and more accurate it must be.

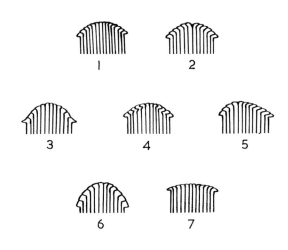

66 Backing forms 1 Correct 2 'Valley' formed by hammering too high 3 'Rabbit' back formed by hammering too low 4 Creasing of back margins by direct hammer blows 5 Asymmetrical shape—backing begun off-centre 6 Over-rounded back 7 Flat back —insufficiently rounded

If backswell is excessive there will be a tendency for the book to slip upwards away from the backing boards when adjusting in the press. If these are dampened by saliva, not water, applied with the fingertips at a few points on the inside surface, slipping is less likely. Should it still occur, the press may be tightened *before* the book and boards have been pressed fully down into it and the book lightly and partially backed so that the position of the shoulders becomes defined. Then it may be lowered to its correct position and the backing satisfactorily completed.

In many commercial hand binderies the traditional lying press has been replaced by the 'hand wheel backing press' in which the two wooden screws have been replaced by one metal one which presses centrally against the right-hand cheek through a solid casting and is operated by a hand wheel. Removable metal backing cheeks are fixed to the wooden ones which allow the book to be adjusted after being placed in the press, all of which results in a considerable saving of time. It has some drawbacks, one of which is that as the cast backing cheeks are almost at right-angles at the backing point —that is 45° as compared with the 60° of the wooden backing boards—it is difficult to obtain a well-defined right-angle to the shoulder.

The 'star' hand backing machine, still in use in hand binderies, has similarities with the foregoing but is all-metal and is fitted with a large roller which is brought over the middle of the book and worked backwards and forwards pressing the back outwards. It requires considerable skill to produce first-class work, and most binders use the hammer to both commence and finish the backing. The use of the roller, turning the whole length of the book in one movement, does virtually eliminate creasing—all too often apparent where the hammer only is used.

Book Boards

Much of the strength of the bound book depends upon the attachment of the boards, but, as with all bookbinding operations, a balance must be maintained. If the sewing has not been soundly executed or if the covering material is not of good quality then the mere excellence of board attachment will be of little avail. The reverse happens more often, and luxurious-looking bindings break away from the still-sound book because of cords that are both too few and too weak. While edition binding does not really concern us here, it may be said that notoriously weak joints are nowadays equalled by 'near-paper' covering material but that at least a balance exists between the two!

Board thickness will have been decided when the backing operation was done, but where a tight-back binding is envisaged, the board surface should be flush with the backing shoulder. With hollow-back work, due allowance for the back linings must be made and the board should project slightly above the backing shoulder (67). If this is not so the back of the book will project above the board surface causing both undue wear there and an unpleasant appearance. In addition, the book will possibly become misshapen under pressure on the shelf.

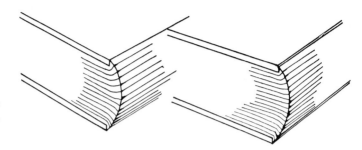

67 Relationship of board and backing shoulder for tight-back binding (left) and hollow-back binding

When boards have not matured and are used in this 'green' state, their behaviour on the book may be unpredictable. If prepared boards are allowed a week in which to dry out the books which they will protect will be better than many, as all too often less than twenty-four hours may elapse between preparation and use. In view of the additional difficulties imposed by the fibre grain in machine-made boards, as long a period as possible must be allowed for drying-out.

Because of grain direction it is better to laminate boards with the grain running in opposite directions where the thickness of the finished board permits this. Where it does not, it is most important that boards be cut with the grain running from head to tail although this must inevitably result in wastage.

The large millboard shears originally made for the purpose of splitting boards may still be found today in hand binderies but have generally been replaced by all-iron board cutters. Whether shears or millboard cutter are used the boards should first be cut sufficiently large to allow for trimming to exact size after lining (see p. 129).

PLOUGHING BOARD EDGES

Before lining, the joint edge must be trimmed quite smooth and at right-angles to the surface. It may seem curious that even today, unless exceptionally heavy board guillotines are available, the best edge results from the use of the centuries-old method of ploughing. A number of roughly trimmed boards are knocked up level along their joint edges and laid on to a piece of wooden board on which a waste mill- or strawboard has been laid to serve as a 'cut-against'.

The pile is lowered into the cutting-press until about $\frac{1}{8}$in projects above the nearside cheek of the press (68), which is tightened with

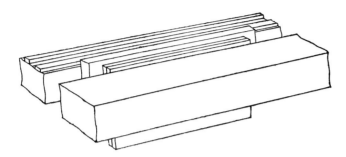

68 *Trimming board edges with the plough*

the press pin. Any adjustment of the position of the pile may be made before tightening by gripping the boards and adjusting from *below* the press cheeks.

The amount projecting above the press is cut away by the use of the plough. Here it should be reiterated that the plough knife used for cutting book edges should not be used for boards. That used for boards should have a rather elongated point, and while it must be sharp the edge need not be as fine as the knife used for book edges. There must be considerable pressure during the cutting operation which is carried out at a good speed. Any slight burr at the edges of the boards when cut should be rubbed down with knife handle or folder.

LINING BOARDS

For full leather bindings the inside of the boards must be lined with paper which serves as a counter-lining and offsets the subsequent 'pull' of the leather covering. A thinnish bank or any thin paper of fairly good quality will serve for this and should be well pasted with medium-thickness paste. It is laid with its long edge flush to the trimmed joint edge of the board and lightly rubbed down with the hands before being given a quick 'nip' in the press between pressing boards. Upon removal boards are stood up, allowing air to circulate freely between them to ensure a good drying-out. When completely dry the boards are lined on both sides with a continuous lining which passes over the joint edge. With this edge nearest the worker the board to be lined is laid on the bench and the pasted paper laid on to its surface with the other pasted portion overhanging the bench.

The surface is first lightly rubbed down and, with the joint edge of the board slightly overlapping the bench, the lining is firmly but gently rubbed to it. There must be no looseness here and adhesion all along the edge must be effected. The board is now turned over and the remainder of the lining brought tightly over and rubbed down. After another very quick press the boards are stood up again and allowed to dry, when they may be cut to size. The second all-over linings not only give a good surface to boards but by causing equal surface tension on both sides add greatly to their rigidity, while the lining of the joint edge is of value later both in cleaning at that point and in laying down the endpapers.

With half- or quarter-bindings only one lining is necessary, and this covers the inside of the board, the joint edge and the area to be covered by the leather on the outside. In practice this is marked first and the paper lining is laid to it and then brought over to the inside of the board (69).

69 *Lining a board for half- or quarter-binding*

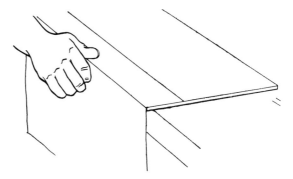

In assessing the final size of boards, considerations will include not only the actual 'square' but the size of the headbands still to be woven and, in the case of books being bound 'in-boards' (where book edges are trimmed *after* boards have been attached), due allowance for trimming. When headbands have been added the boards should project sufficiently beyond them to allow the making of the 'headcap' which is turned over them. When the book is bound and standing upright it should be possible to slide a piece of paper between the headcap and the shelf; unless this is possible, wear there may ruin the binding all too soon.

In contrast to the Victorians who, despite their sometimes brilliant technique, usually considered the finished effect without the best consideration for the life of the binding, today's binder perhaps sacrifices fine technique to common sense. This is particularly noticeable with board edges and corners, which were often accentuated by paring turn-ins dangerously thin. Today the tendency is to use a slightly heavier leather at board edges, which are usually 'cushioned', while corners have their extreme sharpness removed by

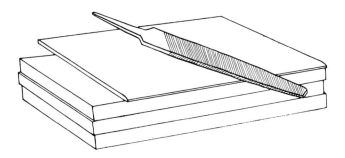

70 *'Cushioning' board edges by filing*

judicious rounding. This improves the appearance and, more important, reduces surface wear at these points. A wood file may be used in conjunction with glasspaper to round the head, tail and foredges of the boards (70).

Very heavy boards may be given a lighter appearance by slight bevelling, and this is especially effective when done on the inside edge. The bevel, which should not unduly reduce the edge thickness, should be a fairly wide one extending to a point level with the book edges when the book is closed. To go beyond this would result in a dust trap and must be avoided. If the width is marked on the board by slightly scoring with a pointed knife against a straightedge it will be found to be not difficult to obtain a clean and accurate bevel using a sharp knife freehand. This method is fairly quick, and any unevenness may be remedied by file and glasspaper. It is not usual to bevel the joint edges of boards, but, where done, it must be on the outside only and the finished board thickness must agree with the backing so that the board surface stands slightly above.

Attaching Book Boards

DRAWN-ON BOARDS

When books are sewn on cords they are usually attached by lacing, when the boards are said to be 'drawn-on'. The slips, which should already have been partially unravelled to prevent their marking the book, are now further opened up with an awl until all the fibres are separate, after which they are scraped by drawing against the edge of a knife held in the hand (71). This results in the removal of

1 *Scraping hemp slips*

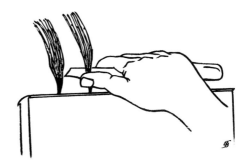

short fibres and the softening of the remainder to a point where they can be moulded to fit in the grooves which will be made to receive them.

With the slips turned back from the book a board is placed exactly in position and marked on the joint edge where the cords occur. The second board is similarly marked. It is necessary to be quite sure that the board positions will result in the book standing upright when bound and this should be checked before marking the second board.

Holing the boards Holes must now be made in the boards a little distance from the joint edge and opposite the points marked. The distance will vary with the size of the book and whether it is to be cut 'in-boards', and may be from $\frac{1}{4}$in to $\frac{3}{4}$in accordingly. With 'in-board' work it is necessary to allow for sufficient movement of the boards after lacing so that they may be lowered level with the point where the book edges are to be trimmed by ploughing.

Holing is done by hammering a printer's bodkin through the board from the outside, the board resting upon a solid piece of lead or on a piece of soft wood. There should be good clearance to simplify the lacing of the hemp later. Reversing the board, a second set of holes is made from the inside a short distance, say $\frac{1}{4}-\frac{3}{8}$in, from the first ones and at 45° to them towards the tail of the book. Displaced board fibres must *not* be cut away from the surface.

V-shaped grooves to hold the hemp cord are cut on the outside surface connecting the first holes with the joint edge of the board. These should be neither too wide nor too deep—certainly not more than half the board thickness—but they must comfortably accommodate the hemp slips when laced. The cutting of the grooves requires confidence, the cut being best made with the knife at an angle that ensures a cut of the correct depth when the centre of the groove is reached (72). A second cut is made from the opposite side and the surplus board should fall out. Remember also that, despite

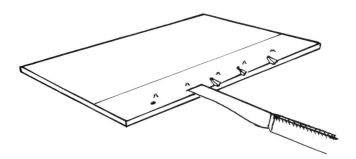

72 *Cutting grooves for hemp slips*

their present appearance, the slips will be only as wide as the original cord thickness at the joint edge of the board, and a groove that is unnecessarily wide at that point may be an embarrassment later. If too shallow, the slips will lie above the board surface and will result in unsightly protrusions when the book is covered and will be subject to undue wear there as a result. If grooves are too deep, in addition to unnecessarily weakening the board they will possibly show as hollows on the finished work.

Using the fingers, the slips are now impregnated with paste almost down to where they emerge from the book. To facilitate threading, their ends only are rolled to a point between the palms of the hands. It is important that the twist does not extend far beyond the ends as this will make it difficult to disperse the fibres in the grooves and to flatten on the inside of the boards. To simplify lacing, the long straggling fibres at the ends of the slips should be cut away.

Attaching the boards With the board held vertically in the joint with one hand, the pasted slips are passed through the holes to the inside with the other and drawn firmly through (73). They are now passed outside again through the secondary holes, again drawn firmly, and the board is allowed to drop into position flat on the book. As the board must be attached neither too tightly nor too

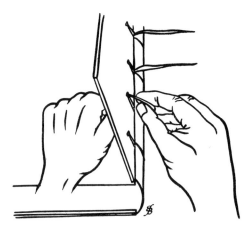

loosely this must be checked before cutting away the surplus hemp slightly above the little mound of board made by punching the holes. If the board is attached too tightly any contraction of the dampened hemp will result in a joint that will remain closed only under pressure and consequent strain. This seems to be a more common fault than a loose attachment, which causes the leather at the hinge to take strain which should be partly borne by the lacings.

The book is now held firmly and the laced board is allowed to rest on the knocking-down iron, the book being at right-angles to it, while the slips are carefully hammered quite flat first outside the board (74) and then inside. Any sudden movement before hammering can result in the board coming away from the book with little hope of successfully re-lacing the cut slips.

When both boards are attached, and this should be done quite expeditiously before the paste dries, metal plates inserted into folds of paper are placed on both sides of the boards, care being taken that the folded edge of the covering paper lies snugly against the backing 'shoulder' on the inside and the joint edge of the board on the outside. The whole is placed between pressing boards flush with the plates and put into the standing press and subjected to extreme pressure.

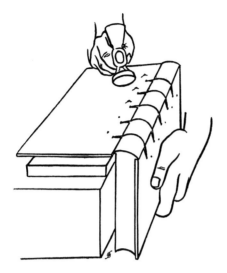

74 *Hammering down the slips after lacing*

There are good reasons why books that are to have their boards 'drawn-on' can be sewn to tapes instead of cords. Experience shows that ultimately there is greater weakness at the joints of a binding than in the sewing, so it is reasonable to think that a better balance can be obtained by sewing to tapes. While this possibly results in less sewing strength, the cutting of saw kerfs (as for recessed cords) is eliminated and reduces damage to the paper of the book. Tape slips must be left longer for lacing, and boards must be prepared

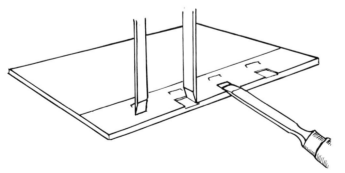

75 *Preparing the board for lacing tapes*

rather differently. A carpenter's chisel the same width as the tape is used to cut slots in them (75), through which the tape ends are passed when lacing. A *very small* amount of the surface of the board must be cut away between the joint edge and the slot to allow the tape to lie flush with it. The surface of the board between the 'entrance' and 'exit' slots on the inside of the board must also be cut away. To facilitate threading tape slips, the rounded end of a metal nail-file will be found useful. Otherwise the procedure is the same as with cords except that tapes do not require scraping. If, when backing the book, the shoulder is made to project the slightest amount above the board, a thin piece of pasteboard may be glued to the surface, which not only ensures a good surface but effectively holds the tapes in position during covering. This thin board must not be affixed until *after* cutting (if in-boards) and headbanding have been completed, as these operations require the lowering of the book boards, which is not possible once the surfacing board is in position.

It will be realised that fewer tapes than cords will be required when sewing.

There is no doubt in my mind that this method provides a stronger attachment of the boards, with possibly freer opening of the book, and has the advantage of causing less damage to the book than sewing to recessed cords. Moreover, in a 'nylon' age, hemp cord is becoming increasingly difficult to obtain, as it was not made primarily for bookbinding and its use for netting has rapidly diminished.

SETTING THE BACK

If the press has been built up with blocks or boards above and below the book, the back may now be 'set'. This is done by coating it with paste and leaving it for about five or ten minutes when the moisture will have soaked into the glue. With a folder or a wooden 'scrape' made from a flat piece of wood (a wooden rule will serve) with its end cut slightly concave and sharpened or bevelled, the back is now cleaned of paste and glue (76), being finally rubbed over with a slightly dampened sponge.

When a standing press is not available the cleaning-off process may be carried out in the lying press and the book then returned to a nipping press to dry out. If the book has been flexibly sewn the bands should be checked and any necessary corrections made with the band nippers, which should be cleaned and dried immediately.

The book or books should remain under pressure at least overnight. The process of setting the back has an extraordinary effect upon the

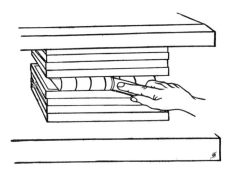

76 Setting the back—removing paste and glue

firmness and compactness of the book and should be done on all bindings that must endure.

WOODEN BOARDS

Where it is desirable to use wooden boards, as in the rebinding of folio vellum manuscripts, it is of the utmost importance that they be cut from timber so well seasoned that there can be no doubt about its subsequent behaviour. Recourse must usually be had to unwanted old furniture for this purpose as most modern methods of seasoning timber are far too hurried. In such cases, the book will possibly be sewn on split leathern thongs which will be laced into drilled holes and secured by the use of glued wooden pegs cut flush with the surface of the board. If, as is often the case, the sides are to be left uncovered a rebate equal in depth to the spine leather thickness and as wide as the leather to go over the boards must be cut beforehand.

SPLIT AND LAMINATED BOARDS

Where books are sewn to tapes their edges are usually trimmed before boards are attached, in contradistinction to some cord-sewn work. Attachment is normally by one of three similar methods, the most common of which is the split-board method. As the name implies, the boards were originally split with a knife along the joint edge, the slips and first back lining—usually mull—being inserted between and the slit sealed by adhesive. Today the 'made' split board is in general use and is very satisfactory, as when making up the opportunity is provided for controlling to a considerable extent the warping of boards.

Making split boards   The making merely consists of glueing or pasting two boards together leaving an unglued margin along the joint edge (77). This may vary in width from 1in to 2in or even

77 A 'made' split board

more according to the type of binding and size of book. Several opportunities for variation occur here according to need. The two boards may be of equal thickness although usually a thinner one is used for the inside, which tends to bring any 'warp' inwards towards the book. In addition, should there be any disturbance of the board surface as a result of the insertion of tapes and back linings it will be on the inside rather than the outside of the board.

Again, the boards may be made of millboard or even of strawboard where doubtful economy demands this. An intermediate course is the use of millboard with a strawboard liner, which although not giving the same rigidity as all-millboard tends to accommodate the tapes and mull less obviously, because of the softer nature of the strawboard.

The boards are made up before being cut to size, and although non-flexible glue is the more usual adhesive used, where a quantity is being prepared for future use and there is adequate time for complete drying-out to take place, many prefer to use paste. The inner board receives the adhesive so that any warp is towards the book: this will also tend to offset the 'pull' of the covering material.

The use of an inner board with the grain running across the book will increase rigidity, but it is advisable to use glue rather than paste and to lightly score, with a knife, the inside board on its *inner* side at the point where it must crease when being opened to receive the tapes and mull. This method should be used with strawboard 'inners' and where, for any reason, a thick millboard is used as an inner board. In either case, if it is thought that undue warping may occur glue should be used in preference to paste.

When quite dried out, the boards may be cut to size; and here it must be remembered that the split-board method of attachment demands a French joint in which the board is set some distance away from the joint. This is made necessary because the connection is now made at least half and usually two-thirds down the board thickness and additional room must be allowed for this. The amount required to be left in the joint will be dependent upon board thickness combined with that of the covering material when folded. Nice judgement on this point is necessary; although too wide a joint gives little support there when the book is on the shelf, it is better to err on this side than make the joint so tight that it prevents free opening of the cover.

Attaching split boards To facilitate the insertion of the tapes and linings into the split, these are thinly glued out on to the waste sheet of the endpaper which is then folded back over them, fitting neatly into the hinge, enveloping them (78). The 'flanges' must

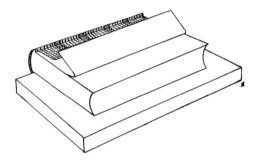

78 *Attaching split boards—making a flange*

firmly adhere, and rubbing down is required to ensure this. When dry, flanges must be cut rather narrower than the board 'split' and shorter than the book by an amount equal to the turn-in of the cover. This does not apply if unlined vellum is used for covering. In this case the flange is left full-length and is slit close to the board to allow the vellum to be turned in.

The boards are now positioned on the book and their position marked by running a fine pencil line on the flanges along the joint edges (79). If the head and tail positions of the book are similarly marked on the boards no error should occur in fitting them.

Once split boards are attached to the book they cannot be re-adjusted to allow for the sewing of headbands and these must be worked beforehand.

79 *Attaching split boards— marking the position of the board for a French joint*

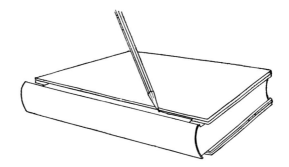

The interior of the split is carefully glued, which is best done by allowing the board to project beyond the bench edge with the 'inner' board well opened up; the glue brush should contain little more than the amount of glue required. With the book lying flat on the bench, its back away from the worker, the board is placed in position with the flange inside the glued split. Do not allow the flange to come into close contact with the glue until the board is correctly placed, when it may be quickly rubbed down with hand or folder. The book is now turned over and the second board dealt with. Metal plates inserted into folds of paper are placed carefully between boards and book, the plates tightly against the fold of the paper and placed accurately against the shoulder of the backing. The book is firmly pressed between pressing boards and the boards are allowed to dry. Metal plates prevent the marking of the book by the creasing of the opened flange, or by tapes if they be thick and the inner board thin. They also assist in sealing the split where the boards overlap the book and where there is otherwise no resistance to pressure. It may be necessary, however, to use the folder at these points to make certain of adhesion.

French medieval bookbinders were, it seems, compelled by edict to reinforce their bindings with back linings of vellum or parchment which were carried to the *inside* of the cover, and so a wider joint was required. This has come to be known as a French joint. This edict was conveniently and variously interpreted, and bindings of the period are found with full-length vellum linings with portions

cut away where the bands project, while others have but a few
narrow strips—sometimes so narrow that they extend to one board
only.

Semi-split boards An extremely useful variation of the split board
is one where the inner flange does not extend the full length but

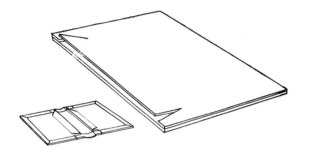

*80 Semi-split
boards*

stops a short distance from the board edges—sufficient to allow the
turn-in of the covering material (80). With the use of a 'hollow'
lining on the spine to which it is later glued, the method permits the
book cover to be made separately while still giving extremely good
attachment of the cover to the book. Because it successfully bridges
the economic gulf between simple casing and binding proper, in
that it permits the making and, if necessary, the gold blocking of the
cover away from the book, the method is of importance. It is
desirable to use reinforced endpapers to give surface strength in the
joint. Boards should be set slightly away from the joint.

Laminated boards The 'laminated' board, especially when used in
conjunction with the 'supported French joint' is one of the few
successful innovations in bookbinding technique of recent years. A
product of the ingenious mind of Thomas Harrison, it sought to
combine the best of both existing methods of board attachment. By
hingeing from the inside of the foredges the two boards used for
split board work it is possible to use either tapes or cords for sewing,
to leave the slips much longer than usual and, with cords, to disperse the fibres over the surface and so reduce thickness (81).
  The inner board is carried right up to the backing shoulder while
the outer is left at the normal distance for a French joint. The result
is greater support for the book in the joint while still retaining the

wider joint on the outside, which permits the covering material to roll open rather than crease, as tends to be the case with drawn-on

81 *Laminated board for supported French joint*

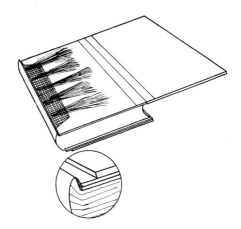

boards. Any objection that the slips—tape or cord—still show in the groove is hardly valid when the extra support given is taken into consideration.

With very heavy bindings it is possible to use three laminations, the thicker outer one providing the semi-French joint while the slips and linings are contained within the two lower ones.

SUMMARY

To conclude the account of methods of board attachment, the following points are made.

82 *Variation of hinges* (left) *and joints*
1 *French joint*
2 *Supported French joint*
3 *Drawn-on (laced) boards*

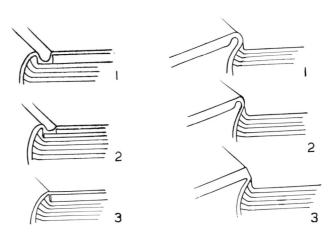

Where the book—especially when large and heavy—will be housed standing upright on shelves, its shape, and therefore life, will be longer preserved if the boards are drawn-on (laced) because of the support given at the joint by the tightly fitting boards.

With bindings that will spend much of their lives lying flat—many reference and public library books and lectern Bibles come within this category—a French joint is preferable.

Where books are large and receive fair usage, but will otherwise be shelved, the Harrison supported French joint with laminated boards will be found to be most satisfactory (82).

Headbands

In medieval books, the core of the headband was a leather thong, in fact an additional band, laced into the boards like the others, and encircled by the sewing thread between the sections. It gave support to the spine, though the extra strength was largely offset by the necessity of cutting the leather of the cover in order to turn it in behind the spine. Headbands were functional, not decorative. Today they give support at the head and tail of the spine, and also contribute to the beauty of the binding. They are made immediately before any back linings are added, and the book covered, and may be woven on cores of vellum, catgut, or occasionally leather. All these, being flexible, conform to the shape of the back when the book is opened; but rolled paper, which has sometimes been used, does not. Even machine-made headbands on tape are preferable—and more honest.

Whether headbands are sewn before or after boards have been attached, their width must always allow for a 'headcap' of leather to be made above them and still be slightly short of the boards in the finished binding. This is of great importance, for should the headcap project, the leather on the book spine will inevitably be subject to unreasonable wear at head and tail and will break down prematurely.

SEWING HEADBANDS

Headbands are worked with the foredge of the book facing the worker. The silks used must be firm and not liable to fray during sewing, while needles should be as thin as conveniently possible but

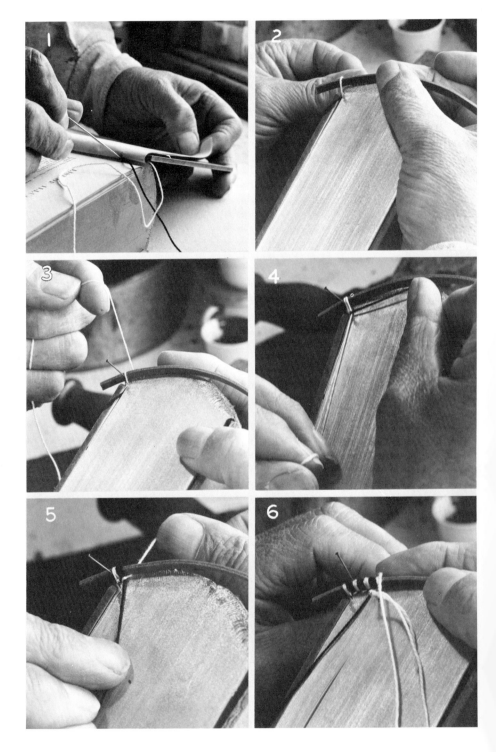

capable of withstanding the pressure necessary when passing them through the sections to the back of the book. A number of different colours may be used but at first it is wiser to limit them to two. Choice of colours is a personal matter, dictated by the nature of the book and its binding. On older books a recessive shade may seem more appropriate.

CORES

If *vellum* is to be used, two pieces—their thickness will depend upon the size and thickness of the book—are well pasted and a piece of bookbinder's linen is sandwiched between them before they are placed in the press under good pressure and allowed to dry.

Catgut. Old cello strings make excellent headband cores, being smooth, strong and very flexible. They require no preparation.

Leather is not as successful, as the silks tend to catch up in the fibres. If treated with paste or thin PVA adhesive, there is less likelihood of this.

Hemp cord should be similarly treated for the same reason. This and catgut give a rounded headband whereas vellum and leather give a squarer, sharper effect.

Whichever core is used, its shape should be lightly rounded by gently passing it over a pencil or folder held in the hand until it assumes the shape of the back of the book. Two pieces are cut about an inch longer than the width of the back of the book at the head and tail.

If two silks only are being used they must be long enough to complete the headband, and this can be assessed only by experience. Tie them firmly together with as small a knot as is necessary for security; usually a reef knot is effective. One silk is threaded through the needle and secured by passing the needle back again through the strands of the silk, and tightening it. This prevents the needle falling off during the sewing.

Opening the book at the centre of the fly-leaves of the endpapers if it is thin, otherwise at the centre of the first section (if not too far from the beginning of the book), pass the needle through from the inside to the back just below the kettle-stitch (83–1). Pulling the silk so that the connecting knot lies nicely in the back of the section,

83 (opposite) *Sewing single headbands*

bring the needle over the top edge of the book and again pass it through the same hole, thus leaving a loop of silk over the top of the edge.

With both silks outside the book at the top edge, if boarded, lower both boards level with the book edge. In this position place it in a small bench press, foredge foremost and at a slight angle towards the worker so that both edge and back can be seen. Any press is suitable but a small one more convenient; in professional craft binderies disused ploughs are sometimes used.

The end of one of the curved cores is placed through the loop of silk (83–2), and with it resting *on top of the book edge* the silk is tightened round it. It can be kept in position by passing a pin through it (the 'made' vellum core lends itself nicely to this) and carefully between the end leaves of the book (83–3). The silk threaded to the needle and at the back of the book is brought over the core to make a second silk on it. It is brought towards the foredge and held firmly by a finger of one hand. The silk coming from the inside of the book is brought directly upwards with the other hand and passed to the right-hand side over the firmly held first one (83–4), passed under the core to the back and gently tightened. This has the effect of pulling the other silk down to the book edge and commencing the bead that lies in front of the finished headband.

A colour change is effected by bringing it over the core again and passing it under the core to the back and bringing it over; there are now two silks of each colour. A third or even a fourth may be added before bringing it to the foredge and tying it down as previously by crossing the left-hand silk over it (83–5). At short distances the left-hand silk is taken down *through*, instead of over the top of the book, coming out slightly below the kettle-stitch at the back to secure the core to the top edge of the book. This tying down must be done with care and consideration for the book, making sure that there is no disturbance of the paper by the passage of the needle. The correct tension of the silk requires that after forming the bead it be kept firm at the back using the finger of the free hand which allows the use of the thumb-nail to press the silks close together at the bead and on the band (83–6). This finger play is essential if the headband is to have a really professional finish. This process is continued until the headband has been woven across the book and tied down at several points along it. To finish off, the silk is passed twice through the last section or endpaper fly-leaves and firmly and securely tied to the other silk at the back of the book.

Taking the book from the press, cut the projecting ends of the headband core with shears. While the silks must obviously not be cut, there should be very little of the uncovered core left behind. Silks at the back of the book are fixed to it by paste or thin cold glue, using a folder and working downwards from the top to tighten them.

Where additional colours are required they are all tied to the silk to be used for sewing down the headband; after the first silks are brought over, all not in use are covered when making the bead and incorporated in it. Some binders bring them from the inside of the book while others leave them at the back, bringing them forward under the core before taking them into the bead. Where a number of colour changes occur, the vellum core can be marked to ensure that any repeated pattern is placed symmetrically in the finished headband.

DOUBLE HEADBANDS

These are an extension of single ones and are very effective on larger volumes.

The method of making is similar, but two cores are used instead of one. They are of different widths, the wider one being placed at the back of the narrower; vellum and catgut make a good combination. When at the beginning the loop is made over the head of the book the front core (catgut) is placed in it from right to left as with a single headband. The second, wider one (vellum), curved to the shape of the back, is also placed very slightly into the loop but from left to right, and with the convex side of the curve towards the worker (84–1). By turning it to the right behind the first core and tightening the silk (84–2), this will now encircle both cores in a 'figure-of-eight' formation with the two cores in their correct positions on top of and across the book edge, where they are held in position with a pin (84–3). From now onwards the headband is woven as for a single one except that each silk, after being passed between the cores and over the book, instead of being brought forward and over the smaller core is brought up and round the wider one (84–4), coming up between them again (84–5) before being brought over the front (smaller) cord to be tied down by the next silk forming the bead (84–6). This is continued until the head-band is completed.

The double headband is difficult to make at first, but if it is borne in mind that the only difference between it and the single one is that after bringing the silk up *between* the two cores it must first be taken over the wider one at the back and again brought up between them before being brought over the front (smaller) core, most of the difficulty is removed. A sewn headband is judged by uniformity of tension and the placing of the silks, especially where the bead is concerned. Weaknesses to be avoided are looseness of tension with silks, and irregularity. Above all, the bead must be neat and lying close to the headband and the book edge.

It is possible to improve a faulty bead by holding the book in one hand with its back on the bench and gently rolling it from side to side, pressing the bead into a better shape with a fine-pointed folder. Looseness in the sewing of the headband cannot be corrected.

MACHINE-MADE HEADBANDS

These are made on tapes and can be cut to the required size. They are not as effective as hand-sewn ones and on aesthetic grounds alone should not be used on good bindings. They are abhorrent to the purist! When used they should have cane centres and be shaped to the book before sticking in position. They are often made with a different width of headband on each side of the tape so that they can be used on books of different sizes. Attachment is simple but needs to be done with care. The headbands having been cut to size and shaped to the book, a small amount of glue is brushed on to the back of the book at head and tail, then the book is removed from the press and held in the left hand, foredge upwards, which gives a clear view of the headband when placed in position from under-neath. With both headbands in position the book is returned to the press back uppermost and the headbands are rubbed down firmly through a piece of tough paper held taut over them to prevent any movement. Adhesion must be 100 per cent to be effective. It is possible for this type of headband to be made by glueing a piece of suitable cloth or $\frac{3}{4}$in ribbon, and laying a piece of soft cord about $\frac{1}{4}$in from a top edge, which is then turned over it and worked firmly round the cord.

84 (opposite) *Sewing double headbands*

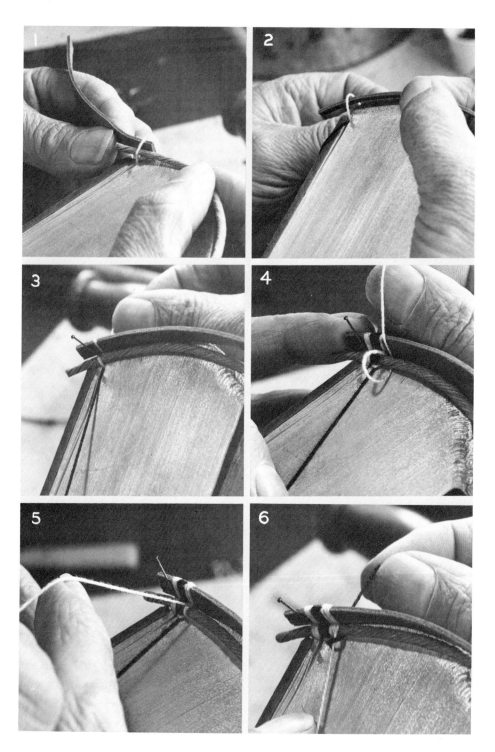

MOULDED HEADCAPS

With library bindings, leather and cloth, the headband is often replaced by a moulded headcap formed by the insertion of paste-impregnated soft string or cord when turning in the covering material at head and tail when making the cover. If the cover is fitted on the book directly after making and tied with thread or thin string round the hinge using a slip knot to hold it temporarily in position, the caps can be moulded to an angle of about 45°. This is best done by holding the book on its spine with its end flush with the edge of the bench and gently rolling it from side to side, using a fine-pointed folder to shape the cap. Buckram and art canvas lend themselves to this treatment; cheaper, thinner cloths are not as successful. When dry, the head and tail of such covers will be found to be firm and strong and yet flexible, while the back edge of the book, covered by the moulded headcap, will look much neater.

Back Linings

Back linings are used on all books with hollow backs, but there are variations in making them according to the style of the binding and size of the book. At first condemned by the bibliophile, the hollow back is now universally accepted, probably because books, being smaller and lighter, do not require the heavy leather of the spine to be stuck directly to the back, which is essential only when books are sewn on raised cords.

A point in favour of the hollow back is that it lends itself more readily to rebacking when this becomes necessary (as it inevitably must at some time) and permits the replacement of the original spine with tooling intact. With so-called 'flexible' or tight-back bindings this can present great and sometimes insurmountable difficulty.

At their simplest, in cloth casings, back linings consist of a piece of 'mull', a coarse variety of muslin lightly sized, and a strip of firm paper. The backed book is placed, back uppermost, in a bench press, projecting about two inches. Using thin hot glue, cover the back lightly by taking up only a small amount on the glue brush and with a dabbing movement working from the centre outwards. Care must be exercised to prevent glue getting into the joints and on to the endpapers. A piece of mull almost the length of the book and about 1½–2in wider is laid centrally across the back, held at the sides and rubbed down firmly with a folder. Work the sides of the mull into the backing shoulders using the tips of the forefinger and thumb of both hands simultaneously—this assists in preventing glue going beyond the back when subsequent coats are added. If the book is to be bound with a tight back, as is often the case with quarter-leather library-style bindings, no further linings are needed after mulling. Where headbands have been added, the mull must extend over them and any surplus be trimmed away afterwards. It is important that perfect adhesion is effected at every point, otherwise the leather spine will be loose there. When lining the backs of leather bindings the first lining of mull usually covers the back only. If flanges of mull are left at the sides they can be cut where cords are laced and each portion carried through the joint to the underside of the board and used as a reinforcement in the joint.

The back is now lined with a piece of suitable paper. Kraft wrapping, unglazed, is very suitable, but it must be of a weight (thickness) appropriate to the size of the book. If too heavy it will impede the opening of it in use, if too light it will not provide adequate support to the back. 'Directional grain' must run from head to tail of the book as it will fold more readily that way when the book is opened. Used the opposite way it will be more difficult to stick to the book and will, if thin, tend to cockle and not fold as readily when the surplus is cut away.

After the mull has been glued in position and before it is dry, the back is again glued, minimally but thoroughly, and a piece of the lining paper rather longer than the book and with its edge cut perfectly straight is laid with the cut edge flush with the backing shoulder and is well rubbed down with a folder. It will be found easier to do this if the folder has been lightly rubbed across the hair; this is always a help when the folder is used. The lining paper must adhere firmly to the book as it will have to flex continuously when the book is in use. Fold back the surplus paper at the other backing shoulder and cut away using a sharp knife.

Taking the book from the press, hold it in the left hand with its back downwards, and cut away the projecting ends of the lining paper, using the shears. Left-handed workers will find this very difficult with right-handed shears and must either learn to use the right hand or obtain left-handed shears. Leave the book to dry, carefully placed between boards and under a light weight. At this stage with simple casings it is usual to mark the width of the back of the book on to a piece of thick paper or very thin pasteboard—again the grain running head to tail—to be cut to form the lining of the spine of the cover, referred to as a 'loose hollow'. The loose hollow is cut to the exact width of the back of the book and at least as long as the *book boards*; some prefer to cut it about $\frac{1}{4}$in longer thus allowing $\frac{1}{8}$in to be turned over when making the cloth case. This makes the spine firmer at head and tail, especially when the loose hollow is only of paper.

THE OXFORD OR ENGLISH HOLLOW

The 'Oxford' or attached hollow is a much better method which can be used on leather or cloth bindings with distinct advantage to the latter. Because it is made *in situ*, allowance is made for any slight variation in the width of the back of the book—and this does occur from time to time.

The method is fairly simple but requires care and accuracy (85).

85 Making an Oxford hollow 1 First paper lining 2 Paper folded back over the book 3 Lining removed from back of book and reversed 4 Next lining brought over to be glued to first lining 5 Rubbed down and surplus folded back and cut away 6 The Oxford hollow returned to the spine of the book

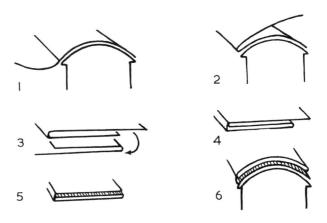

Lining paper is cut slightly longer than the book and at least $3\frac{1}{2}$–4 times the width of the back with the grain running along the length. After 'mulling' a rather more liberal amount of thin glue is applied to the back of the book. The cut edge of the lining paper is laid flush to either the right or left backing shoulder and lightly rubbed down with a folder so that all-over contact is made with the glue.

The lining paper is now folded accurately at the edge of the opposite backing shoulder and again brought over the back of the book. Holding it firmly down in position, it is creased against the original backing shoulder by tucking it into it with the finger-nail. Looseness on the back must be avoided.

The whole piece of lining paper is now carefully removed from the book without further creasing and laid on the bench with the glued area facing upwards and the folded edge towards the worker.

The unglued paper on the far side has been creased to the width of the back, and this is now brought tightly over at the cut edge of the glued area, laid on to it and well rubbed down with the folder.

The surplus paper is folded back level with the edge and cut away with a knife.

This leaves a flattened tube of paper exactly the width of the back of the book, one side being of single and the other of double thickness. Either side, according to whether a single or double lining is needed, may be returned to the still 'tacky' lightly glued back and the whole rubbed well down to it. Provided the glue has not had time to dry out, this results in an absolute minimum of adhesive, which is always desirable as a thick layer would dry hard and inflexible. With practice the Oxford hollow is made both quickly and accurately and is very satisfactory in use. It may be necessary to add another thickness of paper, or even two, to the free portion of the hollow of a leather-bound book, but this is a matter for the bookbinder and one requiring nice judgement. Too thick, and it can be difficult to turn in the leather at the spine; too thin, and the attached hollow may cockle and crease. Before the glue has dried it is well to rub down the headbands to the linings by holding the book back-downwards on the bench and rubbing them lightly yet firmly with a pointed folder. Finally, with the book lying flat on the bench with the back away from the worker, rub down the linings at the joints to ensure good adhesion there.

Reinforced hollow   To give greater strength in attachment of cover to the book, the Oxford hollow may be reinforced by adding bookbinders' linen to the back of the book before making the hollow. Sufficient linen is left on the sides to allow them to be glued back over the hollow after it has been attached. The back only is glued and first one linen flange is brought over on to it and then the other. Surplus linen is accurately folded back where it meets the other piece and with a very sharp knife cut neatly away, leaving no double thickness of linen at any point. If circumstances will allow, the linen can be covered with a piece of lining paper, leaving the back quite level for covering. With large or heavy books the reinforced Oxford hollow adds considerably to the life of the binding. For lighter books mull can replace the linen.

Thought must have been given to the final total thickness of back linings *before the book is backed* in order that they do not project above the boards at the hinges on the finished binding. Should they do so it will be necessary to bring the boards level by glueing a thin board over them. If this is done, any excess thickness of the board can be optically reduced by judicious filing away of the edges at head, tail and foredge.

Unless the board surface has been cut away to recess them, books sewn on tapes laced to the boards will require lining between the tapes to offset the slight projection caused by them.

With very large books sewn on webbings or heavy tapes, the linings may take the form of leather 'clothings' as used in account-book binding. Pieces of leather are cut wider than the space between the webbings or tapes, their edges pared so that when stuck in position the pared edges overlap the tapes slightly. This not only levels the back but adds much to the strength of the binding.

POINTS TO REMEMBER

Back linings must be proportionate to the book, and, while supporting the back, must not seriously interfere with free opening in use.

Paper grain must never be *across* the back; it will not only interfere with opening but can also result in slight cockling of the paper across the back which can spoil the finished spine.

Never use glue thickly—it will dry hard and the book will 'creak' when opened.

Where the backs of books are not 'set' after backing, it is advisable to line the backs as soon as possible; besides supporting the spine, the linings help to keep the expanded back and shoulders in shape.

3

COVERING

Cloth casing—quarter-leather (library style)—cutting and paring leather—half-leather with drawn-on boards—full leather— yapp, vellum and fabric covers—embroidered panels— putting down endpapers—leather joints and doublures

COVERING

A distinction is drawn between books that have boards attached before covering and those that have not. The latter are correctly known as cased books since book and cover come together only in the final stages. When the knowledgeable bookman speaks of a 'binding' he is referring to the former, in which book and cover are an integrated whole. Although there can be no real comparison between them, each has its place and the cased book can be given considerable strength if good methods and materials are used. There should be reinforced endpapers, strong sewing on tapes, firm backing and well-made back linings, combined with a cover made of strong boards and bookcloth such as buckram or art canvas. If the pasting of the book into its cover is done thoroughly and it is allowed to dry in the press, the result will be a book capable of standing as much hard wear as many leather bindings. For heavier library work, quarter- or half-leather, with cloth sides, the tapes and mull inserted into split boards provide an even stronger binding.

The average book collector is usually happy enough to have bindings in half-leather with boards drawn-on, provided the spine is pleasantly gold-tooled.

For the connoisseur, however, nothing but a full leather binding with elegant tooling will do. If it is further beautified with leather inlays or onlays, with leather joints or doublures and perhaps housed in a leather-covered book box, then it becomes a treasured possession and a showpiece to be gazed upon and admired but, too often, seldom used. This, let it be said, is to the detriment of the binding as the natural grease from the hands helps keep the leather in good condition.

Everyone, whether reader, collector, or connoisseur, is entitled to decide on his own priorities in choosing the style of a binding; so too is the artist who regards the book as presenting a problem in design and imposing its discipline in the solution. The one thing that is not justified is slipshod workmanship.

The covering of books is dealt with in order of technical difficulty which represents natural progression from cloth casing to full leather bindings.

Cloth Casing

BOARDS

Normally a book cased in cloth does not have its boards attached to it before covering. These will have been cut to size probably from strawboard or, if the book is a heavy one, from millboard. Greater support is given to the book if they fit comfortably close to the backing shoulder. The protective projection beyond the book edges, known as the 'square' of the boards, is proportionate to the size of the book, varying from about a sixteenth to a quarter of an inch. Board thickness must be considered both from the point of view of the book and from that of the squares. A balance between the book and its binding must be struck, for it is as foolish to use boards that are too heavy for a small book as to use light ones for a large, heavy one. Because of this, the lightness of strawboard as against millboard can sometimes make it preferable for a cloth casing, especially if a thin cloth is used for the cover. It should be remembered that while a light binding will be inadequate for a heavy book, a heavy binding can impose a strain on a light one.

A knowledge of covering materials and their uses is essential, and these are discussed in Chapter 8.

CUTTING OUT CLOTH

The bookbinding cloth is cut large enough to cover the book completely and allow a margin of *not less* than $\frac{1}{2}$in all round for turning in over the board. If the prime consideration is a cover that will fit snugly round the book and in the joints, the cloth is cut with its length along the width of the material. This will result in the warping threads running head to tail as with directional grain in paper, and the usually lighter 'weft' over the spine reducing the likelihood of the cloth stretching at the hinge and of the boards warping there.

If used with the warp running across the spine, the strength of the hinge is increased, but the tendency for the boards to warp there is greater; this can be controlled by lining them inside with pasted paper, which will contract on drying and cause a tension in the opposite direction. Only when dry can the extent of any warping

86 (opposite) *Making a cloth case—glueing the cloth*

or its correction be accurately gauged. While this adds to the labour, the surface tensions set up by cloth and paper do result in a firmer book board.

The piece of cloth is laid with its length *across* the bench on a piece of waste (news) paper large enough to protect it when glueing. Book boards are accurately adjusted on the book; or if this is perfectly square at the base they can be knocked level with the tail; this ensures the boards being level there when the case is made, and is also quicker.

GLUEING CLOTH

Many experienced binders prefer to use hot glue, because its quicker coagulation reduces expansion of the material. The inexperienced, however, may find that a cold glue of medium consistency, that does not dry brittle like those with a gum base, gives more time to finish the operation before becoming too dry. The cold glue Stadex 404, available in the UK, is quite satisfactory if not diluted too much. If hot glue is used it must be fairly thin, and also clean. The brush should be large enough to take up sufficient glue to

cover the cloth at one glueing; with hot glue, a small brush is far less satisfactory.

Turn the brush in the glue-pot between the hands so that the glue taken up is really hot, and wipe off any surplus against a 'glue stick' or wire stretched across the pot. Holding the cloth with the spread fingertips a few inches in from the near edge, with strong, confident strokes brush the glue from the centre outwards and always *away* from the worker, spreading the glue uniformly over the major area and beyond the edges of the cloth (86). Having done this fairly quickly, transfer the finger hold on the cloth to the glued far end, using thumb and finger only, and complete the glueing. If the brush is twisted in the hand it results in a more even distribution of the glue; this requires practice. Returning the brush to the glue-pot, look along the surface of the cloth for any bristles or other impurities; these can be removed with a sideways touch of the point edge of a knife, which must be wiped clean on the newspaper from time to time. Any hairs, lumps, or even small ridges of glue will probably show through the cloth on the finished case.

If the glue in the pot is not clean, spread it freely and generously over the cloth, take up the cloth quickly and lay it glued side downwards on to clean waste paper, rub it down, and speedily remove it from the paper. Many impurities will have been removed from the surface of the cloth and the glue reduced to the correct amount by the use of this method.

MAKING THE CASE

Remove the glued cloth to the bench by gripping it at the near end, lifting it sharply from the waste paper and 'floating' it to the bench. This must be done quickly to prevent the cloth curling under at the edges. Pick up the book, which should have been placed with its boards slightly overlapping the bench edge, the foredge towards the worker, and place it on the cloth, checking that it is squarely positioned. Without moving the upper board, lay the loose hollow accurately against the lower joint of the book (87). The left-hand knuckles are placed on the upper board towards the foredge to hold it firmly in position. With the finger and thumb of the right hand, take hold of the cloth at a point towards the left-hand side (88). By straightening the hand and placing it underneath the cloth this may be curved over the whole length of the side of the hand

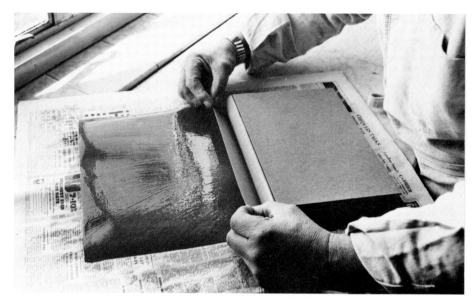

87 *Making a cloth case—placing the loose hollow in position*

88 *Making a cloth clase—drawing the cloth over*

and drawn uniformly and firmly over the back of the book to the front board. As soon as it makes contact with it, the left hand is removed allowing the remainder of the cloth to cover the board. If the cloth is pulled over by the fingers only, it is probable that the unequal tension will result in the finished case being loose at one end, and possibly in creasing of the cloth in its soft glued state. Lifting the back of the cover away from it, remove the book. Assuming that the usual square corners are to be made, with shears cut away the cloth at the corners at 45° leaving a margin equal to about twice the board thickness (89). If the board is a thick one it will be rather less, but there must be sufficient cloth to cover the board edges plus a little to fold in at the tip of the corner.

Holding the case firmly to the bench with the outspread left hand, first turn up the cloth against the edge of the board on the head and tail sides before pulling it over to the inside surface, using fingers and folder as necessary, and rubbing it well down (90–91).

It is important that the cloth be first glued firmly to the board *edges* as looseness here will soon result in its wearing at any unglued point when the book is in use. If the loose hollow is longer than

89 *Making a cloth case—cutting the cloth at the corners*

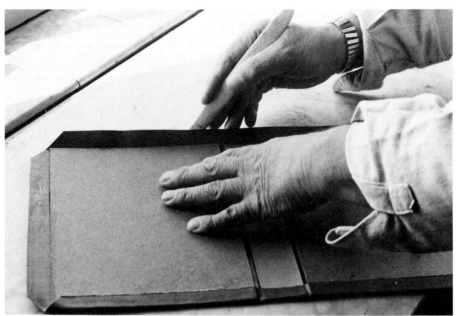

90 *Making a cloth case—turning up the cloth against the board edges*

91 *Making a cloth case—turning the cloth over on to the boards*

92 Making a cloth case—folding the cloth inwards at the corners

93 Making a cloth case—working the cloth into the board edges

the boards it must be accurately turned over, and it may be necessary to crease it with the folder before turning in the cloth at the spine.

For a moulded headcap, there should be no projection of the loose hollow; pasted cord or string, equal to the width of the back, is inserted in the turn-in, which is brought firmly round it with the folder.

The head and tail turn-ins completed, the cloth at the corners of the foredge must be folded in against the board edge, using the finger-nails of the forefingers of each hand (92). The folded glued cloth remaining there should not be flattened but allowed to make its own form as the rest of the cloth is turned in. The side of the hand is sometimes more effective than the folder for this, but it must be used very firmly and this at first can be a little painful. The corners should look neat and tidy with no cloth projecting beyond the board edge at any point.

The case is now turned over and its face side rubbed down with the folder (it may be necessary to work through a piece of plain, tough paper to prevent surface damage) first working on the boards and then into the spine (93). If this has cord in it at head and tail for a moulded headcap it is better to work from the inside at those points.

The book is now laid in the case and the cover brought firmly over to check the fit. The boards are raised at the foredge and the blunt edge of the folder is run along the hinge to ensure good adhesion there (94). The head and tail are now shaped by holding the book spine downwards and rubbing them with a pointed folder as the book is rolled from side to side. If there are to be moulded headcaps these are attended to in the same way by moulding them at about 45°; a piece of thread may be tied round the book at the hinges to hold the cover firmly to the book. A template may be used to ensure that the headcap is moulded accurately and minimally below the board edge (95), which it must be if it is not to take most of the wear when the book rests on the shelf.

If an Oxford hollow has been made when lining the back of the book this is now lightly glued, the cover is drawn tightly over and the spine is rubbed down thoroughly through a piece of clean paper. The book is placed between pressing boards with their edges exactly meeting the book hinge, and a weight is placed on top of them while the case dries.

94 *Making a cloth case— working the cloth into the hinge*

95 *Making a cloth case— moulding a headcap*

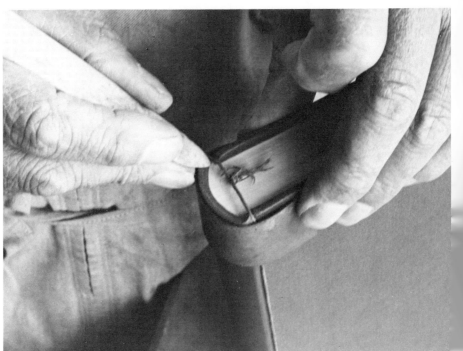

CORNERS

Corners for cloth bindings can vary according to the kind of use the book will receive (96).

The 'University' corner This is much used in library bindings because it gives a strong, slightly rounded corner and is quickly made. It has no pretension to beauty. Instead of cutting away the turn-in of cloth at the corner, the whole piece is turned over on to the board and firmly stuck down; the other edges are turned in as normally. It is unwise to stick the cloth to itself where it is folded over the corner, for this results in a treble thickness of cloth at the board edge, causing a projection which is subjected to greater wear. If the corner of the board is first rounded slightly a fully rounded corner results.

If a neater form of it is preferred, some of the cloth at the corner is cut away but leaving about $\frac{3}{8}$in (according to board thickness) and this is turned over on to the board. The procedure is as before but the result is a slightly less bulky corner.

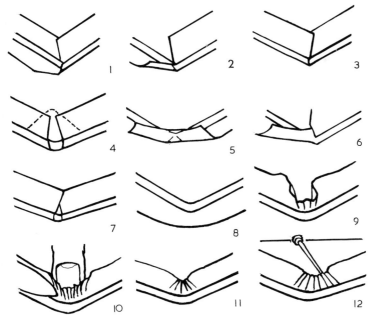

96 *Variations in making cloth corners*
1–3 *Folded corner*
4 *University corner*
5–7 *University corner, alternative form*
8–12 *Rounded corners*

Rounded corners Rounded corners can be really successfully made only with a soft or thin cloth. With the corners of the boards rounded (if a machine is not available they may be cut with a large carpenter's gouge (curved chisel) or with a knife, using a very small coin or the finger-nail as a guide), the cloth is cut away in a rounded form, the cut being rather closer at the corner but still leaving a small amount to turn over. After turning in the cloth on all edges except the corners, lift the cloth there and put the fingertip into the corner and on the board; with a small folder the cloth can be worked round it causing the material to crease. The finger is gradually brought back as the cloth gives to the folder until all of it has been worked fairly flat. Gentle hammer strokes from the *inside of the cover only* will help to complete it. When working the cloth, tend to bring it *away* from the corner to prevent an accumulation there.

With less tractable cloths such as leathercloth which does not lend itself to moulding, the only way is to pleat the turn-in at the corner using a small awl or a large needle to disperse it uniformly. The cloth cannot be flattened there and this must be accepted.

Quarter-Leather

LIBRARY STYLE WITH FRENCH JOINT

This style of binding is designed to give the greatest possible wear at minimum cost. Therefore, instead of the leather extending to a quarter of the width of the boards, as would be expected, it is often reduced to bare essentials, which may be physically effective but results in a binding of mean appearance.

Assuming that the split boards and back linings are already attached, the leather must be prepared. As previously remarked, a craftsman must have background knowledge of his materials, and this is given in Chapter 8.

The leather is cut wide enough to cover the spine and a quarter of the width of the front and back boards. It should be $1\frac{1}{2}$–2in longer than the boards. The centre of the skin is usually used for full bindings, so that leather for quarter-bindings comes from round the outside or from the shoulder, the former being of a rather looser texture and the latter quite the reverse; indeed it is sometimes too harsh at the neck to be satisfactory for lettering or tooling.

97 *Leather binding styles* (top, left to right) *half-leather, foredge strip,*
French joint; half-leather, supported French joint; quarter-leather,
French corners; (centre, left to right) *quarter-leather, paper sides,*
French corners; half-leather, cloth sides, boards drawn-on; full leather,
inlaid, French joint; (bottom, left to right) *full leather, gold-tooled*
leather joint and border with corner onlays; full leather, gold-tooled;
full leather, boards drawn-on, gold-tooled with leather onlays

PARING LEATHER

Paring leather is one of the most difficult operations for the in-experienced. It consists of cutting away from the flesh side of the skin all unwanted thickness at the edges and elsewhere. This is necessary, because leather of full thickness at the edges not only obstructs its turning in over the boards but is cumbersome and unsightly. It is sometimes necessary to reduce thickness slightly at the hinges if the leather there, unpared, would impede the free opening of the cover. If the book has bands on the spine a little of the leather thickness may have to be removed in order to mould it firmly round them.

Paring knives are of two types. That used for edge paring and formerly called a German knife today consists of a steel blade about 9in long and 2in wide at its widest point, tapering at the point of holding. The cutting edge is at an angle to the sides and is sharpened only from the upper side. The French paring knife is broader, shorter, thicker and less pliable and has a rounded cutting edge at the end. Unlike the edge-paring knife, it is fitted with a handle and is more useful for paring away from the edge of the leather. Although the ordinary bootmaker's knife, especially if worn slim, can be used for edge paring it is not as effective as the proper tool. Cutting edges are sharpened in much the same way as carpenters' chisels except that, after a fine cutting edge has been produced it is 'burred' over towards the back by gently rubbing it across the paring stone, the knife being held at a slightly acute angle. Unless the edge has been burred it will tend to cut downwards through the leather instead of over the surface. For paring leather for full bindings most professional craftsmen use a specially prepared carpenter's spokeshave. It will be found safer first to grind away the sharp corners of the cutting blade to prevent their 'digging' into the leather if the tool is held at an angle. The cutting blade must be kept very sharp, and the 'mouth' of the spokeshave, through which it slightly projects, adjusted according to the amount of leather to be cut away at each stroke. The blade edge is not burred as with paring knives.

Paring stones are usually discarded lithographic stones, but a piece of marble or even plate glass may be used. The surfaces must be smooth and clean while at least one long edge should be smoothly rounded. The 'stone' can be fairly large, but it must not be too cumbersome unless it can remain permanently on the bench. The piece of leather is placed face downwards on it and held at one end by the left hand. The edge-paring knife is held in the right hand with the thumb and two smaller fingers underneath and the end tucked into the palm near the wrist; the two remaining fingers are stretched out along the top of the blade to provide the downward pressure needed. With the knife held so that the side is at an acute angle to the leather, with the left hand holding down the leather, at the right-hand end, and beginning a little way along the edge, run the knife forward along the edge of the leather using firm but steady downward and forward pressure. Control is needed to keep the cut uniform, and the knife must be kept fairly flat (98). If too flat and with insufficient downward pressure, the knife edge will not engage but will ride over the leather without cutting; if tilted too much it will cut through it. A slanting cut should be aimed at and continued on all four edges. It will be found necessary to work in reverse to pare edges at the corners. If the knife is not cutting, the reason may be that it is not sharp enough or that the burr at the cutting edge is not sufficiently pronounced.

98 Using the edge paring (German) knife

When all edges are pared, additional attention must be given to the turn-ins at head and tail. With experience the knife can be held flatter to achieve a wider cut, but probably the use of the rounded French paring knife will be more effective. It is held rather flatter than the edging knife, but in much the same way. Because it is so much less flexible than the edging knife it is better to work close to the bench edge to give more room for the hand near the wrist. The leather can be held there by the thumb of the left hand pressed against the leather hanging over the stone or bench edge. This leaves the edge to be attended to flat upon the surface of the stone. The manner of paring away additional leather at the head and tail varies; some work across the width of the leather with the French knife held at a slightly sideways and downward angle towards the edge, while others prefer to work towards the end of the leather (99). This is the position adopted when reducing the thickness of the leather on the spine at head and tail to allow for the extra thickness there when the turn-ins are brought over. When using the paring knife, keep the arm as near to the body as practicable, which relieves the strain on the arm.

99 Using the French paring knife

The use of the spokeshave demands confidence born of experience—sometimes bitter. The leather is held on the stone either by pressing the body against the overlapping piece or by the use of spring clips, which are effective but tend to obstruct.

The spokeshave, very sharp and with the mouth not opened too wide at first, is held in both hands at a slight angle towards the leather surface and also to the edge. The base of the tool must be kept quite flat on the surface of the leather. Take away very little fibre at first, increasing the amount as confidence comes. Let the angle of the cut be too much, and overmuch pressure applied, and the chances are that the blade will cut through or the fibres tend to break and tear away. Once mastered, the spokeshave blade, kept sharpened, is not only effective but a great time and labour saver.

The wise worker will have an oilstone on hand to keep knife edges always sharpened. The time taken to do so is usually less than that wasted struggling with an inefficient tool—and less costly in leather wastage!

COVERING

With the leather now ready for use, the final preparations must be made for covering. Split boards have not had their surfaces impaired, but the edges will probably need reducing a little to lessen the effect of thick boards.

The 'cushioning' of book edges is dealt with on p. 131. Extremely sharp corners on a book cover may look well, but they are more prone to damage. The cutting away of the extreme tip of the board—an extremely small amount—will lessen this risk and yet not spoil the appearance of the book. Rather more may be removed or the corner completely rounded if a University corner is used.

The Oxford hollow must be slit at the joint at front and back of the head and tail to allow the leather to be turned in there. The slit must be cleanly cut for a distance that slightly exceeds the turn-in of leather, a sharp-pointed knife being best suited for this. If the book is slightly opened the hollow will separate from the back linings, allowing the knife to be inserted more readily. Unless cut carefully the paper may tear or even be cut in the wrong place, and this possibility accents the need for a really sharp knife. Library-style bindings sometimes have *false bands* added to the back for effect. This may be considered incongruous on a book sewn on tapes, as originally bands represented sewing cords, but they do not harm the binding and may even improve the appearance of the book on the shelves. As bands more correctly belong to books sewn to cords they are dealt with there (p. 181).

If the top edge is gilded it should be covered to protect it during covering, and this is done simply by turning a piece of cartridge paper over it and securing it with small pieces of sealing tape, making sure that endpapers will not be damaged. The leather is thoroughly pasted. If the atmosphere is warm the paste may be slightly thinned by dipping the brush carrying it quickly into water which assists brushing out. In summertime it is sometimes necessary to dampen the leather first by dabbing it with a wet sponge. When using hide on large books even immersion in water may be necessary. All these methods must be used with good judgement, for while it is fatal for the paste to dry out prematurely, over-damping will allow undue stretching of the leather when working and make it very receptive to marking on the surface during covering.

After pasting, the leather is turned over on to itself so that the paste may soak into it and drying may be retarded. A second pasting may be necessary, but must not result in an over-accumulation of paste on the surface. When this happens the surplus must be removed either with the edge of a folder or with the fingers, leaving a uniform covering. Assuming that the headcaps will be moulded ones, the string or cord is cut to the width of the back and both pieces are impregnated with paste and placed on one side, readily accessible. If the binding is to have a tight back, an Oxford hollow will not have been added and the back must receive a coat of paste before covering. This not only assists in adhesion but is necessary for the head and tail turn-ins to be stuck there. If these are not to obtrude overmuch they must have been well pared.

The leather is transferred to the paring stone and laid lengthwise on it. Taking the book in the right hand, hold it with the back downwards and place it centrally on the leather.

Lower one side on to the leather and draw the remainder over on to the upper board. Stand the book on its foredge and using the palms of both hands draw the leather down on to the spine, rubbing it down with the hand. A check must be made that there is an equal amount of leather on each side and any variation rectified. This can require the removal of the leather, but adjustment can usually be made without this. When the leather is firmly adhering on the spine, that on the boards may now be lightly smoothed out—no more than that. Taking a long folder, press it sideways into the groove between the joint and the board, making sure that there is sufficient there before rubbing down the leather on the boards. This may have moved when the leather at the hinge was pressed into the groove.

For turning in the leather at head and tail various methods are employed. Some stand the book upright with the spine projecting over the far side of the paring stone. Others hold the book upright with its spine on the stone and projecting over the front edge sufficiently to be able to bend the boards downwards. This can result in marking the damp leather at the edge of the stone. Perhaps the best method is to work on a prepared roll of paper laid lengthwise and about centrally on the stone. This may be newspaper rolled not too tightly and held together by fitting a piece of cartridge paper permanently round it. The thicker the roll is, up to about 3in, the easier the turning-in operation, and so a roll of newsprint round a core made from a cardboard tube and held together with cartridge paper provides a useful roll. There is no reason why it should not be covered with soft material sewn round it to prevent damage to the leather when the book rests on it.

The pasted cord or string is accurately placed on the inside of the leather at head and tail and rubbed down with the point of a folder to hold it there during covering. The book is laid across the covering roll with its head or tail projecting 2–3in beyond. The boards are allowed to open flat upon the roll while the book is held using only the palms of the hands, leaving the fingers free. It will be found simpler to stand slightly to one side and allow the book to be held between the body and arm, especially if it is large. With thumbs placed on the boards near to the joints and fingers underneath, except the forefingers which manipulate the leather, the boards are pressed downwards and away from the back of the book. At the same time the thumb-nails are inserted into the hollow where it has been slit, forcing it away from the back linings; at first this is far from easy to accomplish. If the hollow is thick and tight to the back it may be necessary to hold a pointed folder in the hand also and use it to open up the back, after which it can be dropped to the bench. Using the forefingers the leather is turned in over the pasted cord (which must not be allowed to slip out of position) smoothly and without creasing. If the edge of the leather should turn *under* during the process the leather must be withdrawn and straightened. If it should turn over *upwards* it may be possible to return it to its correct position by using a thin, blunt-ended folder. The book is now laid flat on the stone, with the left hand placed between board and book, the turn-in there drawn firmly over using the fingers of the left hand, the folder being held in the right to rub it down in position. During this the book is resting on the wrist and forearm. Having completed one end of the book, examine the spine to ensure that the headcap cord has not slipped and that the turn-in is lying smoothly with no creases showing, before proceeding with the other end. A slipped headband cord can sometimes be worked back into position by careful folder or finger pressure, but any projections on the surface caused by imperfect turning-in of the leather can be remedied only by pulling out the leather and repeating the operation—this time with greater care! It is unrealistic optimism to hope that they can be flattened from the outside.

As soon as the turning-in of the leather at head and tail is completed the book is lightly pressed between rods fitted to clean pressing boards. The rods, which are fitted at the long edge of the board, may be of brass, or may be plastic knitting needles, but they must relate to the width and depth of the hinge groove and be longer than the book. They can be temporarily fixed in position with sealing tape (medical zinc oxide plaster is even better), but as they tend to damage the board at the edge it is better to fix them permanently, using the boards for this type of work only. Brass-edged boards are made for the trade, but often the thickness of brass is unsuited to the groove or the projection is too great or too small. Generally these are used for what is known as a 'nipped' joint in edition binding, where a space is left between board and joint.

When the leather in the hinge has been quickly pressed home, the book is tied round with soft cord, using a slip knot positioned *off* the board. This holds the book firm while the headcaps are moulded with a pointed folder, the book being held with its spine resting on the edge of the stone. Before moulding, the leather at the joints at head and tail should be checked by gripping the book there from the outside using finger and thumb and if necessary forcing the leather neatly into the joint. At the same time turn-ins at head and tail can be flattened, for the tying up will possibly have disturbed them there.

MOULDED HEADCAPS

The moulding of headcaps has already been mentioned under *Cloth Casing* (p. 165) but with leather there are further possibilities. The angle need not be one of 45° although this is excellent from the purely functional viewpoint as the angle makes it difficult for finger-nails to find their way *under* the headcap when the book is removed from the shelf. An alternative is to retain the angle but to flatten the top edge. This can be done by bringing the headcap slightly beyond the board, then standing the book upright at the edge of the stone and placing a strip of plastic or celluloid round the top of the spine, holding it just below the level of the boards, using the finger and thumb. The projecting cap is now flattened level with the plastic template by gently rubbing the folder along it.

If two cords, one thick and the other thin, are used for the core of a moulded headcap, an even better-looking one results. Before turning in the leather the thicker cord is placed close to the book with the thinner one next to it, and when moulding the headcap this is worked down to the front of the thicker one. Careful use of a fine, pointed folder tends to give the effect of the bead produced in a sewn headband.

If dampness has permeated the leather in patches it must be sponged over, otherwise permanent stains may result.

The book is placed between sheets of waterproof paper, then between boards, and allowed to dry under light pressure from a weight on the top board. If the boards fitted with rods are available for use they provide pressure in the hinge during the drying-out period.

Before 'siding' the boards, the leather on them must be cut on the surface only to a uniform width and its edges must be neatly pared. Alternatively a filling may be used to bring the board surface level to that of the leather. This is described under *Half-leather* binding. A line drawn with a fine-pointed folder about $\frac{3}{16}$in from the edge will serve as a guide for paring, which is done with the edge-paring knife. This requires accuracy and care, for the cut must not deviate from the guide line nor must the point of the knife cut into the board if this is avoidable; even the very experienced are seldom 100 per cent perfect in this. It will be found that if the fingers of the left hand are used from the back of the knife to provide pressure, greater control is possible.

If cloth is used for siding it must be cut with the warp running from head to tail of the book; cut in the reverse way the weft, which is seldom uniformly straight, is likely to be cut through at more than one point when the edge is trimmed, and later will fray. The simplest way of cutting the cloth sides from the roll is to mark it at a point $1-1\frac{1}{2}$in longer than the book boards and to measure along the width of the roll a length sufficient to cover the board areas plus the $1-1\frac{1}{2}$in required for turning in. By cutting the two sides in one piece, folding it into halves and trimming away the fold with knife and straightedge, there is complete uniformity of size.

Cloth corners have been dealt with under *Cloth casings* but for greater strength the French corner can be used. It consists of fitting a very small corner of stronger material than the sides before these are added. With cloth sides vellum or parchment may be used, while cloth or bookbinders' linen can be used if the sides are of paper. As these reinforcements must not obtrude, only a very small area of the corner is covered, from about $\frac{3}{8}$in to $\frac{5}{8}$in. With vellum and parchment all edges of the corner piece must be lightly pared, and to the newcomer this is not simple. The paring knife must be sharp and considerable pressure and control are needed, for vellum offers more resistance to paring than most leather.

The corner pieces, having been pasted, if vellum, or glued if cloth, are laid on the bench with their long edges towards the front, and the boards are laid on to them. In this way their position can be judged with accuracy. The edges at head and tail are first turned in, the small projecting pieces at the corner are 'nicked' inwards using the thumb-nail, and, finally, the vellum or cloth is turned in at the foredge. All this must be done firmly and neatly and the face side of the corner pieces well rubbed down. When dry, vellum is very hard, so that the extreme tip of the board should be cut away to avoid the kind of corner that could wreak havoc with the book next to it on the shelf.

The cloth is lightly glued and placed in position on the board so that its trimmed edge abuts on the unpared leather, or slightly overlaps it if pared and rubbed down with the hands. The board is now turned back in the open position and with the shears held at an angle away from the book the cloth is cut away tight to the corners. If anything, the cut can be fractionally inside the corner to avoid fraying there later. When the edges of the cloth are turned in, the vellum corner will show only at the edge of the board and on the inside. While the cloth should be tightly turned in on all board edges, this is especially important at the corners.

The distinct advantage of the French corner is the additional strength it provides without affecting the appearance of the book on the outside. If paper sides are used—even of the best quality—such corners are necessary to prevent damage in use.

VELLUM SIDES

There was a phase in bookbinding history when vellum or parchment sides were popular on quarter-bound books, but the warping of the boards occasioned by the contraction of the vellum on drying made the style unpopular. This could have been avoided if the boards had first been sided with opaque white paper glued in position. Using a protective template over the leather, the paper was then lightly glued out, using dabbing rather than brushing strokes of the brush. The vellum, all its edges pared, was laid down with its edge flush with that of the white paper, quickly pressed and allowed to dry under pressure. The vellum edges were then pasted and allowed to soften before being turned in. This resulted in little expansion of the vellum on the outside but a considerable amount on the turn-ins inside which upon subsequent contraction on drying controlled any outward warping of the board. PVA adhesive would be even more effective, being smooth and white and coagulating quickly; but paste would still be needed on the turn-ins.

SIDING—ALTERNATIVE METHODS

Yet another method of siding (100) is one that not only avoids the possibility of the cloth edge fraying but permits it to be taken right up to the edge of the joint. This produces a very neat appearance and is economical in the use of leather.

The leather is cut with only sufficient on the boards to hold firmly there. Its long edges are pared somewhat thinner by making a broader cut. Pieces of very thin card are cut exactly the same size as the boards, and the cloth is cut about $\frac{1}{4}$in wider than required to cover the whole board area plus turn-ins. When the cloth is glued out, the card is placed on it to within $\frac{1}{4}$in of the long edge which is

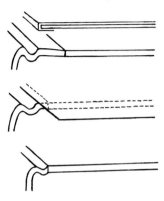

glued and turned tightly over it and the whole surface is well rubbed down with the folder.

The card is again quickly glued all over and laid accurately on to the board with the turned-in edge flush with the joint. The side is well rubbed down, and the cloth is cut at the corners and turned in over the book board. Special attention must be paid where the side overlaps the leather to be certain that it is sticking there.

The effect of the cloth turned in on all edges and the leather showing only on the spine and joints is quite pleasing.

As an alternative to this (101), the card cut to the board size has a

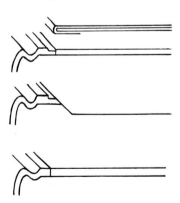

$\frac{1}{4}$in strip cut from its long edge and this is glued flush to the joint edge of the board *before* the leather is put on. This is worked tightly

over the edge of the card strip on to the board. The side is treated as before, but instead of fitting flush with the joint of the book it is tight to the slight projection caused by the piece of card. The effect is a narrow strip of leather showing on the board, but the turned-in edge of the cloth side now lies quite flush with the surface. The appearance depends very much upon the cloth used for siding, but its neatness cannot be denied.

Half-Leather

HALF-LEATHER WITH BOARDS 'DRAWN-ON'

These take two forms, the traditional one having only the spine and corners of the book covered with leather. The other, known as 'half-bound with foredge strip', has much to commend it although seldom used by the trade. As its name indicates, leather covers not only the corners but the whole length of the board at the foredge. Because this strip is quite narrow and the spine leather extends only a small distance over the boards, the total amount of leather required only slightly exceeds that used in traditional half-bindings. Both foredge and corners are given additional strength, while many consider the oblong panel of cloth or paper aesthetically more acceptable than that resulting from the traditional form.

The French joint having been dealt with under *Quarter-leather* binding, the tight one resulting from boards being 'drawn-on' (laced) when the book is sewn on cords is considered here.

BANDS

Preparations are similar, except that bands may be added to the spine for effect. For these, waste leather of suitable thickness, lined with paper to prevent it stretching, is used. The width of these false bands is a personal choice, but they should be proportionate to the size of the book. They can be wide enough to permit gold tooling on them; this applies especially to nineteenth-century volumes. Cutting is done with knife and straightedge while spring dividers may be used to ensure uniform width. The required number, usually five, are cut longer than the width of the back of the book and left attached to a small piece of the leather at one end which allows them to be glued more readily.

Traditional spacing of bands accords with that used with raised bands in sewing. The back of the book, less headbands, is divided into six divisions all equal in width with the exception of that at the tail which is one-third larger, giving a balanced effect on the spine of the finished book (102). If bands are wider than normal this must be taken into account or the tail panel may be too small. Division

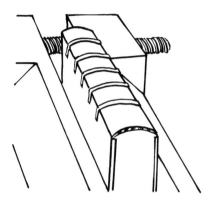

102 Fitting bands to a hollow back

is made by using spring dividers, a mental assessment of the approximate width usually being quicker than an arithmetical one, but it must be checked before marking the book. The lettering of the book must be considered before a decision on bands is reached. If it is necessary to letter along the spine, uninterrupted space must be left there. This does not preclude bands being placed either singly or in pairs at head and tail if this is acceptable. The book is placed,

103 False band, showing angle of cut

back uppermost, in the bench press and the leather strips are glued in one piece before being separated. Each one is placed squarely across the back of the book, the ends being taken on to the boards to hold it firmly while drying. Holding them in position with the thumb and fingertip of the left hand, rub each band down firmly with the folder before removing the book from the press and laying it flat on the bench with a knocking-down iron over the upper band strips while the glue dries. With a knife the surplus is then cut away at the joint shoulder and at an angle that will allow the book board to open on to the bench without falling foul of the ends of the bands (103). If this is not done there will be surface wear at these points when the book is in use.

BACK-CORNERING

Because the joint edge of the board rests close to the backing shoulder of the book, boards must be 'back-cornered' at head and tail to permit the leather to be turned in without impinging on the joint. A cut is made at the back edge of the board at two angles, one to the board edge and the other to its thickness (104). The amount to be removed and the angle of the cut are determined by

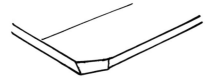

104 *Back cornering*

the width of the leather turn-ins and their thickness where they meet the board edge. Unless these are accurately assessed, a neat joint at head and tail cannot result. The cut may be made either by slipping a small piece of millboard under the board and over the backing shoulder or by opening the board back with the inside resting flat on the bench or stone. Drawing the book back a little, the hemp slips can be lifted out of their grooves, giving access to the face side of the corner without slightly bending the board as in the alternative method. It is the cut at the *inside* of the board that must relate to the thickness of the pared turn-in. The outside allows for the neat tying-up of the spine before moulding headcaps.

Back-cornering completed, any book edges that require protection during covering must be attended to (see under *Quarter-leather* and *Full leather*). Assuming that boards are clean and their edges and corners dealt with, the hemp slips are ready for pasting into their kerfs.

Turning back the board, a small amount of paste is placed on each cord where it meets the board (105), the point of the folder being

105 *Setting the slips into the grooves*

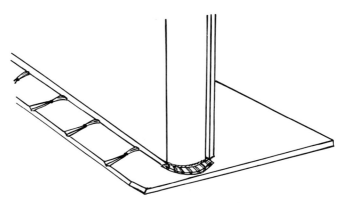

the best medium of application. The board is returned to its former position on the book and adjusted there so that the squares are uniform in width. Always the board *must* project beyond the head-band at the *tail* sufficiently to allow the making of a headcap that is still *slightly short of the board*. Should the headcap project it will later have to take wear that should be borne by the board edges when the book is shelved.

With the board accurately positioned, the hemp slips are worked into their grooves, using the folder point which causes the paste to impregnate the hemp, allowing neat moulding of it and holding it firmly in position when dry. If thought necessary, the book may be pressed while the paste dries, but paper-covered metal plates must be placed on both sides of the boards and quite level with the joint edges of them. Traditionally, books bound in half-leather had a third of the width of the board covered by the leather and the diametric width of the leather corner was equal to this. Today these proportions constitute a 'three-quarter' binding, and 'half-bindings' must be content with a quarter-board width of leather—or even less—with corners proportionate. Whatever the width of leather on the board, it must also be that of the corner at its greatest depth.

With 'half-bound foredge strip' bindings the proportions are optional and are left to the taste of the binder; the width and colour of the panel made when siding have the greatest bearing on this.

The leather is now cut, and templates for both spine and corner
pieces are a help in accurate and economical cutting. For corners it
is useful to have at hand templates of various sizes threaded to a
cord (106–1). When cutting corners there is a natural tendency to
use otherwise-waste pieces round the outside of the skin; but this
must be done with discretion, for book corners get hard wear and to
use poor-quality leather for them can negative good workmanship
elsewhere. Leather for foredge strips is usually about twice the
width of the turn-in and $1\frac{1}{2}$–2in longer than the boards.

Folded corners These corners have the surplus leather already cut
away (the corner template will have allowed for this), but for
moulded ones the extra is required there. Leather corner pieces have
all edges pared, but those being turned in demand wider paring if
bulkiness is to be avoided on the inside of the board (106–2).

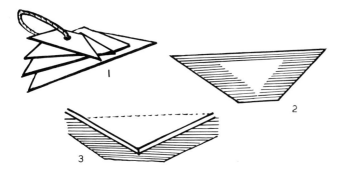

106 *Making
leather corners*
1 *Set of corner
templates*
2 *Leather corner
showing paring
proportions
(shaded)*
3 *Pasted corner
placed in position*

While usually the edge-paring knife only is used, the French knife
will assist in producing a neater corner. For the sake of uniformity
the position of the leather should be marked, and this can be done
by having the amount of turn-in marked on the corner template,
lining it up with the board edge, and pencilling a line across the
board.

Paste the corner pieces, lay them in pairs with the pasted sides
together, and leave them awhile to soak. Place two in position on
the board, checking that the turn-ins are uniform and that the
amount of leather projecting beyond the corner is adequate to
form the corner but not enough to cause unnecessary bulkiness
(106–3). First bring over the turn-ins at head and tail, then, using

the finger-nails, carefully fold inwards the small amount of leather beyond the corner. Place a touch of paste on the face side where it is folded before turning in the leather at the foredge. Corners need careful folding and shaping with the folder so that while the leather is not unduly strained it is firm and tight to the edge of the board. Avoid making sharp corners, for fairly obvious reasons. The edges being turned in, the leather on the face side is gently rubbed down, using fingers and folder.

Corners should be left to dry before proceeding with putting the leather on the spine, for they may be damaged if still damp.

When the corners have dried the spine leather can be fitted. This has been pared as described for quarter-leather French joint bindings and is at first dealt with in the same manner, except that there is no groove at the hinge. While the leather on the spine and boards must be firm, it must not be strained at the hinges. When the leather is turned in at head and tail of a headbanded book, sufficient must be left to form a headcap over the headband. It is better that the amount left be too little than too much, for if necessary a little more can be eased out at the spine, using the thumb-nail. The mere stretching of the leather to produce it will be unsuccessful, for it will contract later. It is more difficult to reduce the amount as, without taking out the turn-in and starting afresh, there is the danger of creasing the turned-in leather inside the hollow and this will show on the surface. There should be rather less leather projecting at the corners if the headcap is to be nicely shaped at the ends. The total overlap should be no more—and certainly no less—than required to cover the top of the headband, and this must be carefully checked in the making.

SETTING THE BOARDS

Before tying up at the hinges, check to see that when each board is opened back its edge lies quite level with the joint shoulder. Particular care is needed at the turn-ins at head and tail where the leather may be too tight, in which case more is worked towards the joint. In reverse, if there is looseness this must be remedied by working any surplus away from the joint. Should the board be dropping away from the shoulder, it must be very gently forced back into position with one hand holding the book and the other the board. These faults cannot be corrected later, and if left uncorrected will cause untidy and unsatisfactory joints. At the worst the leather turned in at head and tail may split, virtually ruining the binding, for the neatest repair there can never be satisfactory.

When the headcap leather is satisfactory, that at the back corners is gently pressed into the cuts there and the book is tied with thread round the hinge. A slip-knot should be used and the thread should be tied off the leather to avoid marking it. The tying-up should be firm but not brutally tight or the thread may cut into the leather at the head and tail. Should the leather tend to crease at the back corners it must be carefully smoothed out with a folder.

SHAPING BANDS

Stand the book on its foredge and gently ease the leather on the spine towards the bands, which can then be 'nipped' with the band nippers, which must be checked for cleanness before use. With the

107 (left) *Using a double bandstick after nipping up the bands*

108 *Using a single bandstick after nipping up the bands*

tail of the book towards the worker the band nippers are opened slightly wider than the bands, placed over them and lightly tightened, drawing the leather firmly against their sides. At first separate movements of the nippers will be found simpler and safer, but with experience and control they can be glided over the band.

Bandsticks After nipping up the bands they are still further sharpened at the edges by gently but firmly rubbing down the leather at each side with a bandstick.

Bandsticks are made in at least two forms (107, 108), one with a groove equal to the band width or, better still, with graduated grooves on each side so that at one point almost any width of band can be accommodated. The other is simply a narrow strip of hardwood, usually beech, that has a sharpened edge on one side, which must be kept smooth at all times. This has the disadvantage of working one side of the band at a time which often draws up the leather on the other side in use. However, this can be controlled by holding it down with a piece of flexible plastic. The edges of bandsticks should be lightly drawn over the hair before use, but they must not be rubbed too vigorously across the leather. Unless they are very narrow, the surface of bands should be rubbed down with the folder to ensure adhesion.

HEADCAPS

To form the headcaps the book is held upright in one hand with its bottom edge slightly projecting over the stone. With the boards held by finger and thumb at the back corners, work the leather neatly into the joint there. The finger and thumb slightly projecting above the board edge will prevent possible damage should the folder slip.

Working from the centre of the book, gently press the headcap over the headband. Place a piece of curved flexible plastic or vellum round it so that its ends come on to the boards and *slightly below their edges*, being held in position by the finger and thumb of the left hand (109). This not only enables the headcap to be firmly and squarely moulded but ensures that it lies slightly below the boards. Should the headband be too wide there is nothing that can be done about it at this stage. When the headcaps have been formed, stand the book upright and check their position by passing a piece of

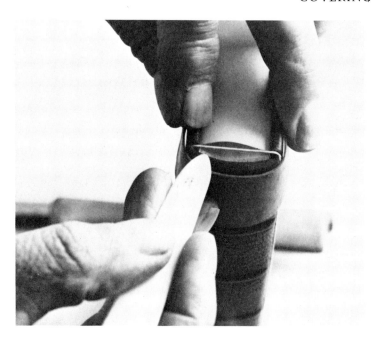

109 Moulding the headcap over the headband against a 'former' to control shape and height

paper between headcap and stone. Unless it passes freely between them the headcap is too high and must be reduced if this is at all possible. Before placing the book between waterproof paper and boards to dry under a weight, very gently rub down the spine leather at the hinges to be sure of good adhesion there, and then sponge the leather surface.

SIDING

Before siding, the width of leather on the boards must be checked for uniformity and trimmed if necessary. The paring of the edges is dealt with on p. 170. With foredge strips the corners must be cut and pared beforehand if they are to be folded.

A neater finish results if the surface of the board is brought level with that of the leather by a filling of paper or thin board. It is cut rather larger than required, and one long edge is trimmed and placed flush to the leather. The cutting point at the corners can be arrived at in several ways. The filler may be folded back level with the leather edges, or a fine pencil line can be drawn on the board at the edge of the leather and the filler worked in tightly and pressed with the finger-nail causing the pencil line to be partially transferred to the underside of it. The method used for cutting cloth sides has its merits here also: the filler placed under the board and flush with the back leather and the corners, cut with the shears to a point exactly at the edge of the leather. If the filler is the same shape as for siding, the leather on the edge of the board must be cut away to allow for the turning-in of the filler.

Always turn in the edges at head and tail before attending to the foredge. The simplest and most accurate way of cutting cloth for traditional half-leather bindings is to cut one piece large enough for both sides and fold it centrally with the face side inwards.

The folded cloth is placed in position *under* the front board allowing $\frac{1}{8}$in beyond the pared leather at the back for cutting away when separating the cloth into two sides. If all corners have been trimmed to a uniform width it is now possible, using shears, to cut both pieces of cloth right up to the board edge at a point very slightly over the pared edge of the corner. Remove the cloth and cut away the surplus at the corners by first turning up the edges level with the cut to mark the cutting point, and carefully cut it away using a knife and straightedge. It remains only to cut away the $\frac{1}{8}$in at the fold, again using knife and straightedge, and to separate the two sides, which are quite uniform, the lower one fitting the upper board and vice versa. Their shape allows them to be placed with accuracy on the boards, but each should be checked before glueing.

Because of the difference in thickness between leather and cloth or paper, care must be exercised when turning in the edges. For this reason leather should not be removed from the *edge* of the board when it is trimmed. With paper sides the ball of the hand will be found to be safer than the folder and equally effective, although difficulty may be experienced in turning in where the board meets the leather.

Full Leather

CUTTING OUT LEATHER

The paring of the leather requires as much care and consideration as the actual covering operation. In the first place it should be free from surface flaws, which usually means that it is cut from the best part of the skin. Unless the spine of the skin is fairly smooth it should not be positioned on the back of the book, for its surface can be unsuitable for gold tooling. The leather at the neck of the skin is often so coarse as to be unsuitable for covering. Depending upon the relative sizes of the book and the skin, it may be better to cut the leather so that the spine comes centrally on the back board where it will least interfere with the appearance of the binding and, in the most fortunate circumstances, will even enhance it. It should not be too close to the hinge because it is less flexible.

Having weighed the pros and cons, place the book in position on the flesh side of the skin and mark round the board edges, using a soft pencil rather than a ball pen. The amount of leather required beyond this will depend upon the thickness of the book board and the anticipated width of the turn-ins. While these should not be too mean they should not be unduly wide, for the greater their width the greater the amount of leather to be removed by paring.

According to the leather thickness, the paring of the edges starts either at the turning-in point marked when cutting the leather or a little further in. Board edges look bulky and ugly if paring is insufficient and, because of the time and effort involved, this is a far more usual fault than that of excessive paring which causes weakness at the board edges and the corners. Once again a nice balance between the two extremes is needed, remembering that the leather on the inside of the boards of the completed binding is not subjected to wear, and neatness there adds much to the book's appearance.

PARING THE LEATHER

General directions for the use of paring tools have been given under *Quarter-leather* bindings; but some additional precautions should be taken. In paring a large area, the spokeshave is, in practised hands, the most efficient tool; but the inexperienced may find that leather cut for full bindings may end as quarter-bindings.

The safety of the edge-paring and French knives is preferable at first. Pare the edges with the edge knife, keeping it fairly flat to produce a wider cut. The French knife can be used to widen the paring and also to lessen the sharpness of the angle of cut at the inside. If this is left, an unsightly ridge on the surface can result. When paring, the leather overhangs the stone where it is held as previously described.

From time to time the pared edges should be run between finger and thumb to assess the thickness and uniformity of paring; this tells the worker much that will affect the surface appearance of the leather. With thick leather it can be necessary to reduce thickness at the spine so that the bands can be firmly shaped, while at the head and tail some additional paring will be necessary in order that the turn-ins do not show on the surface of the spine.

Board preparation has been dealt with under *Half-leather* bindings but a full leather one demands that everything be done with the greatest care and neatness. The board corners must be 'tipped', back-cornering must be done at the correct angles and with restraint, board edges must be smoothly cushioned with perhaps a little filing at the inside edge of the boards should the leather turn-ins be on the thick side. The hemp slips must have been well moulded into the grooves so that the board surface is level there. The hollow will have been slit at head and tail to take the turn-ins.

CAPPING UP

The complete covering of all book edges is advisable when covering full leather bindings. Take a sheet of clean paper about two and a half times the length of the book and twice the width plus the thickness. Place the long edge centrally and tight to the backing shoulder, close the board and turn the book over.

Fold the paper firmly over the book at head and tail, clearly marking the folds with finger pressure. Turning it back again, repeat the process with the paper at the foredge and cut to the shape

110 Capping up edges, showing the sequence of folds

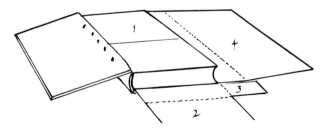

shown in illustration 110. First wrap the book edges at head and tail using sealing tape to secure the overlapping ends. Fold the 'tongues' inwards along the foredge before bringing over the remaining paper and securing it at the edges with sealing tape.

The main points of covering have been dealt with under *Half-leather* bindings, but because of the greater area being manipulated at one time much more care is necessary. Finger-nails have a habit of marking the damp leather, while any hard object, however small, that comes into contact with the surface in this state can have unpleasant consequences. If the paring stone is small it will be safer to place a millboard on the bench and work on that, using the stone as necessary. Have on hand all tools necessary for the work, shears, clean folders, band nippers and sticks, thread for tying up, waterproof sheets to go between boards and book, and clean white paper ready for use on equally clean pressing boards. Because the covering will take so much longer, precaution must be taken to ensure that the paste does not dry before it is completed, by damping the leather and/or using paste that has been moderately thinned as necessary in relation to the atmosphere of the workshop.

COVERING

Examine the leather and place the portion to be used for the front of the book towards the front of the bench. A large brush is best for pasting large areas, and the paste should be liberally and evenly spread, being well worked out over the whole surface and beyond. Fold the pasted leather in halves on to itself to allow for soaking. It must not be left too long before unfolding it again and repasting if necessary. Again fold before use as this assists in dispersing the paste evenly over the surface. Examine it thoroughly, removing any bristles or other impurities, for they will show on the surface later.

Place the book, front board downwards, squarely in position on the leather at the front of the bench and draw the leather over gently but firmly to the upper board (111). Rub it down lightly and stand the book on its foredge on the stone with the pasted leather edges turned outwards (112).

Using the ball of the open hands, draw the leather down on to the spine so that there is no looseness at any point and if there are bands they are clearly defined. This done, lay the book flat on the stone, first having wiped away any paste there. Lift the leather and smooth it out over the boards before rubbing it down with the palms. Do not strain it at the hinges for it will contract there when dry.

If the corners are to be folded, the surplus leather at the corners

111 *Covering in full leather—pasted leather being drawn over the book*

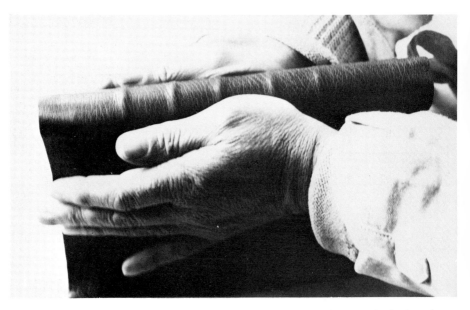

112 *Covering in full leather—working the leather over the back with the book standing on its foredge*

113 *Covering in full leather—turning in the leather at the head*

114 *Covering in full leather—turning in the leather at the board edges*

must be cut away before turning in the leather. This is done by inserting the edge-paring knife between leather and board at the corners and cutting with an angled cut. Sufficient leather must be left at the corner to allow for turning in.

Laying the spine and opened boards on the covering roll, proceed with the turning in of the leather at head and tail, first at the spine and along the edges and then the foredges (113–14). The leather needs careful working, for it must be firmly in position but not unduly stretched. The corners will probably be moulded, and so the leather there will not have been cut away. Proceed with them as described under *Half-leather* bindings. If they are to be folded, the small quadrant of leather at the extreme corner of each must be thinned by judicious paring (115). This requires considerable care, for damage there is not easily repaired. The tip of the edge-paring knife is placed up to the board edge, and while the paring takes place the forefinger of the left hand (which is holding the board to the stone) is used at the back edge of the knife to give extra pressure and control. Some find it easier to work with the board lifted from the leather which perhaps gives easier access. A folded corner looks neater if the smallest sliver of board be cut away from the board at the foredge corner to accommodate the thin leather folded in there and so avoid even the slightest projection at the edge. Be warned that the amount to be removed is very, very slight.

Moulded corners   With moulded corners the leather is left uncut at the corners, but it must be sufficiently pared in order that the turn-ins may not offer too much resistance to moulding. The sides are turned in and then the leather at the corner is moulded against the board thickness and slightly over on to the inside surface of the board. Surplus leather is folded upwards at an angle of 45° to the corner and cut away with the shears about ⅛in above the surface (116), and the foredge turn-in worked neatly *over* the side one. When the leather has partially dried out, but not if it is still quite damp, the over- and under-lapping leather may be cut from the corner at an angle *towards* the foredge and the surplus removed. The join there can now be pasted and rubbed down with the folder (117), tending to work the leather edges tightly towards each other to allow for any possible contraction later, which would expose the underside of the join. Some prefer to cut the mitre when the leather

115 *Covering in full leather— folded corners: paring the leather before folding it inwards*

116 *Covering in full leather— moulded corners: the leather, folded upwards, being cut at an angle of 45° slightly above board level*

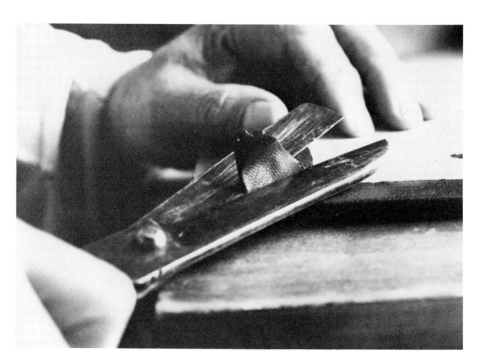

117 *Covering in full leather— after moulding, the leather is overlapped for mitring when dry*

118 *Covering in full leather— 'setting' the boards level with the backing shoulder before tying up*

is completely dry, damping it afterwards to remove the unwanted underlap and then pasting and working the edges together. This takes longer but it prevents any possibility of the join opening, and it should always be done with full bindings. Waterproof sheets should always be inserted between boards and book whenever there is damp leather there.

During these operations the greatest care will have been used to keep the leather surface free from damage by marking, either by finger-nails or by impurities on stone or bench.

Before tying up at the hinges, check the board positions in the joint, correcting any error there (118). For tying up use thick thread, not cord, unless the volume is a large one. The headcaps are now worked (see p. 188).

After the bands have received attention and the surface of the leather has been sponged over, the book is placed between clean paper on pressing boards and allowed to dry under light pressure—a weight placed on the top pressing board.

TYING DOWN BANDS

Where leather used for covering is thick or otherwise resistant to moulding round the bands, and this applies especially to tight-back bindings, it may be necessary to tie it tightly in position while drying. Tying-up boards are easily made from cutting boards by screwing to the wide edge a smooth piece of thin wood which projects $\frac{3}{8}-\frac{1}{2}$in beyond one side. Its edge must be rounded and smooth. By placing a pair of these boards (they must be longer than the book) so that the protruding flanges fit comfortably over the front edges of the book cover, a continuous fine cord (no 3 or 6 seaming cord) can be taken round the book and boards so that the leather at the sides of the bands is held firmly down. Because of the wedge shape of the boards, the cord does not come into contact with the book boards. The cord should be wound at a slight angle to the bands to ensure that the leather is held tightly in position at the band ends.

The book is stood upon its foredge to dry.

The care and thoroughness required during the covering process cannot be overstressed, for any neglect during it can completely spoil the binding once the leather has dried and the damage caused may be irremediable.

MITRING CORNERS

All full leather bindings have turn-ins mitred at the corners, and this is done after the leather has dried.

The book is placed on a pressing board fully twice its size when closed, and the board is turned back on to a 'platform' of smaller boards equal in height to the book's thickness so that it rests comfortably on the surface. Millboards or strawboards may be used to make up any slight difference in height. The pile of boards should be covered to prevent possible damage to the spine of the book.

Mitring consists of cutting away the over- and under-lapping leather of the turn-ins at the corners, at an angle of 45°.

It is vital that this cut is made *inwards* from the overlapping edge of the leather which should be the foredge (119).

119 *Mitring a folded corner*

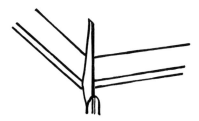

In reverse, instead of a sealed mitre the cut edge of the leather will be exposed.

This is simplified if the trimming-out points are now marked, as they clearly mark the cutting line for mitring (see pp. 193–6). A sharp knife with a level cutting edge, and confidence on the part of the worker, are both needed if the mitre is to be cleanly and neatly effected. With a moulded corner the cut should commence at the point where the leather overlaps, which should be slightly away from the edge of the corner.

To do this the heel of the knife blade is pressed into the leather there and a firm, confident cut made at the angle of the turn-in. Should the knife be unsuitable for this the alternative is to work from the inside and use the point of the blade to make the first incision and draw it towards the joint of the book.

With a folded corner the cut *must* take place from the point where the overlapping leather is folded, even if this should not be directly at the corner. Inaccuracy here will result in either too much or too little leather being removed from the corner. The former will leave a gap and the latter a superfluous 'tongue' of leather which cannot be removed without the error being blatantly obvious.

Both thicknesses of leather at the corner should be completely cut through at one stroke if the join is to be perfect. Next the leather there is dampened and lifted sufficiently for the underlap to be removed. With the upper piece also removed, paste is applied and the mitre completed by carefully working together the leather at the join leaving an absolutely smooth surface.

LEATHER JOINTS

If a leather joint is incorporated in the endpaper, this must be fitted and mitred before trimming out. In this case the mitre cannot be cut from the corner but from the end of the leather joint which is at a distance from the board edge equal to the square.

The cut is made to the marked inside corner of the turn-in, as at the corner, so is not a true 45°.

If the cut was made from the back corner of the board, the joint there would be ruinously weakened. The leather joint is dampened and lifted sufficiently at both ends to permit the cutting away of the under-lapping turn-in *from the surface of the board only*. Do not attempt to remove the leather from the joint at the *edge* of the board (see under *Leather Joints and Doublures*, p. 216).

Trimming Out

Cloth-cased books, and this includes those with pseudo-split boards, are not trimmed out inside the case before pasting down the end-papers. With cheaper library-style quarter-leather bindings, trimming out is omitted unless the leather turn-ins are wide and bulky, when some neatening becomes desirable. If economically possible, this tidying-up process is always worth-while. Much depends upon the uniformity and neatness of the turn-ins and, with leather, on adequate paring there. The thickness of the paste-down of the end-papers has some bearing upon the matter for, if it is thin, almost every unevenness will be visible when the book has been pasted in and pressed.

Taking the narrowest width of the turn-in as a guide, the spring dividers are set slightly within it unless it is exceptionally narrow at one point. Trimming points are marked with the dividers or a line run along using the inner leg of the dividers with the outer leg at the edge of the board (120), and the material beyond them is cut away using knife and straightedge.

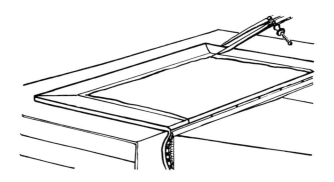

If the variation in thickness between leather and cloth turn-ins is excessive, a narrow paring of the leather edge will partially reduce the difference. Filling-in is done with thin pasteboard or thick paper, its thickness being equal to the inside of the leather. Pieces are cut rather larger than the area to be filled. A trimmed long edge is placed flush with the joint edge of the board, and cutting points are placed on the other edge using the pre-set dividers. When trimmed to size each piece will fit perfectly, even should the boards be slightly out of square. Allowance for some expansion across the paper grain may have to be made when cutting fillings.

If the edges project above the surface of the cloth turn-ins, as they probably will, a slight paring of them on the underneath side, where necessary, is the remedy. After pasting with fairly thick paste and allowing them to dry a little, place them carefully in position and rub well down with a folder, paying particular attention to the edges. Often the filling will fit only one way, so when cutting it is well to mark the joint edge so that it is fitted correctly as cut.

Board Warp

A check should be made before filling in the boards to see that they have not warped as a result of leather contraction on drying. If it has taken place it must be corrected by first lining with bank paper cut slightly smaller than the area to be filled. It is well pasted and left a short while to expand a little before being placed in position, rubbed down with the hand and allowed to dry out completely. Only then can the extent of the correction be gauged. A second lining may be necessary, but the possible contraction of the end-paper paste-down must be allowed for. Board warp is usually on the width of the book, requiring the grain direction of the lining to be from head to tail. Should it be on the length, then the grain must be across the width.

It is important that in such cases the warp be completely eliminated, otherwise the book cover cannot open freely at the joint.

The card or paper used for filling in must be equal in thickness to the surrounding leather. It is cut and fitted as described previously.

Waterproof sheets are inserted at front and back, and the book is placed between boards and under a weight until the board fillings have dried, when it is ready for the finishing operations.

Yapp Bindings

These are limp leather bindings for bibles and prayer books to be carried in the pocket. In order to protect the book edges, the leather projects beyond the limp board all round the book.

The style is named after its designer, William Yapp, who had a bible warehouse in London in the second half of the nineteenth century.

Books to be bound in this way are sewn to thin cords or are machine-sewn without tapes. As most are printed on so-called India paper, the first and last sections are oversewn before end-papers (usually black-surfaced) are affixed to them. Hemp slips are left very short, are teazled before being brought over the back of the book after glueing up, and are flattened by rubbing with the folder. All edges are cut and round-cornered, stained and sometimes gilded.

If no round-cornering machine is available it is possible to produce an acceptable corner by knocking the book to the edges between mill- or strawboards and, using hand pressure at the corners, cutting the corners carefully with a medium-sized carpenter's gouge. It can even be done with a sharp bookbinder's knife, but it requires many small cuts and considerable care. The usual error is to cut too deeply at the base of the book. A small coin serves as a useful template when cutting. Any slight unevenness can be reduced by the judicious use of fine glasspaper.

If there is any backing it must be minute. Machine-made white silk headbands are added, but generally there are no back linings, the cover being stuck directly to the back of the book. Boards are extremely thin (2- or 3-sheet pasteboard) and are cut the same length as the book, but about $\frac{1}{16}$in (2 mm) narrower in width if the book is backed and $\frac{1}{8}$in approx. (3mm) if it is not. The corners are rounded a little more than those of the book. The leather used for this class of binding is usually black-grained morocco or sheep, about 0·06in (1·5mm approximately) in thickness. It is cut to allow for a small turn-in *plus* twice the width of the yapp edge, and its corners must be rounded but leaving sufficient to turn in beyond the yapp edge. All edges are pared, especially at the extreme edges.

When making the case, outward warping of the boards can be prevented, if they are thinly glued. One is placed in position on the leather and the book is laid in position on it. The second one, also glued, is positioned on the book and the leather is drawn over on to it and rubbed down. The width of the yapp edge is marked on the wide turnings of the leather which is creased at those points, using a pointed folder and turning it firmly upwards against a straightedge.

Pasted, it is brought over at all edges leaving the corners to be rounded.

This is best done by working the pared leather there over a thin but firm plastic template with smooth rounded corner and shaped not at a right-angle but at about 80°. With the template in position, the leather at the corner can be moulded round it, and it is removed after the leather has taken the correct shape. Paste can be used as a lubricant when finally rubbing down the leather there, and sponged off later. The turn-ins of the yapp edges are worked carefully against the outside of the thin board to give them a slight pull inwards. There must be sufficient leather on the inside of the board for the paste-downs to overlap it and it must be very thin there. The back of the book is thinly glued before the cover is fitted; the leather at the spine may be lightly pasted also and the leather well rubbed down through protective paper.

When dry the endpapers are pasted down as with a cased book, and it is placed in the press under moderate pressure.

If unaccustomed to making them it is well to experiment with making the rounded corners in order to realise just how much (or little) leather is required there.

Divinity circuit edges are similar to yapp edges except that the overlap of the cover is not continuous. The cover leather is turned in at head and tail and independent flaps are made on the edges of the boards which, like the book, have square corners. The purpose is to allow the flaps to fold flat at the edges.

Vellum Covers

Books to be bound in vellum are sewn to tapes or strips of vellum. Vellum is translucent and needs to be lined with white paper when used for covering. The professional binder works both materials together, but this has hazards for the beginner. He is advised to prepare the book so that it can be covered with unlined vellum.

Unless of very good quality such as hand-made paper, endpapers should be reinforced with thin cambric. The book, sewn to tapes, is forwarded as for hollow-backed library binding, except that the split boards are completely covered with cartridge paper, all edges being turned in over the board. To help control warping, boards must be counter-lined on the inside. The joint edge having been previously marked, carefully cut open the slit without disturbing the cartridge paper there. The back linings must be covered with cartridge paper that extends into the joint to the flanges, being inserted with them into the slit when the boards are attached.

The book is now completely covered with opaque white paper and can be covered with unlined vellum.

Although thin, vellum is extremely hard and the narrow paring required demands a sharp and controlled paring knife. When pasted, it softens but is inclined to curl and must be folded on to itself while the moisture penetrates it.

The book is covered as normally for a library binding but at the French joint the vellum must be firmly pressed into the groove, using rods. Sufficient vellum must have been left for this to be done without stretching it, for then subsequent contraction would negative the purpose of the joint, which is free opening.

Corners may be folded as with other materials, but all edges must be pared. The nature of vellum is suited to the 'boxed' corner which is neater than the folded one but sharper. The vellum, cut as shown in illustration 121, demands accuracy, for the board thickness has to be related to the cuts. The pre-cut mitres have to be cut with care so that finally they overlap. Paring is necessary

121. *Boxed corner for vellum bindings*

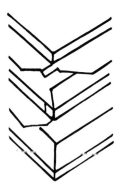

at every edge and must be delicately executed, particularly with the 'tongues'.

Press the rods into the grooves again before tying up the book and setting the headcaps which should be made as narrow as the head-bands permit. Before placing between boards to dry out, check that the vellum is adhering everywhere.

If vellum is to be lined before covering, opaque paper is well pasted and brush-marks removed by laying another piece on it and drawing it off again after a light rubbing down. The vellum is now lined with it, rubbed down and pressed between blotting paper and boards until partially dry. It is then pasted again over the lining when covering may begin.

Warping can be almost eliminated if, instead of pasting the vellum all over, the front board is first glued out using a thin, hot glue that has been spread, not by brushing but by lightly dabbing and frothing it. The book, front board downwards, is laid in position on the vellum and well pressed between white paper and clean boards and allowed to dry completely. The spine and hinge area of the vellum is now pasted out, and the turn-ins are wiped clean of paste and brought over in position on the back board, which has no adhesive on it. Rods are placed on the vellum in the groove and the book is returned to the press and again allowed to dry, which will take a considerable time.

The spine will have been well rubbed down, and the pressure of

the rods in the grooves and the contraction of the vellum on drying
will ensure adhesion there. When completely dry the back board
can be glued like the front one, the remainder of the vellum brought
over on to it, and the book pressed once again. The turn-ins can be
dealt with after drying out by pasting them well before turning
them in. The vellum is expanded only on the spine and turn-ins,
and by contracting there ensures adhesion and controls warping of
the boards. PVA adhesive, slightly thinned, can be used instead of
glue, its smoothness and whiteness being added advantages.

The medieval method of binding in vellum with the book sewn
to strips of vellum and laced through the French joint (122–1)
should be confined to smaller volumes. In reality they are cased,
the cover being added after the book has been forwarded. An
Oxford hollow, reinforced according to the size of the book, is an
advantage and gives added strength at the joint. The slips are cut for

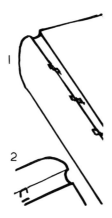

*122 Vellum
binding
1 Vellum strips
laced through the
French joint
2 Cuts for vellum
lacings*

lacing to a width which may vary according to the book size but is
between $\frac{1}{8}$in and $\frac{1}{4}$in. The cuts in the case are made very slightly
below the highest point of the spine where it meets the joint
(122–2) and must be accurately positioned and cut to the exact
width of the vellum slips.

The threading of the slips is simplified if a right-angled cut, no
more than a millimetre in length, is made at the ends of the slits
towards the boards. It also removes the possibility of the slit extending beyond the width of the slip. The re-entry slits are made on the

other side of the French joint at points level with the base of the board. Absolute precision is required if the hinge is not to be damaged.

Only when done with extreme neatness and care can the method be successful. The original method of lacing, at an angle, the vellum cores of the headbands cannot be recommended in view of the weakness resulting at these vital points.

Books bound in vellum should always have boards to control it. Limp vellum bindings are very dainty at first, but with changes of atmosphere and humidity the vellum will inevitably cockle with the passage of time.

The 'turned edge' makes for greater rigidity and helps to control the boards. It requires about $\frac{3}{8}$in *additional* vellum at the foredge of each board where it is creased as shown in illustration 123.

123 '*Turned edge*' *for a vellum binding* 1 *Turned edge made at foredge of board, showing projection to be cut away* 2 *Completed edge, showing the side turn-in brought over to support the foredge*

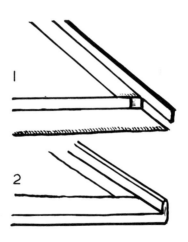

The cutting has similarities with the boxed corner, inasmuch as side tongues are turned in along the board edge at the foredge, but the main turn-in there is not mitred. The vellum at the foredge is creased at a distance from the board that is equal to its thickness plus the 'turned' portion, and is firmly brought up against the board edge. The vellum is turned on to itself at the crease and down on to the board tightly to its edge. The side turn-ins are brought over so that the ends lie flush against the turned foredge and help to hold it there.

The projecting ends of the turned vellum are cut level with the boards. When the cover is dry they are opened slightly and a touch of transparent or white contact adhesive is inserted into them. The fold is pressed flat, covered with a small piece of white paper and held by a little spring clip until quite set.

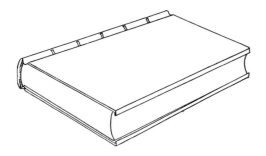

124 *Vellum binding with vellum slips laced through the French joint and with turned foredges*

Fabric Covers

EMBROIDERED BINDINGS

French joints as used in library bindings are unsuitable for fabric bindings, although recourse to them may be necessary if the material is heavy. The book is forwarded as for a full leather binding, but without bands. The Oxford hollow should be lightly reinforced with cambric or mull.

The position of the front board must be clearly marked with chalk on the reverse side of the material. This is most important, for the embroidery will have been designed for its purpose and must be accurately positioned.

Glue the back of the book up to the joint edges, using a dabbing rather than a brushing movement. Lay the book, front board down, precisely in its correct position on the fabric.

Bring the fabric gently and evenly over the glued back, stand the book on its foredge and, through cartridge paper stretched over the spine, rub down the fabric so that it sticks firmly, especially at the joints. Should there be raised embroidery there, the hand must also be used to 'hammer' down the background fabric. Because of the unevenness of the reverse side of embroidered fabric it is not glued to the boards; these are either surfaced at this stage with very thin foam rubber or have cotton wool inserted later. The foam rubber, cut at an angle to the surface, is laid close to the joint, being held in position by a few dabs of glue on the boards. Surplus is cut away from the board edges by undercutting with shears from the face side of the board which should have filed 'cushioned' edges.

The fabric is cut at the corners for a folded and mitred corner, a little PVA or latex being touched on the cut to prevent fraying.

To hold the material in position the turn-ins at the foredges are first attended to, using the same adhesive, fingered or brushed on the board—not the turn-ins. When these are set in position the head and tail turn-ins may be attended to similarly, the material having been folded in at the corners. Headcaps cannot be worked with soft unglued fabric, but, should there be room above the headband, a soft piece of string, impregnated with PVA, may be incorporated in the turn-in there. Although the material must be drawn firmly over the boards it must not be pulled out of position when turning in the edges. Mitred corners should later be neatly sewn, using a button-hole stitch.

If cotton wool is to be used for padding the boards, the head and tail turn-ins will be first attended to. Before the foredges are sealed the cotton wool must be placed in position between fabric and board. This can be done by placing the cotton wool between two pieces of vellum or thin board, rather like a sandwich. When the cotton wool is in position the pieces of vellum or board can be removed singly.

RECESSED EMBROIDERED PANELS

Embroidered bindings look effective but, because of the nature of the fabric, their useful life is short compared with leather bindings. Quite the best way to incorporate embroidery in book covers is to make it in the form of a panel, the material being stretched over a thin board and sewn from behind. It can be inserted into a leather binding which has had a deep recess built into the front board. The covering leather will have been cut to allow for it to slightly overlap the edges of the recess. The leather edges must be pared.

The embroidered panel can be fitted into the recess of the bound book using strong, hot glue dabbed on to the back of it, paying particular care to the edges. It takes care and effort to affix it before the glue cools, working with both hand and folder, the latter very judiciously, over strong paper.

The addition of a gold-tooled border enhances the embroidery as will be seen in Plates 7 and 8.

SILK

Silk cannot be recommended for covering books, its life being singularly short. If used it must be lined with glued paper, well rubbed down and adhering all over, and a case must be made as for ordinary cloth casings. The method used for embroidered bindings can be used, with the difference that after the spine has dried, the boards are glued and the lined silk is laid down on to them and rubbed with the hands. Corners are mitred and turn-ins pasted before proceeding by the normal method used for full leather bindings.

Putting Down Endpapers

Although this operation often takes place after the cover has been tooled, it is essentially a forwarding rather than a finishing operation and for this reason is dealt with here.

Cloth-cased bindings and leather ones with French joints have endpapers put down by merely pasting out the board paper, bringing the cover board over on to it, and pressing the book between pressing boards in the press and allowing it to dry there. With drawn-on boards this is not possible and endpapers must be put down with the boards opened back. The reason for this is that the folded joint of the endpaper and the surface of the board are quite level, but when the book board is opened after covering, the folded leather at the hinge is interposed between them, separating them by the double thickness of leather. There is insufficient paper in the joint to allow for this and so the board must be opened back and part of the paste-down sheet used for the purpose.

CLOTH-CASED BOOKS

Check that the paste-down sheet of the endpapers does not project beyond the book edges and that, if it does, it is not caused by coming slightly away from the joint. Should this not be the cause, the projection must be cut away, using either shears or knife and straightedge. Paste used for pasting out the board paper should be of a good consistency; if it is too thin, the water may penetrate the paper and stain or even stick it to the fly-sheet. Because of the greater absorption of paste by tape slips, and the fact that they are sized, it is not usually necessary to paste under them; their thickness results in greater pressure at those points which adds to the possibility of paste penetration there.

When pasting over the mull a check should be made that it has not pulled away from the backing shoulder and, if it has, it must be returned there, using the finger- or thumb-nail. The insertion of a piece of waste paper under the paste-down (so often indulged in by the newcomer), to prevent paste getting on to the book edges is an unnecessary and bad practice, for its removal can cause paste to be deposited on the face side of the endpapers which can be disastrous. If an Oxford hollow has been used, the cover spine will have been glued to it and the case already firmly fixed round the book, but, if not, the book must be placed centrally on the back board before bringing over the front one on to the pasted endpaper. It is equally important that the fingers pulling it over are free of paste, which could despoil the cover. The book is held in position with one hand while the cover board is brought firmly over with the other, with the middle finger pressing the centre of the board into the joint. The cover can be lightly rubbed down on to the book, and when both endpapers are in position it is placed accurately between clean pressing boards, their edges being level with those of the joint edges of the cover boards.

When placed in the press, the book should be centrally under the screw and a further check should be made that the pressing boards have not moved. It is a worth-while precaution to insert a waterproof sheet of paper between paste-down and fly-leaf to prevent any possibility of their sticking together under pressure. Cloth-cased books with semi- (or 'pseudo-') split boards will have an Oxford hollow, on which the cover spine will have been glued. The tape slips and mull will have been encased in a flange of thin paper, and before the paste-down of the endpapers can be put down, the semi-split must be slightly opened up and cleanly glued or pasted. As each cover board is brought over, the flange—which has been cut slightly smaller than the 'split' area—is slid into the 'split'. Paper-covered tins are placed over both endpapers, which will help to close the 'split' tightly and prevent marking of the endpapers. The book is placed between boards and well pressed. When dry the book is pasted in as normally.

If a number of volumes are being dealt with, a pressing board about the size of the book can be used as a raised platform on which to place the book being pasted in its cover. This ensures a clean surface for succeeding books, even though paste may have found its way on to the bench. Pasting down the endpapers of leather bindings with French joints is almost identical with the method used for cloth casings, the only difference being that, because the boards are set some distance from the backing shoulder, pressure is required in the joint. This may be provided by the use of brass-edged pressing boards or with ordinary ones, slightly longer than the book to allow either a plastic knitting needle or a brass rod to be fixed at the edge of the board. Brass-edged pressing boards are also used with cloth casings where these are to have 'nipped' joints, but while these are very flexible they tend to become loose with use, allowing the book to sag on the shelf.

ENDPAPERS IN LEATHER BINDINGS

As explained previously, the paste-down sheets of endpapers in books with drawn-on boards can be fitted in position only with the cover board opened right back. When working, it is good practice to work with the book placed to one side of a board rather more than twice its area. On the other side is placed a 'platform' of pressing boards equal in height to the book thickness, generously covered to soften any sharp edges. On this the opened cover board can rest while endpapers are being pasted in position. This arrangement ensures a firm surface when fitting the endpaper and also allows the book to be turned round for trimming purposes without unnecessary movement.

First, using fine glasspaper, the joint is carefully cleaned of any hard paste or glue, after which the waste sheet is torn cleanly away. Care is required for this and it is best achieved by tearing slowly from one end, holding the paste-down sheet firmly at the point of tearing, and moving the finger along as necessary. Should any larger pieces of waste remain, flat-ended tweezers will remove them.

Using the finger and thumb to work it comfortably into the joint, the board paper is brought over the board. Because of the extra paper required in the joint, the paste-down will be short on the foredge and the head and tail must be trimmed to equalise the margin. This is done by setting dividers to the width of the margin required, allowing one leg to overlap the board edge, and marking the amount to be cut away from the paste-down sheet. The surplus may be trimmed away using a knife and straightedge, by placing either a thin piece of millboard or a tin plate under the board paper, cutting only as far as the base of the backing shoulder. This is more accurately done if cutting is commenced at that point, which will require either ambidexterity on the part of the worker or working *away* from the body when cutting one edge. There are three ways of dealing with the shaping of the paste-down at head and tail, where it fits into the joint. Originally it was cut so that it came over the joint and on to the board edge, level with its surface (125–1).

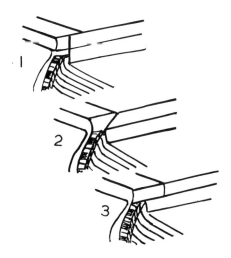

125 Three methods of cutting board papers at the joint
1 Paper cut level with board edge
2 Angled cut
3 Paper turned into the back linings

It tended to come away there in time and a more sensible shape is one cut at an angle so that the outside edge of the board paper that is stuck to the board edge is level with its base and the inside is level with its surface (125–2). With hollow-back linings the trimming can be continued right up to the joint fold of the endpaper, and the surplus cut away leaving just sufficient (about $\frac{3}{16}$in) to turn into the hollow (125–3). This requires care for the paper has been softened with adhesive, and the hollow should be slightly opened beforehand to receive the turn-in of paper. The rubbing down of the paste-down on to the board is done with a folder through cartridge paper. The finger and thumb are used, again through paper, to ensure complete adhesion in the joint (126). Unless this is done carefully and thoroughly, there is the possibility of the paper coming away when the board is closed after the adhesive has dried, causing what is known as a 'pencil box'. This is difficult to rectify, as the only access is via the ends of the joint, where it may be possible to ease a dull-pointed knitting needle to release the remainder of the paper in the joint, working from both ends. Having done this, and using a thinner knitting needle, adhesive (paste or PVA) may be worked into the hollow and the paper again worked into the joint.

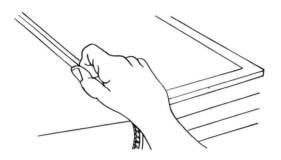

126 *Rubbing down endpapers into the joint*

If, for any reason, the board paper may be inclined to stretch if pasted, it is better not to use paste in the joint but to finger PVA there; this will minimise stretch there and also effect quicker adhesion. Should there be no need to expand the board paper to control warping of the board, PVA may be used all over. Where there are a number of books being dealt with at the same time, it will be necessary to stand them upright after putting down ends so that less space is required. The boards are held in the open position with small pieces of card in which are cut away two slightly wedge-shaped pieces, into which the top edges of the boards will fit. If the leaves of the book tend to spring open they can be held closed by the same method, but using card cut with an aperture big enough to take the book thickness.

Leather Joints and Doublures

As previously mentioned, it is usual to attend to leather joints and doublures after covering has been completed so that they may be tooled if need be. Joints are put down with paste, worked into position and allowed to dry, as with endpaper paste-downs. They have to be mitred, as do leather corners, but with the difference that the cut cannot be from the edge of the board but must be from the end of the leather joint. Because it finishes at a similar point to the corner mitres at the foredge, the mitre is not one of 45°. After cutting, the leather joint is dampened at the ends and lifted there to allow the underlapping turn-in to be removed, but on the board *surface only*, otherwise the joint will be weakened. The leather is again pasted and put down, when it will meet exactly with the turn-in where mitred.

The French word *doublures* has no English counterpart for it invariably refers to leather linings inside the boards of a book, whereas its literal translation is merely 'a lining' which is quite inadequate from the point of view of fine bookbinding.

While doublures may incorporate the joint, they are usually added after this has been put down. The leather used should be thin, certainly no thicker than 0·06in, or it will look bulky when in position. The trimming-out of the board and infilling it with a soft thick paper must be done with complete accuracy to leave a good surface. If the whole surface is to be lined, a piece of firm hand-made paper, cut very slightly smaller, its edges sand-papered to zero, and the tips of the corners rounded, is first mounted on it to produce an absolutely level surface. When dry it may be necessary to very lightly glasspaper this at certain points, while the adhesive (PVA or paste) must be completely free of any impurity which would destroy the perfectly level surface. The doublure leather requires all-round paring to zero and, unless it is the same as the cover leather, will need to have its edges trimmed to tidy them, but the finished product must be only very slightly smaller than the area it has to cover. To prevent any movement of the leather when trimming, sealing tape may be used on the flesh side and removed afterwards, using care.

If the doublure is not to completely cover the surface of the board, leaving a border of the cover leather, it must be pared to a thickness exactly equal to that of the turn-ins and be rather larger than the area to be covered. It can be placed in position and secured there by the use of sealing tape extending on to the turn-ins, the outside border being marked with dividers. Both leathers can now be cut together with a bevel sloping towards the board centre. The sealing tape should be removed immediately afterwards to prevent any possible marking of the leather surface.

Leather joints are better if sewn in with the book, but if this is not considered necessary a 'one-piece' doublure and joint can be effected if, when making the endpapers, the lining of the fly-leaf (there being no board paper) be left unpasted for about $\frac{1}{2}$in at the joint. The doublure is cut to allow sufficient extra width to line the joint, plus about $\frac{1}{4}$in to overlap on to the unpasted portion of the fly-leaf, beyond the backing point; the fly-leaf lining can be put down over the leather overlap after this has dried (127). The paring

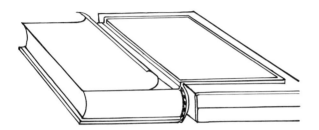

127 *Putting down a one-piece doublure*

of this particular piece of leather must be very fine so that it shall not obtrude when lined. The ends of it must be cut back at an angle so that it is not seen at the edges. A further neatening can be produced if the leather joint be cut so that it conceals the exposed ends of the headband.

If leather joints are added after the book has been covered, allowance for them must have been made before forwarding by the addition of blank sheets equal in total thickness to the leather. These can be loosely inserted in the endpapers and forwarded with the book, being removed only when the leather joint is put down. It is a worth-while precaution to neatly reinforce the outer folds of the endpapers from the inside with a narrow strip of jaconet. This will take any strain imposed there by the leather joint when the book is in use.

4

FINISHING

*Tools—lettering—gold and blind tooling—gold stamping foils—
machine blocking*

FINISHING

Finishing comprises all the work necessary to decorate the book after covering has been completed. It includes the polishing of the leather to make the surface uniform for tooling where this is necessary, designing the cover, tooling, and lettering it.

Tooling consists of impressing heated metal tools and stamps into the leather and gilding the impressions with gold leaf, unless they are to be left 'blind'.

Polishing irons are of two types, as shown in illustration 128, that with the cylindrical crosspiece being used for flat surfaces and the other for the spine of the book. The edges should be smooth and rounded, and the working surface kept polished at all times.

Tools and Letters

FINISHING TOOLS

These consist of stamps made of non-ferrous metal, usually brass, set into wooden or asbestos handles. The head, often larger than the shaft, may be a plain solid unit or its face may be engraved. The faces of larger tools should be very slightly convex so that they may be rocked gently from side to side to make a uniform impression.

Pallets Pallets are best described as segments of fillets or rolls set into handles and are used mainly for tooling the spines of bindings. A set of line pallets could comprise ten or twelve, varying in length from $\frac{1}{8}$in to about $1\frac{1}{2}$in for use in building linear designs.

Fillets Fillets are used for running continuous lines and are solid metal discs or wheels, usually 2–3in in diameter and set into a forked metal holder; the perimeter edge is the thickness of the line. Two or three of different widths are required. Sometimes the edge is cut away for a short distance and the two ends are angled in opposite directions for making mitred joins at corners. While fillets can be obtained with two or even three lines, only when time is of importance are they necessary, as single lines can be repeated when required.

221

128 *'Cockerell' electric finishing stove, and some finishing tools* (Back, left to right) *glair, benzine and petroleum jelly, miscellaneous finishing tools, spine polishing iron, spring typeholder with brass type set up, 'roller' polishing iron (for board surfaces), handle letters (in box), improvised finishing tools*

Rolls These take the same form as fillets except that the edge is engraved with a continuous border design. Such designs are also to be found on pallets for tooling on the spine.

Gouges Gouges are arcs made from concentric circles set uniformly apart, except the smaller ones, which must provide for sharper curves. When in use they are always sighted from the concave side. In the past, binders often had several sets of gouges to produce

(front, left to right), *decorative roll, pallet, gilder's cushion and knife with gold leaf book and cotton-wool pad, pallet, single-arm fillet cut for mitring*

different curves, the flatter ones being cut from larger circles and the rounder ones from smaller circles.

Unit tools   The individual unit tool has existed since gold tooling was introduced. The faces of such stamps may consist of geometric or floral elements: they may be simple or complex, when each tool is a complete design in itself. On such tools the design is invariably in outline above the surface, for gold-tooled impressions, but sometimes in 'intaglio', with the design cut below the surface to be impressed into the leather leaving the design raised above it. This type of tool is normally used for blind tooling. In effect, the composite tool is a 'time-saver' as it produces a large design which does not have to be built up from smaller units. In the last century they were most commonly used for quickly decorating spine panels by the repetitive use of corner and centre tools. This type of tooling was used, and at an incredible speed, for tooling inexpensive half-bound leather bindings, but these have only a limited vogue amongst collectors, especially for sets of volumes.

There is still room for the carefully designed tooled spine if only for its effect on the bookshelf, but an individual approach is desirable. The newcomer can exercise his ingenuity by personal use and arrangement of unit tools, especially combined with gouges and lines. It is only necessary to see work by Douglas Cockerell and Katharine Adams to realise the possibilities.

Because of the skilled work involved in the engraving of such tools, most binders are dependent upon those cut in the past, and so the alternative to high cost is the second-hand market, and there must be literally thousands of such tools that are no longer used by their owners.

Today 'expressive' designs are no longer framed by the book edges, and while tooling is as meticulous as ever, there is much more freedom in design and many craft binders make finishing tools to specific requirements, often using scrap metal. For this purpose a set of locksmith's key files, which are small and fine, in flat, rounded, circular and triangular forms, will be necessary as will a metal drill and a small metal vice in which to hold the tool being made. When controlled and well-executed the results are not only exciting but usually individual and personal to the binder. This 'freedom' has coincided with greatly increased traditional engraving costs—or may have resulted from them!

Lettering tools   At least four alphabets of different sizes of the same type face are necessary, and these may range from 10 point to 20 point (there are 72 points to an inch). These will serve for books of average size, but very small or large books will demand smaller or larger type.

Most types are based on the Roman alphabet, but with the change in book-cover design to stronger and more powerful linear work, many binders feel that the sans-serif letter, modernised by Edward Johnston and further improved by Eric Gill, is more appropriate; while it has great legibility it can look out of place if the cover design is not equal in strength.

Although bookbinders' letters, usually of brass, are made for use as type to be screwed into a special typeholder (and this saves time when lettering spines), most craft binders prefer handle letters in which each character has a wooden handle and is 'struck' separately, giving much more freedom of arrangement. For spine lettering, type is sometimes preferred for smaller letters. Letters, whether type or 'handled', are marked with a line or 'nick' to denote the head or base of the letter and so show plainly which is the right way up. With type, the nick is at the base of the letters and can readily be seen when placing them in a typeholder, while with handle letters it is on the upper side, as the characters are sighted from the head of the letter.

BOOKBINDERS' TYPE

This is sold in founts of 100 characters made up in proportion to their usage; thus there are at least four of vowels and only two of such letters as J and V. Brass 'quads' and 'spaces' are required for separating lines and words, and also individual letters, which, because they are impressed *into* and *below* the surface of the leather or material, should be separated by a 'hair space' whenever possible. In use, in the typeholder, there should always be a metal space at each end to avoid damage to the type. The use of 'lower case' characters is inadvisable in hand bookbinding because of the difficulty of sighting them.

Small founts of printers' type made of lead with some antimony, known as 'sorts' or 'card founts', can be purchased very cheaply by comparison with brass type, and offer a larger range of type faces. However, they require the greatest care and attention when being heated, if they are not to melt on the finishing stove. I still have, and use from time to time, founders' type that was purchased forty years ago—but I cannot claim that some letters have not been melted during that period. If printers' type is used, brass spaces, not lead, are required. The golden rule is to control the heat of the stove, never allowing the type to come into actual contact with the heating plate, and checking the heat of the type frequently, cooling it as necessary.

With handle letters there is one tool for every character including ligature vowels (Æ), ampersand (&), comma, full point and hyphen. Sometimes the letter O is used for the numeral 'nought', but quite often it is rather wider than desirable.

Care is always necessary in the heating and use of finishing tools, for overheating will soon cause handle letters to loosen as the hot 'tangs' burn away the wood of the handle from the inside. Tools should be replaced on the stove with care so that only the metal head rests on the heating plate, and where this is grooved, as with the 'Cockerell' finishing stove, that it rests in the groove, so avoiding damage to the edges of the engraved face.

Preparation for Tooling

Before tooling a leather book cover, the surface must be quite clean and is usually lightly polished to remove irregularities. Polishing irons must be polished with fine emery paper and then with a piece of soft leather on which a small amount of powdered abrasive such as Bath brick has been sprinkled. Until experience has been gained, the polishing iron should be only slightly heated, for an overheated tool can do irreparable harm. Pressure must be light at first, increasing later, and the iron should never be allowed to rest at one point but should be kept gently moving. The sequence of polishing is usually first the inside borders, then the spine, using the flat polisher, and finally the boards of the cover using the cylindrical polisher.

When polishing the inside borders, the cover must be supported, preferably on a prepared block of wood with one long edge concave to take the spine of the book. To polish the spine the book is placed in the finishing press between leather-covered boards or thick millboards lined on one side with surgical lint. These may be used for resting the book upon when polishing the cover boards. The long wooden handle of the polishing iron is rested upon the shoulder, which gives control over the tool when polishing. It is quite essential that the cylindrical polisher has softly rounded edges so as not to mark the leather in use. Again, pressure must be very light at first, being increased as the surface of the leather becomes firmer; the polishing movement is a circular one similar to that of the french polisher in woodwork.

Heavily grained leathers such as Levant morocco or pigskin are often better for tooling, especially if this is to be considerable, if their surfaces are first 'crushed'. For this, a block or a pile of pressing boards in the press is covered with a pad of blotting or other suitable paper (thin telephone directories serve well). The leather on the cover board is dampened and it is placed on the block with the book hanging downwards in front. A pressing board covered with plastic laminate or similar material is placed over it, taking care that the edge is tight up to the hinge of the book, and the press platen is brought carefully down on to it. Firm pressure is required for only a minute or so before the book is removed. Should the leather have been too damp the board may tend to cling to the cover and must be allowed to dry out. If, by some mischance, a spot of adhesive should have been left on the board or cover, the result can be serious. Do not try to remove the board immediately, but, easing it gently, endeavour to moisten the leather where it is sticking, using a long-bristled but thin brush. Better still, make certain that everything is clean before commencing the operation!

Lettering

The lettering of the title, author and other details is, logically, of the greatest importance. Common sense demands that lettering on the spine should be clear and legible. Where possible it should be across the spine, and this often poses problems where words are long and spines narrow. Often the only possible solution is lettering along the spine, which, as the book stands upright on the shelf, can hardly be said to be immediately legible. The alternatives are either to split words, which can sometimes be amusingly disastrous, or to use a 'condensed' letter. Neither is completely satisfactory and so it is left to the wit of the finisher to find the best method. A 'binder's title' is not necessarily that of the book as it appears on the title page, often being a condensed version of it. For example, *The Posthumous Papers of the Pickwick Club* would never be lettered otherwise than as *The Pickwick Papers*. Such abbreviations are an aid to the bookbinder, but must be used with knowledgeable discretion.

In the nineteenth century attempts were made to solve the

problems of lettering the spine by the use of condensed type faces. In some, the fine Roman letter was debased into compressed forms with disproportionately thin and thick lines, neither beautiful nor legible. The types designed by William Morris and his followers were more suitable for tooling, but it was still found necessary to divide long words, or even to introduce letters of smaller size to fit a word across the spine.

It is sometimes possible to accent the main words in a title by using a larger type for them and a smaller for less important ones, especially where these have more characters. Both types must, of course, be of the same face. Good judgement combined with an appreciation of lettering is necessary for this to be successful.

Letter spacing is important and, because of the different geometric forms that comprise the alphabet, spacing between them must be such that optical uniformity is achieved. In the word LAMP, for example, all spaces between letters are the same, but because of their different forms, optical spacing is uneven. This should be corrected by bringing the L and A close together, and setting the A and M slightly further apart, with the M and P even more so—LA M P. Accidental mis-spacing can result in such anomalies as NO YES for the poet NOYES.

The arrangement of lettering for titles requires thought and nice judgement to obtain good balance. Where several uniform lines of letters can be arranged there is no problem, nor is there when, with three lines, the upper and lower ones are of approximately equal length, with the centre one shorter or slightly longer than the others. Allowance must be made for the optical space left, and the lettering positioned either slightly higher or lower in the panel. Put into geometrical terms, when the lettering is rectangular in form a slightly wider space is left at the base; this also applies to the lozenge, or diamond, form. When it is triangular in shape it is necessary to lift it considerably to offset the greater optical space at the top; should it be an inverted triangle then the reverse applies.

For important work, lettering should be set out on good-quality bank paper before tooling through it in 'blind' on the book. Carbon deposited on the tool face by holding it at the tip of a candle flame gives a clear impression in black—but remember that the tool must be wiped clean before tooling with gold leaf. Where the book has bands, a strip of bank paper as wide as the space between the bands is cut. The width of the spine is marked centrally on this, and the paper is then folded to show the median line of the panel; round this the lettering can be arranged. Pallet lines close to the bands must be allowed for. Spacing between letters, words, and lines of the title must receive thoughtful attention, for it must separate them sufficiently for legibility but not estrange them. To use a large letter which results in lines of lettering almost touching one another is bad; far better to use a smaller and so leave adequate space. The first and last letters of a line should leave space on either side, for should they overlap the spine edge they will not only not be seen on the shelf, but will ultimately become illegible as the gold leaf is loosened with the continual opening of the book cover.

Setting out spacing of lines of letters in a panel can be effected by impressing the edge of a letter 'I' according to the number of lines required, always allowing for pallet lines and slightly additional space at the base of the panel. The positions having been marked, thin parallel lines at right-angles to the sides can be marked with a fine pencil at the head of each line of letters. With this guidance, it is not difficult to arrange each line centrally by counting the number of letters, plus spaces, and making due allowance for letters of greater or narrower width than usual, impressing the middle letter centrally and working outwards towards the edges. Sealing tape is now usually used for fixing paper patterns to the book cover, but with good work it is safer to wrap a band of good-quality paper round the book from head to tail, secure it by joining the ends with sealing tape, and stick the pattern to it when tooling the spine. With rebacked books having old leather-covered boards, this is an essential precaution.

The book is placed within leather- or lint-lined boards and put into the finishing press. The spine should be at a slight angle towards the finisher so that the head of the finishing tool can be clearly seen for the accurate positioning of the impression. Finishing tools are gripped in the hand by all four fingers, with the thumb resting on the end of the handle, and are guided into position by placing the thumb-nail of the left hand against the tool, the hand steadied against the finishing press (129). Fairly long thumb-nails are an advantage! Alternatively, a short, slender piece of wood (a pencil would serve) with a V-shaped cut at one end, in which the hot tool rests, can be used.

The heat required varies with the leather being tooled but, as a general guide, the heated tool should just cease to 'hiss' when placed on a wet cooling pad. This may be a piece of sponge rubber or a pad of cloth thoroughly soaked in clean water and placed in a shallow saucer.

Variations are caused by the type of leather being tooled, and the speed with which the finisher strikes the tool, after checking its heat. The amount of metal at the head of the tool also has a bearing on the time factor, for the greater the amount, the longer the heat is retained. The important thing is not to use overheated tools at any time—they can always be reheated and re-impressed. It is not possible to tool satisfactorily on leather that has been burned. It is fairly easy to strike letters geometrically formed on the square (H, N, etc) and inverted triangle (V and W). It is less simple with those founded on the circle (O, S, etc) because the tool must be kept quite square; most difficult of all are the narrow letters (I, J and L) and with these the eye has to be trained to strike them with the upright stroke at right-angles to the guide line. Nothing looks worse than letters leaning either forwards or backwards. When striking a tool its head should just touch the base of the guide line; the tool should be impressed evenly on the surface, and then given slight all-round pressure, which ensures that every part of the face of the tool is impressed. With experience, the movement is automatic and is executed so quickly that no variation is noticeable to an onlooker. A watchful eye should be kept on letters with enclosed areas, such as A, B, O, P, Q and R after checking tool heat on the cooling pad, for they sometimes pick up, and hold, water, which the metal heats. If impressed, the leather may well be scalded and harm done which cannot be rectified.

When all impressions have been made, the paper pattern is removed and any indefinite or slightly incorrect impressions corrected by re-impressing the tool.

TYPE

If type is used for lettering the spine, words are composed in reverse, ie from right to left, and laid on the bench, base uppermost. A spring typeholder is adjusted so that the opening is wider than the type face. Using sufficient finger pressure to hold the letters together, each word is picked up separately and slid into the type holder,

129 *Lettering along the book spine*

with the base of the letters uppermost and towards the adjusting spring and plate, and moved to the right-hand side. A 'quad' or brass space, its thickness equal to that of the type, is placed next to it, and the next word or line inserted. The space after each line must be sufficiently wide to prevent the following line fouling the spine when the previous one is impressed. When the holder is almost full (a 4in holder will usually take two long, or three short lines) a check is made that each letter is the right way round by seeing that the 'nick' on each piece of type is uppermost. Spaces are inserted between words and letters as necessary and the projecting ends of the type carefully straightened by lightly resting them on the end of the press and gently shaking them into position. The type may now be screwed firmly in the holder by tightening first one screw and then the other alternately. Check that the type is quite level. When lettering book spines with type, some prefer working from the side of the book, while others have the tail of the book facing them. Each method has its advantages and disadvantages. When working from the end of the book, the spine with lettering is seen as it will appear on the shelf, and centring each line of type is fairly easy; but there is a tendency for it to curve when impressing. When working from the side, on the other hand, positioning is less easy but it is simpler to keep the line of type square across the spine. The choice is the finisher's.

Gold Tooling

When all tooling impressions have been made, the leather may be prepared for gold tooling. Leathers are porous in varying degrees and must be prepared accordingly. With the exception of good-quality goatskins, leathers require 'filling' with thin paste, known as a paste wash. Paste is thinned with water and sponged over the leather surface and allowed to dry. This 'filler' prevents the gilding size (glair) from being absorbed into the leather. It is insufficient for calfskin, which is extremely porous and requires a coating of warm size; some bookbinders even precede this with a paste wash. 'Glair' is the traditional gilding size, and is made from the white of egg (albumen); it is more fully dealt with under *Materials* (p. 376). It differs from that used for edge gilding, being much stronger and made with vinegar. It is carefully painted into the impressions with a fine sable brush, and allowed to dry. When dry, the surface of the impression should look bright and glossy; if dull, a second coat of glair will be required. This will have depended upon the effect of the paste wash and the strength of the glair. Neither should be too thick, for should a slight coating of paste remain on the surface of the leather, subsequent gold tooling will ultimately come off as the surface paste disperses. If glair is too thick it will dry brittle and will chip. There are no 'short cuts' in successful finishing.

It is an inexplicable fact that while the surface of the leather must be apparently dry, the fibres below must contain a modicum of dampness if gold tooling is to be bright and clean. Because of this, the paste wash must be such that the leather is well dampened by it, or the cover may be sponged over with water or vinegar beforehand, and only as much tooling glaired as can be completed at one session.

While the glair is drying, finishing tools may be cleaned and their face surfaces polished by holding them upright and rubbing them lightly on a piece of soft leather, flesh side uppermost. Rouge may be sprinkled on the leather but harsher abrasive powders can cause undue wear on the engraved face of the tool. The faces of new finishing tools sometimes need 'softening' at the edges on the leather to remove any harshness there, but it must be done with discretion. Bright gold tooling can be achieved only if the faces of the finishing tools are clean and polished.

The handle letters having been arranged round the finishing stove, either alphabetically or as required for the particular book being lettered, the gold leaf may now be cut into suitable sizes for laying on to the glaired impressions.

Handling gold leaf has been dealt with under *Edge gilding*. It is cut to suitably sized pieces that will adequately cover the lettering, and the areas over which it will be placed are lightly greased with either petroleum jelly (Vaseline) or coconut oil. The latter is thought to reduce the possibility of staining the leather, but tends to dry out in a warm atmosphere. If petroleum jelly is used, a very small amount is placed on the back of the hand and a small pad of cotton wool is worked over the jelly so that it is equally distributed on the cotton wool, and a minute amount is then rubbed over the tooling area. A second piece of cotton wool is flattened and folded over at one end. This is rubbed lightly on the forehead which imparts sufficient grease to cause the gold leaf to adhere when the pad is touched on to it. Placing the gold leaf accurately over the impressions is simplified if the smallest amount of its edge is visible when taking it up on the pad. The gold is now gently pressed in position; if the atmosphere is dry, lightly breathing on the area will help it adhere more readily. Should the gold leaf split, and this usually happens at the edges of the impressions, a second piece must be laid over it. Because of this possibility, finishers usually use single-thickness gold leaf, applying two layers. For finishing tools with large, solid faces, it may be necessary to apply further thicknesses of gold leaf to obtain solid impressions. The actual striking of the finishing tools has already been described.

The gilt impression should look quite bright after tooling; if it is dull it is possible that the tool was insufficiently heated, and it must be re-impressed at the correct heat.

With type, if this method of preparation has been used, there is a tendency to strike the first letter of the line a little deep if it is struck first. By sighting the second one and striking it before coming back to the first, this tendency is lessened.

When all the tooling has been completed, surplus gold may be removed and collected by the use of a 'gold rubber' which has been softened by the addition of paraffin. These rubbers often tend to become sticky and one wonders if it is not just as well to forego the slight amount given for the salvaged gold, and use a soft pencil eraser, which seems to serve equally well. Should any tiny scraps of gold still remain, they, with any trace of grease, will be removed by wiping over with benzine on a cotton-wool pad. If, as the result of using too cool a finishing tool, or, more rarely, insufficient pressure, there are faulty impressions, small pieces of gold leaf may be laid over them by first breathing on them, and they may be re-tooled, provided it is done immediately. If this is unsuccessful, re-glairing will be necessary. If faulty impressions are not clearly defined, some finishers touch the face of the tool on to a lightly greased pad and pick up small pieces of gold leaf on the face of the tool, touching down any overlap of gold on to the side of the tool with a clean piece of cotton wool, to leave the edge sharp and clear. The purist will have none of this, arguing that the finished impression is never as bright, so yet again the method becomes a personal one. With lines of type, or pallets, strips of gold leaf are sometimes picked up in the same way. As this is done only on the score of economy, it seems reasonable to suggest that atomised gold on polyester film, which is only a fraction of the cost of gold leaf, serves for this class of work.

On half- or quarter-leather bindings, lettering panels, or even the whole spine may be sponged with glair, and gold leaf laid directly on to the leather. Guide lines for lettering can be marked by drawing a piece of thin silk across the gold at pre-marked points and, if handle letters are used, their positions can be marked with a point of the dividers. The glair used should have a few drops of milk added to it to prevent frothing. The glaired surface should later be varnished, for spiders have a penchant for albumen glair but not for bookbinders' varnish!

If rolls have to be used for inside borders, guide lines are marked by impressing one leg of a pair of dividers along the border while the other runs along the outside edge of the board, which ensures that it is parallel to it. The surface is prepared and glaired for direct gold tooling and gold leaf is laid on to one edge at a time. The roll is held with the handle resting against the shoulder and moved along steadily, with even and firm pressure. Because roll designs are continuous, to stop them at a particular point requires an artifice such as a strip of vellum placed at a point equal to its thickness, beyond the stopping-place. Usually a 45° angle is required but it can be a right-angle if a corner tool is to be used. Another method is to wipe away the gold leaf at the stopping-point, but this not only means re-glairing where the roll overlaps at the corner but, unless a piece of vellum is used to prevent it, will result in blind impressions where it passes over the already tooled border. Gold tooling with a roll is quite final, for it is seldom possible to re-impress it accurately at any given point, although a commencing point can be marked on the side of the roll.

For corner mitring with a fillet the choice is either to have a small piece cut away from the perimeter and the two ends angled in opposite directions, or to stop the fillet before the corner is reached and complete the line with a small pallet that has mitred ends. Nice judgement is needed with the first method, for the fillet must be stopped slightly away from the corner, and the wheel turned forward to a point where the distance to the cut angle agrees exactly with that still to be traversed.

Blind Tooling

This differs from what should be known as 'blinding-in' when the heated finishing tool is merely impressed into the leather before gold tooling. With blind tooling proper, the tool is used cooler and the leather surface dampened. Greater uniformity of colour will result if the tool is kept cool and impressed many times into the damp leather, rather than increasing its heat and allowing the leather to dry. As the tool loses heat it will be necessary to slightly reheat it, but, once designs have been impressed with a hot tool they tend to resist re-damping, which may be necessary if the blind tooling is to be successful. The effect is less pronounced on darker coloured leathers than on lighter ones, particularly natural and tan; it is less effective on white, if effectiveness is judged by sharper contrasts.

A highly polished tool can produce a good permanent polish in the impression, but some binders prefer to use an equal mixture of white wax and lard, lightly smeared on to the flesh side of a piece of soft leather on to which the cool tool is pressed. The preparation is made by first de-salting the lard by heating it, when the salt will come to the surface and can be skimmed off. The white wax is also heated, and the two are mixed together and allowed to cool. Pour the mixture into a wide-necked shallow pot fitted with a screw top. The heating of the two substances should be done with care, as both are inflammable. Once made, the mixture does not deteriorate and will last for many years. The method is not used by all binders; some prefer to build up the polish by the use of the cool tool only.

Lines may be blind-tooled by first running the fillet over the dampened leather against a wooden straightedge; on no account should a steel one be used on the damp leather, or an iron-mould stain will result. By placing a peg of wood between the fillet wheel and its metal holder, it can be slid, or 'jiggered' along the line which will produce a polish. A short piece of line can be used with equally good results.

If the remainder of the blind tooling has been done with 'intaglio' engraved tools, which leave the design standing above its immediate surround, a specially made tool, with a wider face in which a groove equal to the width of line required has been smoothly cut or filed, should be used. The sides of the groove will depress the leather, leaving a raised line centrally between them.

Gold Stamping Foils

In the 1930s Messrs George M. Whiley of Ruislip introduced atomised gold on polyester film, primarily for industrial gold-blocking machines. Since then foils have been improved and in addition to pure gold include simulated gold, coloured aluminium, and matt and glossy pigments in many colours. In addition, they may be obtained specially prepared for use on various materials and surfaces including vinyls. In view of the extremely high price of gold, and the fact that atomised gold is about sixteen times thinner than the thinnest beaten gold and therefore very cheap by comparison, it is much used by hand bookbinders for cheaper grades of bindings.

Originally, natural suspicion about its suitability and permanency was understandable, and this, combined with the inevitable difficulties that come with new materials demanding new techniques, caused it to be ignored by many binders. It now has a place in hand binding, but there are limits to its usefulness. To obtain solidity and clear definition it needs a smooth surface which excludes grained leathers and bookcloths having coarse or open texture. It is a reasonable assumption that the pressure required to produce the necessary smoothness for a solid impression results in the fracturing of the ultra-thin gold deposit plus the fact that between the face of the finishing tool and the gold is the polyester film, which, although extremely thin, must slightly aggravate the position as regards definition, especially when only hand pressure is used. With practice, remarkably good results can be obtained on polished leather, the fibre of which is soft and receptive, and binders often 'piece' cloth casings with leather for this reason.

Line pallets can be used successfully on book spines because they can first be impressed in blind; with the foil held tightly over them, the impressions are clearly visible for tooling again. This does not apply to lettering, although some finishers maintain that by first tooling in blind and fixing the stamping foil over the impressions, if the worker first breathes on the foil and presses the finger firmly over and into the impressions, these will show sufficiently for an experienced and quick finisher to accurately re-tool them through the foil. For direct tooling, guide lines may be lightly drawn against a strip of vellum or plastic with a good-quality ball pen if the foil is firmly secured in position. With regard to permanency; although many years must pass before a final judgement can be made, experiments carried out many years ago still look as good as when executed. The reasons for this could be that pure gold does not deteriorate no matter how thin; and that because the gold impressions are *below* the surface of the leather or bookcloth they are not subjected to wear by rubbing.

Provided the colour required is obtainable, and there is a good range, pigment foils can be of considerable value to the fine bookbinder. In the past there has been no such convenient method of applying colour to tooled impressions, and they are being increasingly used. Despite all that has been written about stamping foils, their main use lies in industry rather than in the craftsman's workshop; but it is foolish to ignore their uses. They will never completely replace the traditional method of gold-tooling fine bindings, for apart from the fact that atomised gold does not have the beautiful smoothness of beaten gold in the finished binding, there is the near-insurmountable difficulty of successfully tooling an intricate design by hand with them.

Machine Blocking

Although it was in the 1830s that the blocking press came into use, from medieval times larger areas were impressed with designs in blind, using engraved metal, or even wooden, blocks. These were used cold, being placed in position on the dampened leather of the book cover, which was then pressed.

The early blocking presses were called 'arming presses' because their main purpose was to impress on to book covers the owners' heraldic arms. Heat was supplied by inserting pre-heated iron bars in the platen of the press. Upon its introduction, gas was used; today, electricity is used almost entirely. With the introduction of stamping foils, blocking presses are fitted with automatic roll feeds, and heating can be fairly accurately adjusted to the individual requirements of the particular work. Because the hand bookbinder is sometimes called upon to impress heraldic arms, access to a blocking press is desirable. As, usually, only one final impression is required, and that on a completed bookbinding, preparations must be such that success is assured. Experimental boards (only the area to be blocked need be covered with leather) must be prepared, and they should be of similar thickness to that to be blocked.

The block, usually of brass and $\frac{3}{8}$in high, is fixed to a mounting plate which should be warmed before having stout brown paper glued to it. The back of the block is treated similarly and any surplus paper is cut away at the edges. A piece of strawboard is cut to the same size as the book, and the block, with its back glued, is placed on it in the position it has to occupy on the book. Board and block are accurately and squarely placed on the bed of the blocking press so that the block is quite central. Gauges at back and side are set, and the bed is brought up into contact with the platen for a short while. When the bed is lowered, the block will be securely attached to the plate. An impression is taken on a piece of thickish paper or thin white card; should it be uneven at any point, 'make-ready' will be necessary. This consists of tearing—not cutting—pieces of paper of suitable thickness and pasting them where the impression is weak on the board, until a uniform one is obtained. Heated impressions are next taken on the experimental boards and the leather prepared as usual for gold tooling. When ready, gold leaf is laid on.

With blocking, the three important factors are heat, pressure and 'dwell' (the length of time the block is in contact with the leather). Heat should be that normally required *at the point of contact* and this can be higher than indicated on a press thermometer, should one be fitted, necessitating experiment. Pressure, being applied by mechanical leverage, can be unwittingly made greater than is necessary for blocking on leather, and experience is required to assess it. 'Dwell' should be the minimum required; if excessive it will result in gilt impressions being dull, and in the in-filling of small open areas. All three factors must be considered together, not in isolation, always having regard to the type of surface being blocked and the nature of the design. It will be realised that perfect blocking is a matter for the experienced professional.

Plate 1 (opposite) *Edgar Mansfield*, Dance and the Soul,
$8\frac{5}{8}$in $\times$ $8\frac{1}{2}$in (22cm $\times$ 14cm)

PAUL VALERY   DANCE AND THE SOUL

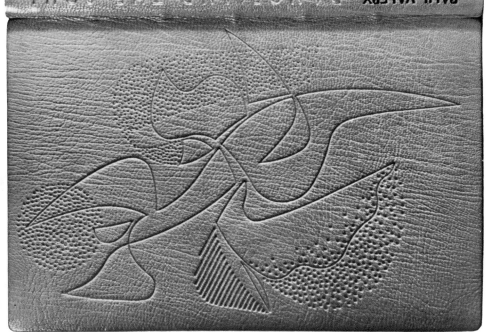

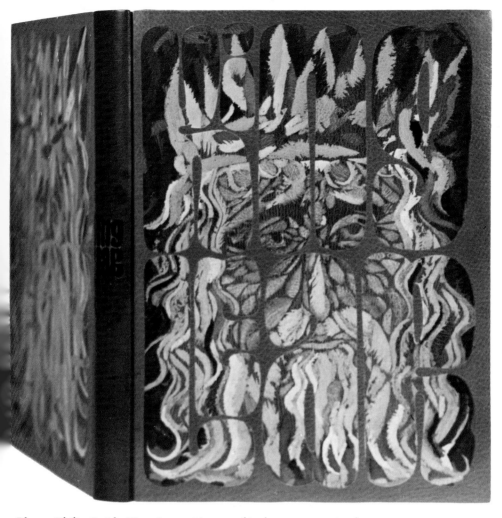

Plate 3 Philip Smith, King Lear, 18in × 14¼in (45·7cm × 36cm)

Plate 2 (opposite) *Edgar Mansfield*, Shorelands Summer Diary,
12in × 9¼in (30·5cm × 23·5cm)

Plate 4 Philip Smith, Pilgrim's Progress

Plate 5 (opposite) *Paul Bonet*, Dionysius Halicarnaseus,
$11\frac{7}{8}$in × 8in (30·1cm × 20·5cm). *Dark blue morocco, gold-tooled*
'Irradiant' design; leather doublures, gold-tooled with all-over design

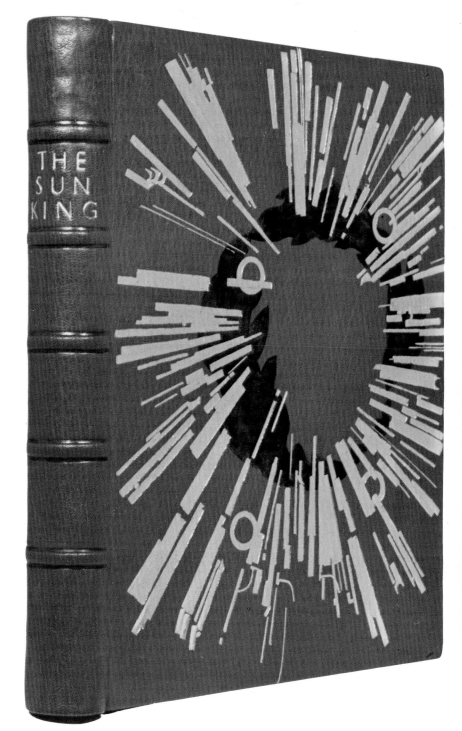

Plate 7 Kathleen Stuart-Harris, English Embroidered Bookbindings.
Embroidered panel $8\frac{3}{4}$in $\times$ $6\frac{1}{4}$in (22cm $\times$ 17cm)

Plate 6 (opposite) *Ann Tout*, The Sun King

5

COVER DESIGN

Finishing techniques—board decoration—cover design in the twentieth century

COVER DESIGN

Cover design is inhibited in many ways. When a book is to be rebound, its nature, and its period—wherever this may lie in the five centuries over which the craft extends—must be considered. So, too, must the wishes of the owner, though they may conflict with the better judgement of the binder; for even a craftsman of national repute seldom feels able to refuse a valuable commission. Only when the designer bookbinder has complete freedom of expression can his design be truly personal.

With older books, traditions of design should be respected; mere copying is not suggested, but the design should be in keeping with the book and sympathetic to its period; anything quite out of period is unacceptable.

Until the earlier part of the twentieth century, hand-tooled book cover design was purely decorative and unrelated to the book's contents. Finishing tools were made in almost completely standard patterns, and their very nature generally restricted decoration to geometric arrangement, although occasionally with considerable individuality. One thing was constant; the design was inevitably framed, often by a border round it, and always by the edges of the board. Today no such restraint exists, and designs often extend over the whole cover—and even beyond; for much is left to the imagination.

Spines

The spine treatment of bookbindings is so much controlled by its proportions, raised bands, and lettering, that there is less scope for imaginative treatment.

With the natural beauty of the grain of the leather, especially if polished, gilt lettering only, and bands accentuated by blind pallet lines, give a quiet dignity that is very effective, provided the workmanship is of a high order. Spines of half-leather bindings have nearly always suffered from over-embellishment as though they were trying to compensate for the book's nakedness elsewhere, but admittedly the gleam of the gold on the bookshelves usually excites the onlooker.

PIECING

Coloured lettering pieces not only provide additional colour but also have the effect of separating sets of volumes, and with today's improved adhesives (in this case, PVA) are permanent, which was not the case when paste was used. With cloth-bound books any form of elaborate tooling is out of place, but the addition of a lettering piece can improve the appearance, if only by adding a second colour. The very thin leather used for these labels can be obtained already reduced to the necessary thickness, or goatskin may be pared down. Their size, if the amount of lettering permits, should be that of the panel that would have resulted had the spine been divided for five bands, and they should occupy the position of the second panel from the top. It is inadvisable to use sheepskin skiver in view of the much shorter life of its surface. More than one lettering piece may be required on library bindings because the author's name should be separate from the title, and other details may be required. Dividers are used to mark the width of labels from top to bottom and where a number are needed, the pared leather is cut into strips. The long edges are finely pared and the width of the individual labels is gauged by laying the leather across the spine and marking it at the edges. Should it overlap them, it will tend to come away when the book is opened; if too short, the effect is poor. The two ends of the label, cut at right-angles to the edge of the leather, are also pared. After checking for size, the back is thinly covered with PVA adhesive and the label is placed in position before being rubbed down with a folder through paper stretched firmly across the spine. After the paper has been removed the edges can be lightly pressed down with the finger and the label left to dry. Unless labels are large, the finger may be more effective than a brush for spreading the PVA. Single or double gilt pallet lines across the spine seal the edges of the lettering piece and improve its appearance.

MITRED PANELS

Mitred panels give considerable dignity to a leather spine if well executed, but the work is not simple for the amateur. Line pallets with mitred ends are required and these may be of either single, double or even triple lines. Using a two-line pallet, lines are marked against the bands, which leaves one of them away from the band.

The head and tail lines are marked with a folder against a plastic or vellum template. To mark and tool the vertical lines, the book must

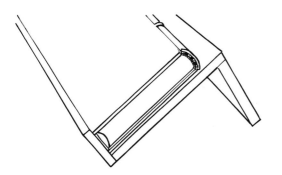

130 *'Cradle' for tooling vertical lines*

be placed at an angle, and this is done by making a 'cradle' for it (130) or by screwing a suitable piece of wood at the cut-away portion of the finishing press, against which the book, on a piece of millboard, can rest (131). Vertical lines should be near to the

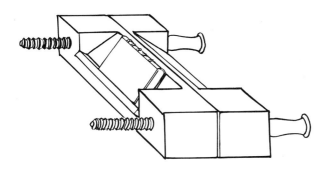

131 *Alternative method of 'cradling', using block fitted to finishing press*

joint edge but not so near that they will be affected by the opening of the book cover. They are first marked with a folder against a straightedge and tooled with a heated pallet. It is not often that an angle pallet of exactly the correct length is available, and care has to be used when extending a line made by a shorter one so that it is in alignment and the mitred end is exactly placed. This also applies to the running of the lines across the spine where they must exactly meet the mitred ends of the side lines. The marking up must be accurate, especially if more than one volume of a work is involved, for the panels must be not only perfectly square on the spine but uniform when placed side by side. If desired, decorative additions to the panels are made by the use of corner and centre tools, with, possibly, thin decorative pallets on the raised bands.

The 'run-up' gilt back, formerly a feature of school prize bindings but seen less today, was but a quick method of trying to simulate the mitred panelled back. The vertical lines were marked, the leather prepared for gold tooling, and gold leaf laid on where required. The vertical side lines were first tooled for their whole length and surplus gold on the outside of them was removed by the finger covered with a piece of cloth. This prevented pallet lines across the spine from overlapping them. Tooling for this type of work was 'direct', ie no blind impressions were used and the whole spine was glaired, being varnished after the gold tooling had been completed.

TIES

These form an attractive finish to a half-bound leather binding and consist of the pallet lines on either side of raised bands being extended on to the book boards, their ends meeting at a central point a short distance from the joint. A leaf or other simple unit, preferably slightly triangular in shape, is tooled three times at the 'tie', one continuing in the same direction and the other two at right-angles, one left, the other right. They may be either in gilt or blind according to the treatment of the spine.

The sides of half-bindings are neatened (and accentuated) if blind or gilt lines, single or double, are worked at the edge of the leather where it abuts on the cloth or paper sides. With blind lines, a creasing iron may be used, or even a short line pallet, provided the advancing end is lifted slightly clear of the leather. The leather should be quite clean, and sponging beforehand is advisable. For gold tooling, the preparation must be as usual, the gold leaf being cut into narrow strips and either laid on to the impressions or picked up on the fillet. If a roll is used, tooling must be direct, no previous impression being made.

Board Decoration

Decorative patterns consisting of geometric arrangements of lines, gouges and smaller unit tools, that are too intricate to be tooled directly on the leather, must have working patterns prepared.

Strong, thin bank paper is cut to the exact size of the board and the tools are impressed in black, after the face of each has been held in the tip of a candle flame, which leaves a deposit of carbon on it. It is sometimes convenient to divide the board surface into equal geometric parts by first folding the paper lengthwise and across the width, creasing it, and lightly pencilling in the crease lines. Should a central symbol be envisaged, the second fold will have to be made at the centre band on the spine, which will give an *optical* centre. Further folds can be made from these to produce rectangular areas, or, if lozenge-shaped ones are required, can be made by drawing lines from the corners of the four rectangles already marked. By making lines that bisect the diagonals where they cross, the pattern paper is further divided. From these guide lines repeat patterns may be built according to the fancy of the finisher.

Carefully planned lettering can be very effective on the board of a full leather binding, either as a border round all four sides or as a centre-piece, possibly enhanced by the judicious use of simple units arranged round it to form a circle, oval, or other shape. Douglas Cockerell was supreme in the controlled and elegant use of inter-twined lines and gouges with leaf and flower forms; above all else he used space to accentuate his pattern. Although every generation must have the freedom to express itself as it may, beauty, of whatever period, will always be a joy for ever.

'Expressive' is the term used in this second half of the twentieth century to describe bookbinding design that is no longer in bondage to yesterday. Like the artist, the designer-bookbinder uses abstract form, often with exciting effect. His designs not infrequently cover the whole book cover, and yet with each separate area, back and front board and spine, still individually complete in itself.

Abstract Design

Because bookbinding design could never have the freedom that painting had, and which, in the 1880s, produced the Impressionist school which discarded minute detail and elaborate finish, the advance to abstract design was all the more spectacular and challenging. Some may feel that the word 'abstract' has been taken so literally that what is left is too demanding of mental effort to be fully understood—or appreciated—by the viewer. To the uninitiated it is all too often a matter of guesswork rather than deduction to elucidate the deeper meaning behind the artist's design, although the colour may attract.

Because of this, the author introduced the subject of abstract design to youthful bookbinding students by having them make two or more 'natural form' drawings of units or articles that had a reference to the book for which the cover was being designed. These were then traced separately and placed over one another, and each was moved around until an interesting outline resulted. A further tracing of the whole was made and lightly transferred to drawing paper and each student was made to ponder on which detail could be eradicated without destroying the identity of the particular item. At first the results were quite extraordinary, but by continued experiment the confusion of the intermixed designs was reduced to a point that resulted in one that could be reproduced by on- or in-laying and gold tooling. What was equally important was that the student had begun to realise the subtleties of abstract design, starting at the right end—the beginning! This is only suggested as an experimental approach for those who have never inquired into abstract form and design.

Cover Design in the Twentieth Century

The history of bookbinding is, in the main, the history of book-cover design. This is almost inevitable, for although binding techniques develop there is much less change in them than in the decoration of book covers. In consequence there are many sources of information and an abundance of illustrations dealing with book-cover design of earlier periods. In the first part of the twentieth century, too, art and craft magazines kept those interested up-to-date with changes and trends; but today such sources appear to have diminished.

With the resurgence of interest in the craft of bookbinding, the time has arrived to make a permanent record of the work of the present era. To do this in detail is a task beyond the scope of a single chapter. Here, therefore, after a cursory backward glance at the past, a look is taken at present trends in book cover design and the work of those whose names are closely connected with it.

In Britain, gold tooling was not practised to any extent until the beginning of the seventeenth century, although specimens as early as the mid-fifteenth century exist. The bindings of the Mearne school are the first outstanding landmark in English gold-tooled designs, and even here the French influence is present. Samuel Mearne is not known to have bound books but as Bookseller and Stationer to King Charles II he was responsible for the 'Cottage Style' bindings produced between 1660 and 1683 (132), the style being copied profusely. The 'drawer handle' bindings from the same school show much ingenuity in the repetitive use of one main tool (133). In the next century, Roger Payne showed equal dexterity and individuality and, most will agree, even greater artistry in his gold-tooled bindings. They are renowned for the simplicity of the decoration, for most have large open areas which set off the delicately tooled designs often comprising corner pieces and borders (134). Equally interesting to posterity are his accounts, which throw light upon his careful forwarding. Descriptions of him always stress his insobriety and consequent poverty, and suggest that but for them he might have been an even greater binder. What is often over-looked is that they may well have been partly responsible for the admired simplicity of his designs, since he was too poor to buy many tools and was often reduced to making his own. He did not have sufficient tools to produce fulsome designs even if he had wanted to! Who knows?

During the nineteenth century, English bookbinders were re-inforced by many continental binders, particularly Germans, who settled in the country and who without doubt made a useful contri-bution to the craft and raised standards of workmanship.

Vellum bindings decorated in colour were produced by the 'Edwards of Halifax' family towards the end of the eighteenth century, when a method of making vellum transparent was patented by James Edwards. Paintings of scenes and portraits were executed on the reverse side of the vellum, showing through on the face side after the book had been bound (135). At the end of the nineteenth century Bagguley of Newcastle produced his 'Suther-land Tooling Process' which was used very effectively on vellum, the coloured designs being tooled with great delicacy. About the same time Cedric Chivers of Bath reintroduced bindings with paintings under vellum that were marketed under the name 'Vellucent'. They cannot be confused with the 'Edwards of Halifax'

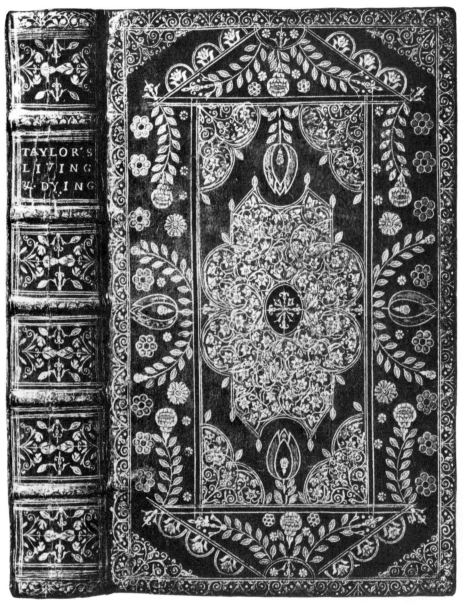

132 'Cottage Style' binding, c. 1682. Red morocco. $7\frac{3}{4}$in × $4\frac{5}{8}$in (18·6cm × 11·8cm)

133 (opposite) 'Drawer handle' binding, 1677. Red morocco. $7\frac{1}{2}$in × $4\frac{7}{8}$in (19cm × 12·5cm)

134 *Roger Payne*, Plutarch, 1744. *Red straight-grained morocco*

vellum bindings if only because of the period differences. The Edwards bindings have greater dignity, the colours being less harsh, while the almost classical designs contrast sharply with the paintings in the Vellucent bindings, which are usually in the Pre-Raphaelite style. Ann Tout of Weymouth, England, a comparative newcomer to the craft, has recently been experimenting with vellum, and one of her vellum bindings is illustrated (136), unfortunately not in colour; in the absence of transparent vellum, one with translucent qualities has had to be used. Another of her bindings, in full leather, for which she made the finishing tools, is also illustrated (Plate 6).

The disciples of William Morris, especially T. J. Cobden-Sanderson, who with Emery Walker founded the Doves Press in 1900, brought a new individualism into book design (137). His use of units tended to be an extension of Payne's, but records show that his designs were related to passages within the book.

His own student, Douglas Cockerell, followed him in the main, but allowed his conventional plant forms to virtually 'grow' and usually gave them plenty of space to do so (138). He used 'intaglio' blind tooling to better effect than had been seen before and introduced tawed (alum-dressed) pigskin for the purpose. Although some of his forwarding methods are not as suitable today, his standards set an example for all time. Whatever changes may come in bookbinding design, the innate beauty of Douglas Cockerell's will ever be appreciated. Although Katharine Adams worked with Cockerell for only a short while, her work (139) belongs to the same school and its quietness and intrinsic loveliness will have the appreciation and approval of posterity.

In France, always in the vanguard of bookbinding design, a completely new approach was made in the early twentieth century, mainly inspired by Marius Michel (1820–90). He was followed by Georges Cretté and later by such brilliant designers as Pierre Legrain, his son-in-law Jacques Anthoine-Legrain, Henri Creuzevault, and the giant of them all, Paul Bonet (Plate 5). The new French school completely divorced itself from what had gone before and was nearly a quarter of a century ahead of the 'Expressive' school in Britain. Sybil Pye, almost alone, broke away from the prevailing English style, using an abundance of geometric coloured leather inlays. Her designs combined linear tooling with that of geometric shapes occasionally grouped together (140).

135 *Binding by Edwards of Halifax. Transparent vellum.* $7\frac{1}{2}$in $\times$ $4\frac{7}{8}$in (19cm $\times$ 12·5cm)

136 *Ann Tout*, Rubaiyat of Omar Khayyam. *Translucent vellum with 'turned' foredge. Painted under vellum and tooled with Palladium.* $6\frac{3}{4}$in × 4in (16cm × 10cm)

137 (opposite) *Cobden-Sanderson*, Poems from Shelley. *Blue smooth morocco.* $7\frac{7}{8}$in × 5in (20cm × 12·8cm)

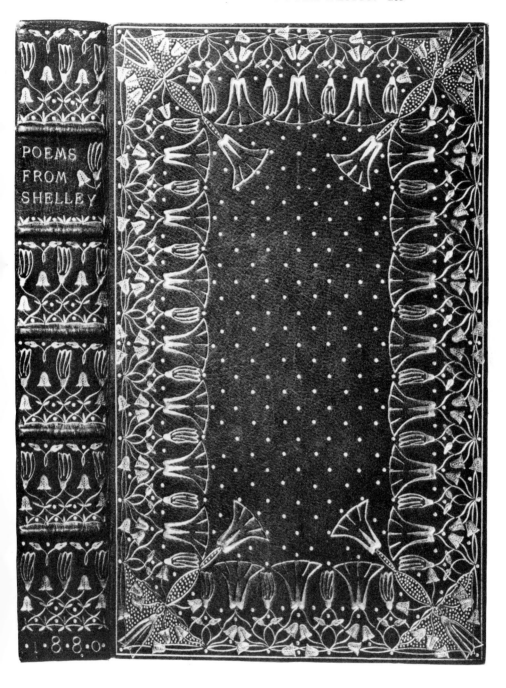

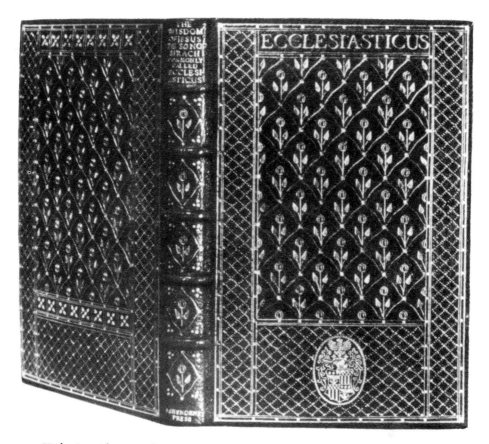

139 *Katharine Adams*, Ecclesiasticus. *Brown morocco, gold-tooled.*
$11\frac{3}{8}$in × $7\frac{1}{4}$in (29cm × 18·5cm)

138 (opposite) *Douglas Cockerell*, Pictures at Hagley Hall. *Red
Niger morocco, black onlaid shield and leaves gold-tooled.* 11in × $6\frac{1}{4}$in
(28cm × 16cm)

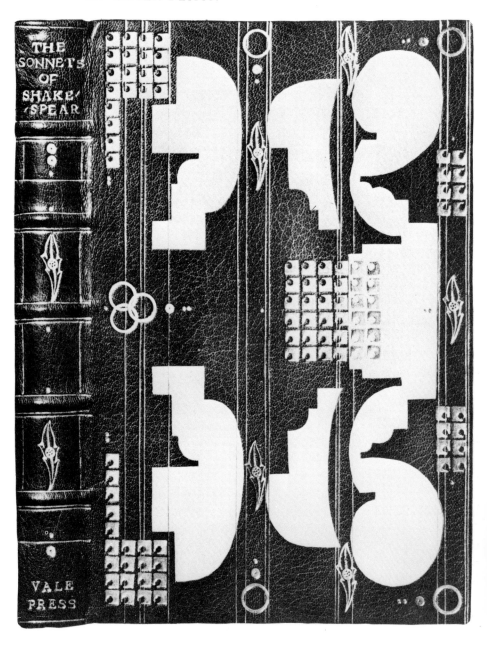

140 *Sybil Pye*, The Sonnets of Shakespeare. *Black morocco, fawn inlays.* 8¾in × 5⅞in (22cm × 14·9cm)

The Gregynog Press, founded in 1922, produced what were then considered to be advanced designs by several designers including Blair Hughes-Stanton and also George Fisher, who did the binding (141). It was the Festival of Britain in 1951 that turned national traditional design inside out, and gave everything, from architecture downwards, a 'new look'. From the few bookbinding exhibits, about a dozen, no great change was obvious, but the photographic files of bindings not exhibited, seen by comparatively few people, contained a few photographs of work by a virtually unknown bookbinder, Edgar Mansfield. It was he who was to change completely the approach to bookbinding design in England, and his appointment as Lecturer in Design at the (then) London School of Printing, which included bookbinding, showed excellent judgement on the part of those responsible. Today he is known internationally and may justly be considered to be the founder of the present school of binding design in England. No binder could give more thought and study to the design of a single book than he, and his workmanship is impeccable (Plates 1 and 2).

Edgar Mansfield is ever in debt, as he constantly admits, to William Matthews, another stalwart of bookbinding in England. His contribution to the craft lies not only in his superb workmanship but in his influence as a lifelong teacher of the subject (142).

Sydney Cockerell, brilliant son of a brilliant father, has latterly concentrated much of his craft effort on vellum bindings, aided by Joan Tebbutt. Apart from his contribution as a bookbinder, the craft is indebted to him for his remarkable revival of the art of marbling.

A high proportion of British bookbinders are members of the Designer Bookbinders, a title which succeeded that of the Guild of Contemporary Bookbinders, founded in 1955 as an offshoot of the earlier Hampstead Guild of Scribes and Bookbinders. Under the initial presidency of Edgar Mansfield, followed by that of Ivor Robinson and Bernard Middleton, it has done much to encourage interest in bookbinding both in Europe and America. The friendly rivalry engendered by exhibitions in many parts of the world has been an incentive, not only to maintain standards, but to improve them.

Bernard Middleton is equally well known as a fine bookbinder and as an erudite author of books and articles upon the subject. His

History of Craft Bookbinding Technique is a splendid piece of research that required years of study and inquiry, and is the most complete book of its kind. As a book restorer he has few equals, while his fine bindings reflect his quiet nature and often consist of simple units repeated with amazing accuracy and delightful results (143).

Ivor Robinson has built an enviable reputation as a bookbinder and was a worthy successor to Edgar Mansfield as president of the Designer Bookbinders. His one-man exhibition at the Galleria del Bel Libro, Ascona, Switzerland, was the first accorded to an English bookbinder and meant giving up a whole year entirely to the preparation of exhibits. Previously he had a similar exhibition in Stockholm where he lectured and demonstrated. After many years of experiment, he has produced an individual style in which symbolical design spreads over the book cover. With no more than half-a-dozen small line pallets he builds designs composed of restless lines which ignore board edges. His larger bindings have a magnificence in a curious, reticent way. His binding of *King Lear* (144) which measures $18\frac{3}{8} \times 14$in, is a good example of his more recent work and clearly shows the accuracy of the tooling with short pieces of line.

Without doubt, one of the cleverest bindings of today is that for the Ganymed edition of *King Lear* executed by Philip C. Smith (Plate 3). The book is identical with that bound by Ivor Robinson, and the two bindings provide splendid examples of different styles by two quite different but equally good craftsmen. Ivor Robinson proclaims his individualism by using traditional methods to produce contemporary design, while Philip Smith, who is also a painter, uses the highly personal technique he has developed of using 'feathered' onlays to provide colourful designs far less divorced from painting than traditional inlays and onlays. The design for *King Lear* necessitated extremely ingenious preparation which is explained in detail in his book, *The Lord of the Rings and other bookbindings*. The binding is one of superb design and workmanship. Philip Smith has also devised 'marbled inlaid leathers' which he calls 'Maril'. These are 'reconstituted and sectioned inlays' and give the impression of leathers of different colours that are stuck together, rolled or otherwise shaped, and, when dry, cut through sectionally. Impressive and exciting effects are produced by their use, especially in conjunction with feathered inlays, as can be seen in his exceptional

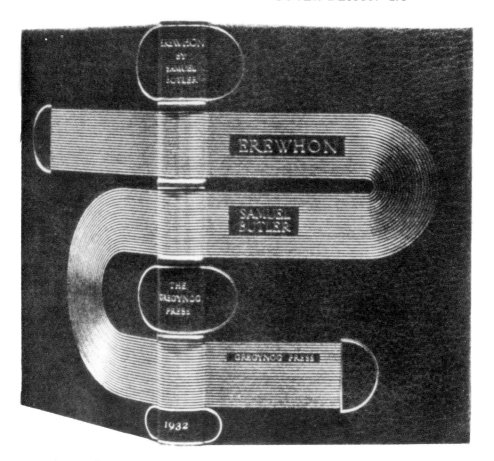

141 *Blair Hughes-Stanton*, Erewhon. *Brown morocco.* 9in × 6¼in
(23cm × 16cm)

'book wall' comprising six volumes of Tolkien's *The Lord of the Rings*, displayed in a walnut case (145). A set of four volumes of Yeats's *Works*, dealt with similarly, provides the opportunity to examine the workmanship more closely. In this case one can but admire the use of a French joint which indicates a combination of functional realism and artistry—too often a rarity.

Most bookbinders have an individual style of cover decoration even though they are designers, but in England today in many cases it seems to be a reflection, sometimes an extension, of the Mansfield tradition. There is no suggestion of copying, but of working along

142 *William Matthews*, The Car Snob.

143 *Bernard Middleton*, Twelve Books. *Red and black morocco, green circular onlay with recessed black centre, gold, silver and black tooling.* 18½in × 12¼in (46·5cm × 31cm)

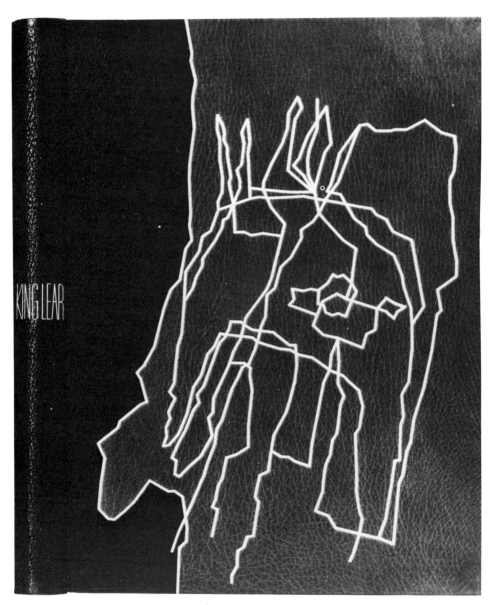

144 *Ivor Robinson, King Lear. Brown and black morocco, tooled gold and blind, black suede doublures.* $18\frac{3}{4}$in $\times$ 14in (46·5cm $\times$ 35cm)

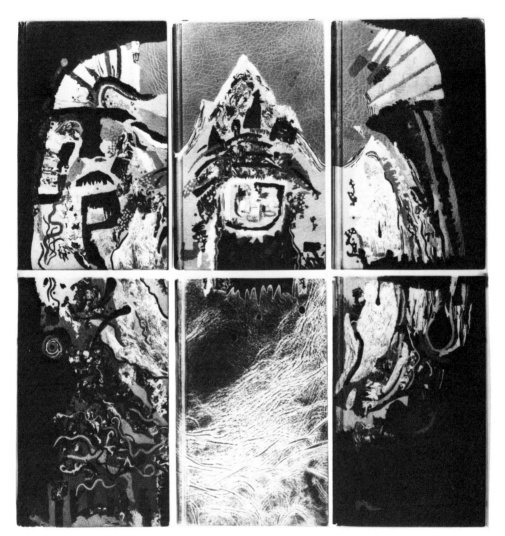

145 *Philip Smith*, The Lord of the Rings. *Six books assembled as a 'book wall'. Binding in various coloured moroccos and silver kid, mainly black and grey, with feathered onlays and coloured marbled inlays ('Maril'). Each book* $9\frac{1}{8}$in $\times$ $5\frac{7}{8}$in (27cm $\times$ 15cm)

146 *Jeff Clements*, Roman Imperial Coins. *Amber morocco over sculptured boards.* 9⅝in × 9⅛in (24·5cm × 24·2cm)

the same lines. Three examples illustrated, in which the beauty of the leather is accented, are those of Jeff Clements, Trevor Jones and Anthony Cains, the two former being senior members of the Designer Bookbinders and established British bookbinders. In *Roman Imperial Coins*, bound by Jeff Clements (146) the powerful decorative units suggest the subject-matter of the book, but do not in any way detract from the sheer beauty of the leather grain. Trevor Jones' binding of *The Odyssey* (147) comes into the same category, although here the induced graining of the leather makes a splendid and appropriate background to the superimposed design. In a slightly different way, Anthony Cains in his binding of the *Pergamon Atlas* (148) has used induced graining round the blind-tooled symbol of the Orb of the World, the old conception of the division of the earth—and has done it very effectively. The exciting effect of leather inlays, contrasting sharply with the cover leather, is exemplified in Edward Gray's binding of *Art in the Ice Age*, bound in 1963 (149). The *Little Book of Prayers*, bound by Ian Ross (150) is a sublime example of an inlaid abstract design that makes its point without demanding extreme mental exertion. Hilary Barnett's *Country Houses of Dorset* (151) shows ingenious use of continuous inlays heightened by gold tooling to give an effect of perspective.

Onlays give greater freedom in design, and, now that stronger adhesives can be used, no longer look impermanent without tooled edges. Elizabeth Greenhill's *Fables of Esope* (152) with its multi-coloured onlays combined with simple tooling, is a vigorous and satisfying example of the method. Another is Arthur Johnson's *Extinct Birds* (153) which has a delightful humorous element as an added attraction. Sally Lou Smith has used the traditional onlay outlined with gold tooling in a modern style very much in keeping with the book, Whitman's *Leaves of Grass* (154).

Gold tooling in the traditional manner will always be effective but, to be completely successful, demands great accuracy and skill. The *Chichester Bible* bound by Sydney Cockerell (155) is a quite splendid example of bookbinding in all its aspects, while the simple tools required for its decoration show clearly that their disposition can make a centuries-old method acceptable to modern taste. The not dissimilar design of Ann Tout's *The Sun King* (Plate 6) is further proof that expensive engraved tools are not essential to contemporary bookbinding design. Simplicity in design must not be confused with simple design, and this is exemplified by Bryan Maggs' *The Hundredth Book* (156), which demanded considerable skill to tool the two 'noughts' which tie the design to the book's title. Similarly, James Brockman shows the use of the straight line by superimposing one set of radiating lines over another in his binding of *Majorca Observed* (157). *Christ and the Apostles* (158), winner of a Harrison award, is in full scarlet goatskin tooled simply but very efficiently in black and gold; it is the work of Brian Robinson.

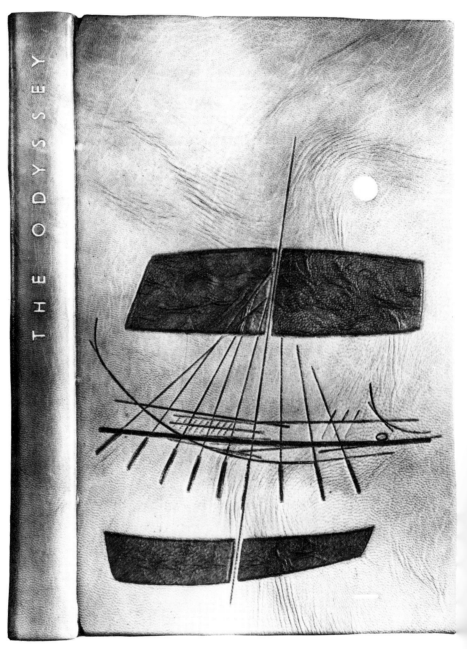

147 Trevor Jones, The Odyssey. *Modelled rust red, native dyed goatskin, grey-blue onlays, blind and gold tooling.*

148 *Anthony Cains, Pergamon Atlas. Undyed goatskin, raised and moulded decoration, blocked in blind, leather joints, green goatskin doublures.*

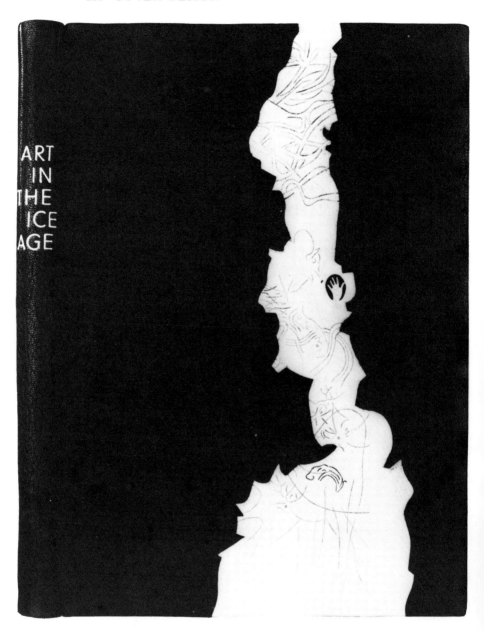

149 *Edward Gray*, Art in the Ice Age. *Black Levant morocco, chrome yellow recessed Niger inlays, tooled olive green.* 12in × 10in (30cm × 25·5cm)

150 *Ian Ross*, Little Book of Prayers. *Biscuit Niger goatskin inlaid olive green.* $7\frac{1}{4}$in $\times$ $4\frac{3}{8}$in (18·5cm $\times$ 11cm)

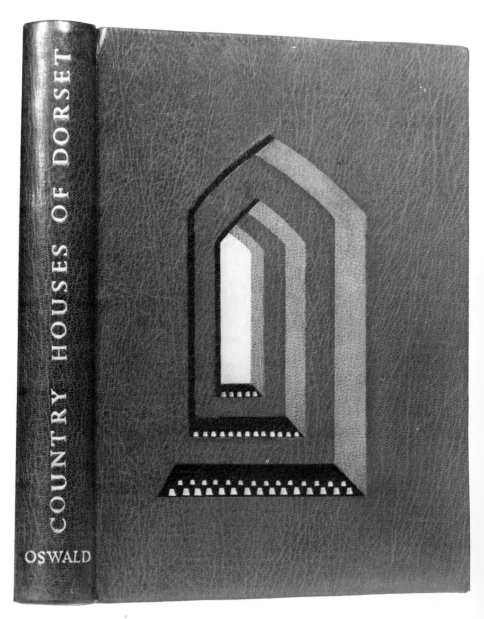

151 *Hilary Barnett*, Country Houses of Dorset. *Dark red Niger goatskin, inlaid black, tan and chrome yellow. Back board inlaid khaki. Tooled blind and gold.* 9¾in × 7¼in (25cm × 18·5cm)

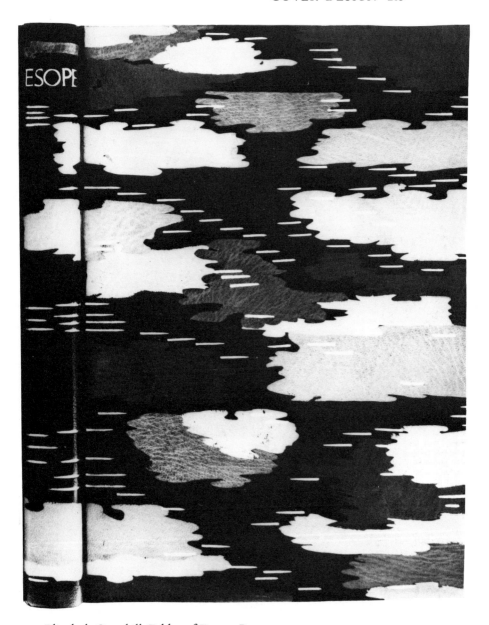

152 *Elizabeth Greenhill*, Fables of Esope. *Brown morocco, multi-coloured onlays, brown 'Oasis' doublures.* 12¼in × 9in (31·1cm × 22·9cm)

153 *Arthur Johnson*, Extinct Birds. *Green Levant morocco spine, sides of Spanish marbled sheepskin, design onlaid in pink, white, light and dark blue, crimson, yellow and natural leathers.* $15\frac{1}{8}$in $\times$ $11\frac{7}{8}$in (38·5cm $\times$ 30·3cm)

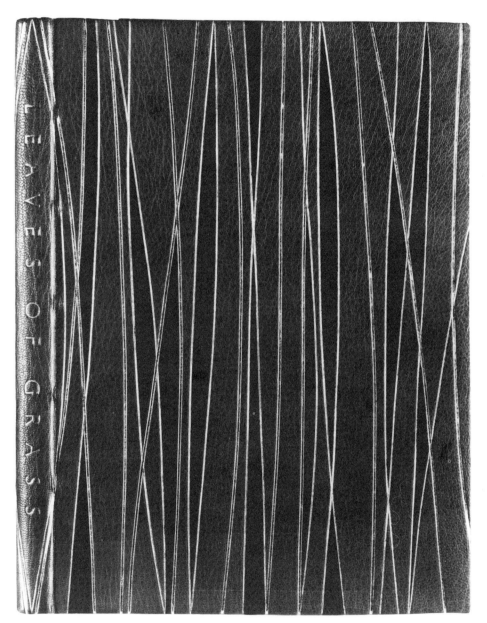

154 *Sally Lou Smith*, Leaves of Grass. *Light green morocco, onlays of olive and dark blue, tooled gold. Dark blue morocco doublures, light green onlays.* $9\frac{3}{8}$in $\times$ $7\frac{3}{8}$in (26cm $\times$ 18cm)

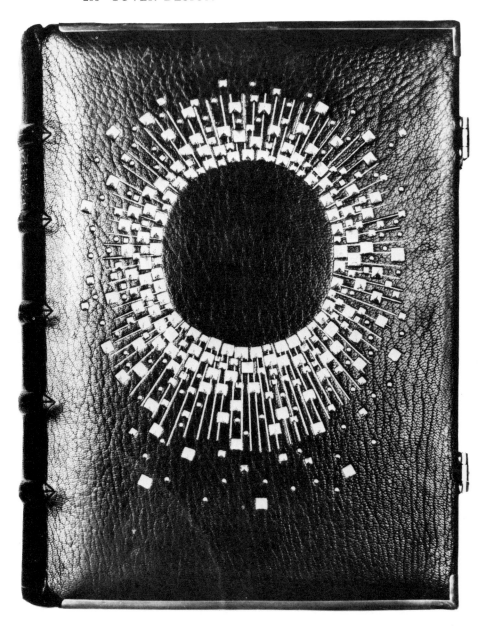

155 *Sydney Cockerell*, Chichester Bible. *Dark blue Levant morocco,*
gold tooling, silver-gilt nails, oxidised silver clasps and board edges.
$13\frac{5}{8}$in × 10in (33cm × 25cm)

156 *Bryan Maggs,*
The Hundredth
Book. *Brick red*
French morocco,
gold-tooled.
14½in × 10in
(36·8cm ×
25·5 cm)

157 James Brockman, Majorca Observed. *Sage green morocco, gold tooling.* $9\frac{5}{8}$in $\times$ $6\frac{5}{8}$in (24·5cm $\times$ 17cm)

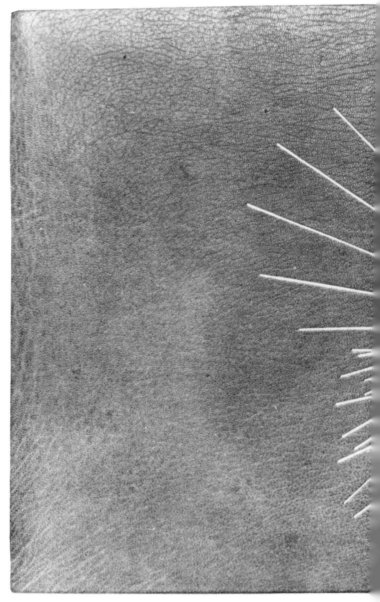

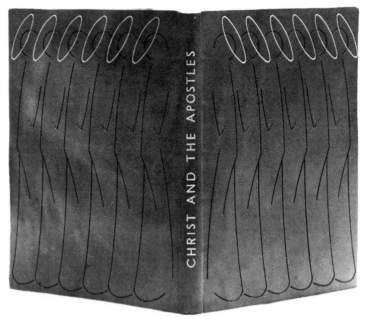

158 *Brian
Robinson,*
Christ and the
Apostles.
*Crimson Niger
goatskin, tooled
black and gold.*
10in × 7½in
(25·5cm ×
19·2cm)

One particular method of cover decoration that has been almost
completely neglected for nearly three hundred years is the use of
embroidery. It was singularly unsuitable for full bindings because
of the comparatively short life of the background fabric used for
the book cover. By the combination of the two crafts, needlework
and bookbinding, with leather for the binding material, embroidered
panels are once again being used as cover decoration. In the two
examples shown (Plates 7 and 8), the books, bound by the author in
Niger goatskin, have deeply recessed panels in the front boards
into which the embroidered panels are fixed. The decoration is
widely different, that by Kathleen Stuart-Harris being finely
embroidered in period style as befits the contents of the book
English Embroidered Bookbindings (Plate 7). The other, *Royal Palaces
of England* (Plate 8), contrasts sharply in the decorative treatment
of the panel by Mary Collins depicting the White Tower of London,
which includes collage of white and gilt kid and other materials.
Both bindings are splendid examples of the embroiderer's art.

From the foregoing it would seem that every possibility of cover
decoration has been exploited, but no doubt man possesses the
ingenuity and skill to find still further variations.

6

MISCELLANEOUS ITEMS

Inlaying and onlaying—insets and 'sculptured' boards—single-section bindings—unsewn binding—guard books—slip cases and chemises—book boxes and pamphlet cases—portfolio cases—pockets in books—books on stilts

MISCELLANEOUS ITEMS

Inlaying and Onlaying

In the days of Thomas Wotton, 'the English Grolier', in the sixteenth century, colour was introduced in bindings by painting the tooled and interlaced strapwork. The sprinkling and marbling of calf also added colour to the bound book, as did the infamous 'tree marbling' in the late eighteenth and nineteenth centuries.

Today, inlaying and onlaying of coloured leathers provide much more colour, some of it very exciting, on leather bindings. At the beginning of the century coloured onlays were stamped out of thinly pared leather with a punch, the outline of which was identical with that of the brass fleuron or leaf or other form by which the onlay was afterwards gold-tooled. The method was fairly simple, but it required almost paper-thin onlays. After blind tooling was completed, the open area within the outline tooled impression was pricked up with the blade of a small penknife or a needle. The punched (or cut) onlays, laid on a piece of well-pasted glass, were picked up, one by one, by the point of a bone knitting needle that had been touched into the paste, laid in position on the blind-tooled impression, and pressed into it with the finger, any paste that exuded at the edges being later taken up with a damp sponge. From time to time the cold finishing tool was impressed over the onlays, sealing the edges. Before drying out, the book board was placed in the press on a block or a pile of pressing boards with a pad of blotting paper placed on top of them. A celluloid sheet was placed over the board and covered with a pressing board. The press platen was brought down firmly but carefully for a few seconds only, before removing the book from the press. This ensured that the onlay was adhering firmly to the cover. If necessary, the cold finishing tool was again impressed over the onlays. When all onlays had been dealt with and had completely dried out, the board could be gold-tooled in the usual manner. Because of the extreme thinness of the leather onlay, tooling had to be done with minimal heat to avoid burning it. For the 'decorated' cover as against the 'expressive' designs of today, the effect is still quite pleasing.

Onlays are now used much more bravely, and the 'feathered' edge, used so successfully by Philip Smith, gives an effect of leather being used as paint. In this way the designer-painter effectively uses his skills to produce stronger and more exciting colour effects. Each has his personal method; some use emery cloth or glasspaper to feather the edge, whilst others use fine files to produce stronger effects.

Inlays provide greater areas of colour for backgrounds and it is important that their thickness should agree exactly with that of the leather of the cover. If they are too thick, judicious all-over paring will be necessary, and if too thin, the cut-away area to be inlaid must be raised by the use of paper or thin board to produce a uniform surface.

When designing for inlaid work, it is important to bear in mind that it is unwise to cut the cover leather for inlays close to the board edges, although inlays can be turned over them to the inside of the cover. The position of the hemp slips must be considered when preparing the design, for to cut them when inlaying could wreak havoc to board attachment and therefore to the binding.

An inlay is merely the removing of an area of the cover leather and replacing it with an identically shaped piece of another colour, or perhaps texture. But it is not quite as simple as that! Not only must accuracy be 100 per cent but the inlaid leather must slightly over- or underlap the edges of the cover leather. Choice of lapping is dependent upon whether it is considered that the edges of the inlay are more secure if lapped under those of the main leather. It can be argued that one of the two edges must overlap and so nothing is gained by underlapping the inlaid leather, whereas by overlapping a trimmer edge results. Some binders temporarily stick the piece of leather to be inlaid on to the cover, and cut through both leathers simultaneously at right-angles to the surface. While this ensures a perfect fit, it can result in minute openings appearing later if contraction of the leather takes place, whereas with the lapped edges one leather is attached to the other at the edges, which virtually eliminates the possibility. If an angled cut is made it must be towards the centre of the inlay so that the edges of this will overlap those of the main leather. If cut in the reverse the inlay will be slightly smaller and cannot possibly overlap the bevelled edge of the main leather.

Where a number of inlays, all flush to the surface of the book cover, are to be used, an accurately drawn design on paper is necessary. From this, secondary ones can be traced which will provide templates for the various inlay shapes and can be stuck to the face of the inlaying leathers. The whole inlay should be built up from the outside edge of the design so that only the outer edges of the inlays need to be accurately cut at first, the remainder of the inlay being left larger at this stage. The whole of the inlaid area is first cut away, with the bevel towards the middle, the unwanted leather is removed, and the exposed board and bevelled edges of the main leather are painted with thin glair. The first outer inlay is pasted, laid in position and carefully rubbed down with the fingers and allowed to dry. The outline of the next inlay area is marked on it, using the original template, the surplus is cut away and removed, and the board and leather edges are glaired. The next inlay is cut to shape on its outer edges and placed in position. This process is repeated until only the centre inlay remains, and this is cut all round to its final shape and fitted into the last uncovered space. All leather used must be of uniform thickness.

If thought necessary, the book board can be pressed after each inlay has been fitted, but it is very important that any paste on the surface of the leather be completely sponged off before this is done.

If the binder prefers it, the inlays may be underlapped, each piece being cut very slightly larger than the template or tracing and fitted into position from its outer edge.

Edgar Mansfield, who has examined and analysed the subject more than most contemporary bookbinders, divides it into five parts:

> Inlay with tooled edges,
> Inlay without tooled edges,
> Recessed inlays,
> Sunk inlays,
> Recessed onlays.

In the first, all lines outside the inlay areas are deeply tooled, the 45° angled cut is made with a scalpel at the *inside* (inlay) edge of the tooled line, and the leather is removed. A tracing is taken from the *outside* of the tooled line, transferred on to thicker paper and cut. From this the inlay may be accurately cut, the flesh side pared at an angle of 60° (not 45° as before), and the edges feathered. The surface board may have to be raised or lowered as necessary to

159 *Edgar Mansfield*, Through the Woods. *Three-dimensional plan for the binding design*

160 *Edgar Mansfield*, Through the Woods. *Completed binding.*
Native-dyed morocco with colour and tonal variations, inlaid on four
levels in chrome and lemon yellow, black, stone and neutralised green.
$10\frac{3}{8}$in $\times$ $7\frac{1}{2}$in (26·5cm $\times$ 19cm)

bring the inlay slightly above the level of the surface. The board and edges are painted with thin glair, and the inlay leather pasted and applied while the board is still damp. Gentle hand pressure is required, but as the damp inlay will contract later, to allow for this its surface should be left to project slightly above the dry leather surrounding it. The sharp edge of a folder can be used to press the feathered edge to the base of the tooled line. The inlay must be quite dry before the outline is tooled.

If the outline is not to be tooled, it is accurately cut away with the inlay, at 60°. The tracing will follow the outside edge and so will be slightly larger. Again the inlay should be slightly above the cover level; the reverse looks terrible. The edges are gently pressed with the finger, or even by rubbing the edge of the scalpel across them at right-angles.

The 'recessed inlay' lies slightly below so that its edges are flush with the bottom of the tooled line or are curved downwards to it. This is achieved by slightly lowering the board surface.

The 'sunk inlay' demands that the book board be made of several thin boards, the various recessed areas being cut from them before making up. It is wise not to cut these boards to the finished size *before* cutting the recessed areas, but to complete the inlay design, glue them together, and then cut to size. When covering, the leather is pressed into the first depth, and it may be necessary to cut it diagonally across to release tension there. If it is cut very slightly smaller, the original piece of board removed to form the recess can be inserted, to ensure adhesion of the leather at all of the different levels.

Mr Mansfield uses 'recessed onlays' for lines not less than $\frac{1}{16}$in in width. Those not wider than $\frac{1}{8}$in are tooled deeply and the surface scraped, using a steel knitting needle sharpened to a chisel edge. Initially wider ones are outlined by tooling one side first, setting a pair of blunt-pointed dividers to the total width and marking it by sliding one leg along the line while the other marks the parallel one which is then tooled. The central leather is either shaved off or completely removed.

The onlay leather may be pared as thin as possible if sealing tape is stuck to the face side. The strips are then cut and the edges feathered. The sealing tape is carefully removed and the leather pasted and placed in position.

Edgar Mansfield almost invariably designs his inlays as part of the tooled cover, and so they are outlined; this provides for continuity and also sharpens the effect (159, 160).

These notes on inlaying and onlaying are only the essence of Edgar Mansfield's methods, and his book *Modern Design in Bookbinding* is essential to those who wish to pursue the subject further and also to study his bookbinding designs.

The choice of a knife for cutting inlays seems to be a personal one but it is essential that the blade be narrow. The fine blade of a small pocket knife, if properly sharpened, can be used. My preference is for one with a $\frac{1}{4}$in or $\frac{3}{8}$in diameter cylindrical 'pencil' handle which also holds reserve blades. One with a blade resembling a plough knife in miniature is most adaptable and can be turned in the hand for cutting sharp curves.

Insets and 'Sculptured' Boards

When an inset is to be recessed into the board of a finished cover, the cover must be made from two thin boards, the upper one having the area needed for the inset cut out before being glued to the other and pressed.

When making the cover, the material is worked into the recessed

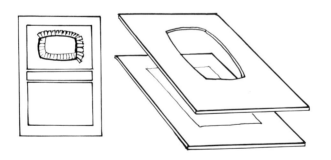

161 *Recessed panel for a cloth case*

area. If the piece of board cut out has its edges slightly reduced, it can be used for compressing the covering material into the recess by pressing before the adhesive has dried. A bevelled cut will be found to be more effective when cutting the recess.

With cloth, a better method is to partially make the cover *before* glueing the two boards together, and to turn in the material round the cut-out shape. This will require radiating cuts to be made in the turn-ins after the central portion has been cut away (161). The item to be inset will have been glued in position on the lower board before the upper one is glued, using a 'dabbing' stroke with the glue brush. The two boards, glued together, can be subjected to moderate pressure in the press before completing the cover by turning in the edges of the covering material.

The method is useful where a gold-blocked portion of the original cover is to be incorporated in the new. Normally, if in good enough condition, and thought to be worthy of preservation, the decorated sides and spine of the original case are removed and mounted so that they can be bound in at the end of the book.

Sculptured boards are used nowadays to give a three-dimensional effect to the cover design with full leather bindings. According to the complexity of the design, two or more laminated boards may be needed. Such bindings present problems not only in design but in construction, for the attachment, and possible weakening, of the boards must be considered. Covering leather will have to be expanded when working it into recesses and paring will probably be necessary at those points. For perfection, complete coloured 'mock-ups' in pasteboard will be required, and no one in England has been more successful in reaching this standard than Edgar Mansfield, as can be seen by the photographs of his work (160, 161).

Single-Section Bindings

The problem of binding single-section booklets becomes more important as the number produced increases. This particularly applies to such items as those issued by government departments, and local studies, which are often important to archivists as well as collectors.

When quite thin they may be housed in pamphlet cases but this method often hinders classification. Thicker pamphlets do not lend themselves to multi-section bindings and tend to lose themselves on bookshelves. This makes it important that they can be lettered on the spine.

It is a simple process to case a pamphlet of one folded section.

The wire stitches or threads removed, it is placed in two folds of paper for endpapers with linen reinforcement affixed to the outer one, about an inch wide on each side of the fold. It must adhere strongly and should be of good-quality, but not necessarily thick, linen. Opening the pamphlet to the centre fold, it is held upright with its back on thick waste board, and sewing holes are made with a fine awl through the centre of the fold.

Unless the pamphlet is held upright when making the sewing holes they will not emerge centrally at the back of the booklet, resulting in sewing that is not in alignment and so obstructs the opening of the leaves. Pre-made holes are not required when sewing thin pamphlets, and sewing can take place at the edge of the bench.

The number required will vary according to the size and thickness of the pamphlet, but it must always be an odd number. This becomes automatic if the first hole is made centrally and an equal number are made on either side of it. Holes should be equidistant, the end ones being far enough away from the book edge to allow for trimming (162).

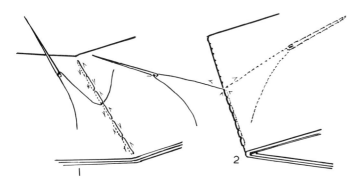

162 *Single-section binding*
1 *Pamphlet stitch, showing direction of stitches (dotted lines indicate unseen threads)*
2 *Saddle stitch, using two needles and completing each stitch in turn*

Sewing commences at the outside of the pamphlet if the spine is to be lettered and from the inside if not. It is a simple 'figure-of-eight' stitch working from the central hole outwards, returning again using the same sewing holes which completes the 'figure-of-eight' stitch.

The return sewing passes the central hole and, completing the other end, is brought back through the central hole so that the long thread there lies between the two ends of the thread, which are drawn tightly and securely tied *over* it, drawing it into the fold. The thread must be tightened during the sewing, pulling it along the back to avoid tearing the paper. If the booklet is thick, a reinforcing guard at the back of the centre fold will resist tearing of the paper there in use.

The book edges having been trimmed (knife and straightedge may be used if it is thin), boards are cut allowing a small square and a margin of $\frac{1}{8}$–$\frac{3}{16}$in at the back edge. A piece of thin board is cut the length of the boards, its width being *exactly* that of the total thickness of the book and boards combined. If cut wider, the booklet will tend to turn sideways under pressure on the shelf and defeat the purpose of the hard back, which is to show the lettered title. The cover is made as normally for a cloth casing, except that the hard spine strip must be stood upright, on edge, when the cloth is drawn over. If this is not successfully done, the finished spine will be at an angle. Lettering is done, using handle letters, before the book is pasted into its cover (163-1).

163 *Single-section binding*
1 *Hard spine, lettered*
2 *Saddle spine*

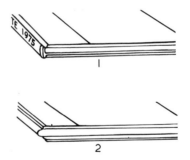

Should lettering not be required, sewing must commence from the inside, the hard back being dispensed with and the cloth drawn directly on to the back of the book (163-2). This makes for easier opening, and possibly longer life, but the omission of lettering on the spine will result in much unnecessary handling. Half-foredge strip and quarter-cloth bindings are much used for this class of work on the score of economy.

'RETURNED GUARD' SINGLE-SECTION BINDING (164)

This method—another 'Harrison' invention—provides for a cloth or leather binding of a single-section book worthy of a place on any collector's bookshelves. It is as involved as the previous method is simple but is well worth while where economy is not vital.

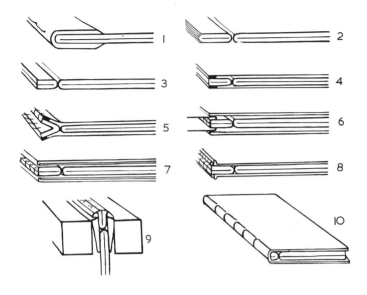

164 *Single-section binding—'returned guard' method*
1–3 The stubs to form the returned guard sewn to the section, returned backwards, and trimmed
4 Protective sheets tipped to stubs
5 Stubs and protective sheets oversewn
6 Protective sheets returned back and endpapers tipped
7 Protective sheet folded back over endpapers
8 Protective sheet and endpapers turned outwards to form joint shoulders
9 Back being formed in the lying press
10 Completed book

Sufficient blank paper, similar to that of the book, the same length and $1\frac{1}{2}$–2in wide, is folded in half. Its total thickness must equal that of the book round which it is placed. Sewing holes are made from the inside as with the previous method—perhaps more of them to make a secure, permanent sewing—and the whole is sewn together, commencing from the outside. The fold of paper that has been added is turned back in the opposite direction to the book so that book and 'returned' guard appear to be sewn together back to back. The returned guard is trimmed parallel to the book to a width of about one-and-a-half times its thickness. Protective sheets of paper the size of the book including the guard are 'tipped' at front and back, level with its back edge. When dry, the two halves of the returned guard, with the protective sheets, are each oversewn neatly along their edges and the protection sheet is thrown back. In that position endpapers are tipped on it at both sides flush with the back edge of the guard, and when they are dry the protective sheet is brought over them to the front again. The book edges are now trimmed.

The protective sheet, which has now formed a zig-zag joint, is turned upwards at right-angles against a straightedge, the amount being equal to the thickness of book boards to be used.

Backing boards are placed up to the upturned edge and, with the book, lowered into the lying press. Because there is no backswell to aid backing, a piece of white string is stuck along the opened zig-zag using PVA and letting it set. The back can now be shaped by backing, using the hammer judiciously. The ends of the string are cut

165 *A returned-guard single-section binding. Full light blue Niger goatskin, tooled gold*

away and edge decoration applied—the book must be put into the lying press for this.

Machine-made headbands and back linings can now be added, using linen instead of mull to give additional strength at the joints.

The cover may be in cloth or leather, quarter, half or full bound. Leather headcaps can be formed in the normal manner and bands added if justified and if lettering permits (165).

Unsewn Binding

The 'caoutchouc' method of unsewn binding introduced by Hancock in the 1830s failed because the rubber perished in a comparatively short time. Polyvinyl acetate provides an adhesive almost imperishable and equally flexible, and to a certain extent makes unsewn binding practicable. It has not replaced sewing and for worth-while book production there seems no likelihood of its doing so. For ephemeral publications, especially paper-wrapped 'paperback' editions, it has virtually replaced sewing because of speed of production and cost.

The problem arises of what is to be done with the important book obtainable only in an unsewn edition, and which is in need of rebinding. To guard all the single leaves into sections is not only time-consuming but results in a back so swollen as to make

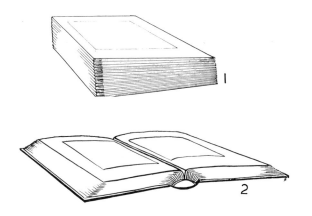

166 *Single leaves guarded to form sections, showing* (1) *swollen back and* (2) *tendency of leaves to fold at edges of guards*

binding difficult and unsatisfactory (166). Oversewing into sections eliminates backswell but is tiresome, while, often, the quality of the paper and narrow back margins make the method unsuitable.

A return to unsewn binding is the only recourse, and although some doubt about its permanence still remains, with care it is possible to produce a fairly durable book. Back margins should be fairly wide, and the paper fibres with the grain running from head to tail to make opening easier. Art paper does not lend itself readily to the method because of its high clay content which is fibreless and heavy.

If back margins permit, the original adhesive may be cut away, but no more than absolutely necessary. Knock the book up squarely between waste boards and place in a bench press with the back projecting about an inch. Using either a small tenon saw or coarse file, roughen the cut edges to produce a fibrous surface more capable of absorbing the adhesive. With the book square at all points place it at the bench edge, the back facing outwards. Holding it at the back with one hand, twist up the leaves at the foredge with the other and, slightly easing the pressure at the back, return them to the flat position on the bench. This will have the effect of fanning the edges at the back and these can now receive a fairly generous coating of PVA. Return the book to its original shape by knocking it to the foredge. If it is to be rounded, use the method for gilt-edged Bibles described under *Rounding* (p. 110).

Press together the leaves at the back, using the fingers, and place the book under a weight for a while. While it is drying cut a strip of bank paper, grain lengthwise, $\frac{1}{4}$in wider than the back of the book.

Alternatively, the trimmed book may be placed in a bench press with the back projecting about 2in and the leaves turned over the edge of the press in order to apply the PVA. Uniform pressure can be obtained by the use of a small piece of wood at the back of the book.

Brush it over with PVA and, placing it $\frac{1}{8}$in on the back edge of the front leaf, bring it over to the back so that there is also $\frac{1}{8}$in there. Carefully rub the lining to the back of the book and leave it to dry under a weight. This not only serves as a thin lining but allows the endpapers to be tipped on the narrow overlap, removing strain from the first and last leaves (167). When dry, endpapers are trimmed to the book size and the edges coloured, if newsprint, all round, and with pigment poster colours rather than stain to provide a little more protection from the light which 'yellows' mechanical wood-pulp paper. A second back lining of bookbinders' linen that projects about $\frac{3}{4}$in over the sides may be added. Cut thin boards to size

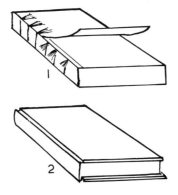

167 *Unsewn binding*
1 *Fitting endpapers*
2 *Completed book*

leaving a small margin at the back edge, as there is no backing, for the free opening of the book. The case can now be made, using a flexible loose hollow. It will be found easier to letter along the spine if it is left to dry flat and is curved again—over the rounded edge of a long backing board—before pasting-in the book.

Another improvement that can be made is to cut saw kerfs in the back of the book before glueing up (168), and afterwards to

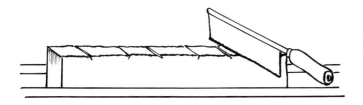

168 *Unsewn binding—sawing kerfs for hemp*

insert fine hemp rubbed well into the kerfs. Paper linings will have to be slightly cut to allow them to be taken round the hemp slips; with linen, holes may be made with an awl and the slips threaded through them.

The slips are scraped so that they can be pasted down flat to the case when pasting-in. This strengthens both back and joints, essential to heavier books.

169 *Unsewn binding—using an improvised press*
1 *Book shaped with back resting in curved former* 2 *Press reversed, rounded back of book facing upwards*

169 *Unsewn binding—using an improvised press*
3 *Back fanned outwards for glueing (using PVA)* 4 *Glued back
fitted with 'stretch' linen*

A special form of PVA is marketed that permits backing satisfactorily and is excellent where quantities of books are to be bound in this way.

It is possible to improvise a small bench press that pivots on to interchangeable formers which give the back of the unglued book a true rounded shape (169–1). The press, tightened, is turned over, leaving the rounded back accessible (169–2) and which, with a strip of wood at the back, may be pressed over, first one way and then the other, giving a much better penetration of the adhesive (169–3). The back having been pressed together, a strip of specially woven expandable 'stretch' linen is rubbed down to it. Later the book may be backed (169–4).

The main difficulty with unsewn binding is to obtain a sufficiently strong attachment of boards, and heavier linings flexible enough not to put a strain on the unsewn book. The fact that endpapers can only be 'tipped' on is another unsatisfactory feature.

Guard Books

Where books are made so that additional matter may be added later, compensating guards, equal to the estimated extra thickness, must be incorporated. Because they do not have the solidity of an ordinary book, they present certain difficulties during forwarding.

Paper used for the body of the book should be of a quality suitable to withstand the extra weight thrown upon the leaves later. Heavy cartridge or cover paper is suitable, the latter obtainable in a variety of colours. The folded sections, with sufficient extra paper to make the guards, and the prepared endpapers, are trimmed *before* sewing.

170 *Sewing on a continuous guard*

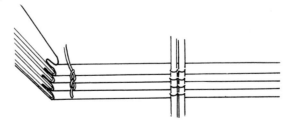

Endpapers are better if made with cloth joints, or well reinforced and sewn with the book, using 16/3-cord or even 4-cord linen thread to tapes or webbings according to the size and weight of the book. If both sides of leaves are to be used for additions, two guards between each conjugate pair will be necessary. If it is justifiable, those on the outside of the sections may take the form of a continuous guard which effectively prevents glue entering too far between sections and gives added strength there (170).

Forwarding can vary, but that used in quarter-leather library style is most suitable. If sufficient clean paper such as newsprint is available, the book may be carefully packed with it after sewing, and in this case edge trimming and subsequent operations follow the normal course. Without such 'packing', it is still wise to use clean offcuts of paper, cut to the book's length, to equalise the thickness of the back of the book for about 2in across the width. This prevents the book from becoming over-rounded and also permits backing, which would not be possible otherwise.

Whether the cover is to be entirely of cloth or to have a leather spine, back linings should be well reinforced, using an Oxford hollow.

Split boards must be accurately fitted, well rubbed down and each separately pressed between boards. A block of boards equal to the width of the book will be necessary so that the book itself may overhang at the front of the press while the book board is being pressed. Extreme care will be needed to ensure that no movement of the board takes place. A wide elastic band placed round the paper of the book near the back, or banding it there with a wide strip of paper, will prevent packing falling out. Covering is as already described in Chapter 3.

Semi-split boards may be used if a cloth case only is required, in which case the spine of the cover will be firmly glued to the reinforced Oxford hollow. A reinforced headcap is strongly advocated whether the cover be of cloth or leather.

As the whole book cannot be pressed at once, each board paper is thinly glued out (or PVA may be used), a paper-covered metal plate is placed under it and the cover board is brought over and rubbed well down on to the endpaper before pressing it (without the remainder of the book) between pressing boards in the press.

SKELETON GUARD BOOKS

Skeleton guard books differ only in that, instead of full-size leaves, these consist of wider guards, on to which additions such as letters, pamphlets, etc, may be affixed by tipping. By this method, economy of paper is effected but additions do not have the protection and support given by full-width leaves.

Guard books must be firmly built if they are to retain their shape in use and boards should be as substantial as the binding permits.

Slip Cases

These attractive adjuncts to good books and bindings serve several worth-while purposes. They protect the binding and add to the presentation of the book; if the book fits snugly within them they help to control its shape. Yet another useful purpose is served when more than one volume is contained in them, since they reduce the likelihood of a volume being lost.

The simplest form of slip case consists of three pieces of millboard, two of them forming the ends, with the third creased and folded to fit round them on three sides (171–1, 2). As it is important that

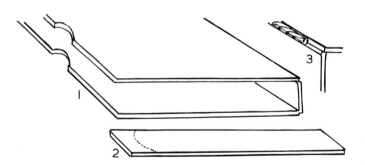

171 *Simple slip case*
1, 2 *Assembling the parts*
3 *String glued into the open cut*

the case fits exactly, the book is used for measuring rather than a rule. First the board for the end pieces is selected, then a thinner millboard, long enough to go round the book, and its width only slightly more than the book's length, plus the total thickness of the two ends. Both pieces of board are now lined on one side with suitable paper, pressed, and allowed to dry under a weight to control warp. Surplus lining paper is cut away at the board edges.

Directional grain must be on the width of the larger millboard, which must be cut quite square at one end. The book is placed on the lined side with its hinges level with the squared end. The position of each corner of the book board is lightly marked on the millboard and the book is removed. With a square, check that both points are on a line at right-angles to the edge; if they are not, re-mark them level at the further one. This is necessary because all folds of the slip case must be at right-angles. On the reverse, the unlined, side of the board, lightly score along the right-angled line using a pointed knife. The cut must not exceed half the thickness of the board. Turn up the longer side against a straightedge, place the foredge of the book up to it and, very precisely, mark the overall thickness of it at head and tail. Repeat the scoring, making sure that it is at right-angles at the furthest mark, and again bend the board. By placing the book within the folded board, the hinge position of the second book board can be accurately marked. Remove the book and cut away the surplus board. A piece of string glued into the open cut will have the effect of neatening the final appearance (171–3).

The front edges of the case should be gently chamfered so that they do not project above the surface of the book; this neatens the appearance not only there but also where they join the ends. For convenience in removing the book from the case the front edges of it will also require shaping, either to a long gentle curve or a thumb-shaped one. The former must be marked out and cut with a knife and the latter cut with a carpenter's gouge.

Return the book to its position within the folded board and, with spring dividers, check the distance between the *inside* of the boards and cut the two end pieces to that width, and long enough to cover the spine of the book when placed within the case. To allow for the slight creasing of the outer board where folded, the smallest amount must be cut away from the corners of the end pieces of board.

Using hot glue or a contact adhesive touched along the edges of these pieces, fix them accurately in position, rub the outer cover down on to them, place a knocking-down iron over the whole case and leave to dry completely. With care, plastic sealing tape may be used to hold the case temporarily in position while drying. With slip cases for heavy books a thin linen reinforcement extending over the ends to the sides may be necessary to strengthen the joins.

Before covering, the ends of the case must be shaped to agree with that of the spine of the book; this is placed in the case and the spine shape is lightly pencilled in. Remove the book and cut the case ends by first removing any large surplus and then cutting away small pieces with a knife until the correct shape is achieved. Glass-paper or a fine file will be required to smooth the edges.

If the slip case is to have cloth-covered edges and paper sides, proceed as follows. Cut a piece of suitable bookbinders' cloth $\frac{1}{2}$in wider than the thickness of the case and long enough to cover it completely plus 1in for turn-ins at the front. The cloth is cut up the roll and not across its width; if it curls unduly, draw it over a smooth edge to straighten it.

Using thin, hot glue (or a suitable cold glue) glue out the cloth and lay it on the bench. Place one end of the slip case *absolutely square* on to it, leaving a $\frac{1}{2}$in turn-in at the front edge (172), and fix the cloth by rubbing down the end to it from inside the case.

172 *Assembled slip case placed on glued cloth strip*

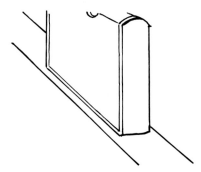

Holding down the other end of the glued cloth, bring the case over tightly so that its back is placed on the glued surface. Take up the case and rub this down with the hand, making sure that there is no loose cloth at the corner and that the case is centrally on the cloth. Finally bring the remainder of the cloth, squarely and tightly, over the last side and rub it down.

Taking the case in one hand, use the thumb of the other to fold the glued edges of the cloth tightly on all sides. At the corners fold the surplus cloth upwards, cut it away with the shears slightly above the board surface and fold in as when making corners on cloth book cases (173–1).

Check that the cloth is sticking everywhere and that corners are neatly and tightly folded. The cloth projecting at the rounded ends is cut in a semi-circle and, if necessary, lightly re-glued. Radiating cuts are made inwards with the shears, stopping the thickness of the board away from it. With careful use of the thumb the cut cloth can be moulded over the curved edges to the inside (173–2), but care is required in both cutting and folding the cloth at the points where the case sides meet the curved ends. If the folder is required it must be used with care or the cloth threads will separate.

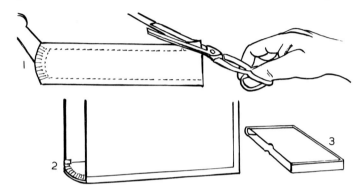

173 *Slip case*
1 *Cutting cloth when making the corners*
2 *Turning in cloth on curved surface*
3 *Completed slip case*

For siding, paper with a firm surface is cut $\frac{1}{2}$in wider than the case and shorter than its length by the thickness of the boards at the ends. This thickness governs the width of the margin of cloth left when the linings are placed in position and rubbed down. Before turning-in the front edge, the paper must be cut in much the same way as the cloth at the ends of the case to allow it to be turned in neatly at the curved edges. The newcomer is advised to experiment first on waste material. The radiating cuts are turned in gently but firmly with the pad of the thumb and it will be found necessary to cut away a small piece of the paper at the corner when turning at a thumb-shaped semi-circle. The curved shapes are turned before the straight edges.

Because it is not possible to turn edges in on a concave curve without small areas of the board being left exposed, the narrow lining required for neatening the inside must be cut to allow for this, by positioning it close to the edge on the inside, marking the semi-circle with finger pressure, and cutting the shape before fixing it in position. This also applies to the curved ends of the case, except that they can be placed on to the lining and a pencil line drawn round them.

A number of points need to be stressed in making slip cases. Accuracy is essential, a loose-fitting or a tight one being equally bad. The slightest allowance only is needed for the turn-ins of paper; perhaps a little more for cloth, but very little. If scoring and folding is not at right-angles, the slip case will be hopelessly out of square. When assembling the case, all edges must be flush, and are better for being lightly glasspapered at the edges before covering.

For larger or more important books, slip cases should be covered in full cloth and made from separate pieces of millboard rather than one piece scored and bent. The cutting of the various pieces must be done with accuracy; to this end, all pieces of the same width (such as back and ends) are cut in one length and separated, ensuring uniform width.

If the case is made with the sides to overlap the ends and back, it is a good thing to stick a piece of thin millboard over the back, cutting it *in situ*, which not only neatens it but makes for a firmer join with added strength.

The cloth, $\frac{1}{2}$–$\frac{3}{4}$in wider than the length of the case, is cut long enough to go right round the case with sufficient for the two turn-ins at the front. It should be cut along the roll, which reduces stretch when pulling it round the case and makes for neater turn-ins at the edges. The cloth may be glued out in its entirely and drawn over the case in one operation, but with larger cases this requires speed born of experience. The corners are cut as previously, turned tightly over the edges, and a folded mitre is made at the back corners. The front edges may need the glue to be 'freshened' with a thin second glueing after the cuts have been made for the turn-ins at the thumb semi-circle. Everything must be done that little bit more neatly than with paper siding, for cloth is less co-operative when turning-in at rounded edges. Cloth for the case ends is cut to allow $\frac{1}{8}$in margin on three sides with a turn-in at the front edge. The corners at the back should be slightly cut away to lessen the possibility of their lifting.

REVERSED SLIP CASES

Occasionally slip cases are reversed on the shelves in order that a rounded and lettered spine can be incorporated. This requires that a rounded slip of wood be fixed to the closed side before covering. 'Flat' rounded wood about $\frac{1}{4}$–$\frac{3}{8}$in thick can be obtained from most timber stockists, and a few lengths of different widths should form part of a bookbinder's stock. A piece as wide as, or slightly wider than, the thickness of the case is cut exactly its length. When fastening it to the case with glue, it is well first to glue it lightly, allow to harden, and give a second coat of strong glue to make it adhere more readily. Alternatively a contact adhesive can be used. Any small projection of the wooden spine above the sides must be removed with a carpenter's plane.

If the complete glueing-out of the cloth is frightening to the newcomer, one side and the spine of the case may be glued and the side laid to the cloth, this rubbed down, the spine covered and the cloth well rubbed down. This gives more time to ensure that it is firmly and tidily fitted. When glueing the spine the glue should be taken very slightly to the back of the case to prevent unwanted glue seeping into the edge when the second side is glued.

The remainder of the cloth is laid on to the second side and also well rubbed down. The cloth edges can now be cut in the 'star' form at the front edges and corners for folded mitres, all of them glued and all turned in neatly. Front linings are added as before.

CHEMISES FOR USE WITH SLIP CASES

For full leather bindings, especially those tooled and inlaid, a chemise which fits round the book is essential. It provides protection against rough handling and strong sunlight when the book is shelved. Its use is not limited to this, for it is equally important for the protection of early editions in worn bindings and for paper-covered items contained in book boxes.

It consists of a separate light cover made to fit exactly over the book it protects (174) and may be covered in either leather or cloth, or a combination of both.

For use with a slip case the front edges are turned and made at right-angles so that they fit firmly over the board edges of the book. The chemise must be made and fitted before making the slip case.

Thin board, such as chipboard or pasteboard, is used for all except larger books and is cut to the actual size of the binding, the grain running from head to tail. Absolute uniformity of height is ensured if all five pieces of board required are cut from one piece of board whose width is exactly equal to the length of the book.

Material for the turn-in at the front edge must allow for it to be turned completely over the turned edge and on to the main board (174–1).

In the making, the turning over at that point must be done with the front strip at right-angles to the main board (174–2) to ensure that it remains permanently in that position (see *Vellum Covers*, p. 205) so that the front edge of the binding is gripped firmly by it.

174 Book chemise
1 Make-up with turned foredge
2 Details of making
3 Chemise fitted to binding, showing grip at foredge

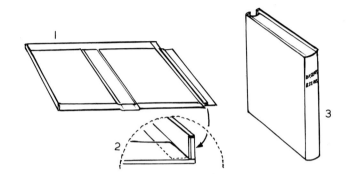

The chemise is lined on the inside with pasted paper linings which will not only prevent an outward warp but tend to draw it to the book at the edges. If the spine of the book is rounded, the chemise should be allowed to dry out so that its shape conforms to that of the book. Using a book block for support, the essential details are lettered where the chemise covers the spine (174–3).

Book Boxes and Pamphlet Cases

These come in a variety of forms, from the fairly simple cloth-covered millboard type to the Solander book box, leather-covered on a cabinet-made wooden base. These latter owe as much to the cabinet-maker as to the bookbinder, possibly more. Their construction is so beautifully elaborate and involved that, together with the fire-resisting moulded pull-off case, it cannot be discussed here. The reader is referred to Thomas Harrison's *Fragments of bookbinding technique* for full details of their construction.

The two main differences in the construction of millboard book boxes are that one has a fixed back with a fall-down front, and the other a fall-down back. Experience has shown that the latter has greater durability.

SIMPLE BOOK BOX

One of the simplest forms consists of two three-sided boxes, one made to fit over the other, contained within a cover (175).

On a piece of thin or medium millboard, flush to one of the long edges, is marked a rectangle that is only very slightly larger than the closed book, *including* the rounded spine. With spring dividers set slightly wider than the book's thickness, the box sides are marked

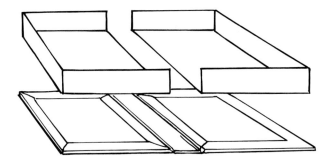

175 *Simple book box, the two halves ready for glueing into the cover*

on the three sides and the surplus board is cut away. On the reverse side the points at which the sides will be folded are marked and with knife and straightedge scored half-way through the board. The square pieces at the corners are cut right through and removed. The sides are turned upwards from the reverse side by first firmly marking the point of bending with a pointed folder against a heavy metal straightedge and then turning the board against it. The importance of accuracy will be realised, for without it the sides will not be uniform in height. To secure the corners, glued linen reinforcements up to an inch in width are placed both outside and inside, those at the outside being turned over on to the base and to the inside of the box.

The 'lid' is next made to cover the lower half, allowance having been made for the thickness of linen reinforcements and covering material. The base of the lower half can be used to mark out the upper half, by drawing guide lines slightly away from its edges. Its sides will have to be slightly wider than those of the lower half.

Two boards, uniform in size, fitting flush with the open end of the 'box' but allowing a suitable 'square' on the other edges, are cut, together with a hard spine cut to the same length and its width equal to the overall thickness of box and boards. Cloth joints will be added on the inside of the spine and allowance for this made by placing a piece of thin board against the inside of the hard spine, temporarily increasing its thickness. When making the cover, the two spine pieces must be held squarely in position when drawing the cloth over. The cover is made as described in Chapter 3 and the spine covered with cloth on the inside, the cloth being worked into the joints and on to the front and back boards.

The two halves of the 'box' have their edges covered with cloth or paper in one piece and turned over on to the base and neatly into the inside. The lining of the inside begins with the sides, for which three pieces of suitable paper are cut. Their width is that of the side at the inside, which, when placed in position below the top edge, allows for a similar amount of paper to overlap on to the base. All three pieces are cut to the inside length of the sides. Because those at head and tail of the box are set away from the edges, there is an overlap on to the base and the long side. A slight diagonal cut at the bottom corner will facilitate the folding of the lining there. The front lining will fit exactly and allow the slight overlap on to the base. The base lining is cut slightly shorter than the inside length of the box and its width is reduced by the amount the end linings are set back from the inside edges.

When dry, the two halves of the box are glued in position within the cover. This is done by heavily glueing the base of the 'lid' portion and placing it, accurately positioned, on the front cover, the open side towards the spine, rubbing it well down and, if possible, pressing in the press using suitable pressing boards to fill it and provide pressure inside the lid. When this has set, the lower half is glued and placed in position inside the upper half, and the cover is brought over on to it. The box is opened and the lower half pressed as with the lid portion.

Where scoring and bending of the boards is possible, a stronger and neater join results if the opening made by scoring and bending is filled with glued string.

With larger book boxes of thicker millboard, the various pieces required are cut separately and assembled by glueing at the edges in much the same way as does the woodworker. Contact adhesive will be found especially useful for this, as drying time is greatly reduced.

The front and back boards are made to overlap the sides and should be wider by the thickness of the board to allow for a mitred hinge. Where a greater strength is required, a single-piece linen reinforcement may be glued and fitted round the three sides of the box and neatly turned over on to the back board.

The solid spine is cut to fit the open sides exactly and, as with the front and base boards, its long edges are cut and filed at an angle of 45°.

USE OF FILLETS

An improved form of box results if, instead of the two halves completely overlapping one another, they are made exactly the same size but only half the width so that they meet edge-to-edge when closed. By glueing a fillet of board that projects rather less than half the total width of the sides, inside the lower portion of the complete box, the upper half is guided squarely into position and held firmly there (176). Allowance for the total thickness of the fillets must be made when setting out the box.

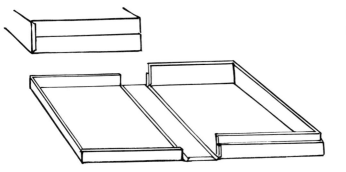

176 *Book box with fillets*

The two halves may be covered before fitting the fillets, or the completed box may be covered with a single piece of material. In this case the newcomer is strongly advised to do the covering by stages.

The base of the lower half is glued and placed in position on material large enough to cover the box completely, not forgetting the sides, and well rubbed down. The base of the upper half is next glued and that half is placed in position on the lower. The solid spine is placed temporarily in position with extra thickness of paper or thin pasteboard to allow for cloth linings, and the covering material is brought over and rubbed down.

By this method the material for the sides, while still unglued, can be worked into position and turn-ins accurately marked and cut before glueing and fixing. If the fillets are to be covered at this stage, very careful cutting will be necessary to secure a neat finish.

In order to make satisfactory turn-ins at the spine, it is necessary to cover the four open ends of the sides for about $\frac{1}{4}$in quite separately before covering the remainder. This leaves sufficient material to turn over into the joints at the spine.

Rounded spines can be added to book boxes either by the addition of half-round wooden moulding glued to the millboard spine or used independently as the spine. When turning in the covering material at head and tail, it will be necessary to cut it at a number of points unless it be leather when it can be moulded.

Another method of making a rounded spine is to cut the half-round moulding so that it fits inside the box spine, which is curved round it and secured to it before covering. If this is done, the open ends of the box sides must be extended and cut in a curve precisely matching that of the half-round moulding (177). The method is more appropriate to a cabinet-made box which is leather-covered, but it successfully prevents dust entering the box at the spine.

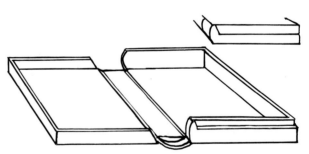

177 Book box with rounded spine

Where leather is the covering material, bands may be added and the spine tooled.

Thomas Harrison's warning might be heeded where book boxes are concerned. 'Individual boxes can never be done cheaply. Millions, yes, but not one.'

Portfolio Cases

The bookbinder is often called upon to make many articles connected to bookbinding only by the similarity of the materials and techniques used in their production. Portfolio cases are an obvious example. The case consists of a base board with flaps hinged to it, inserted in a cover made like that of a book (178).

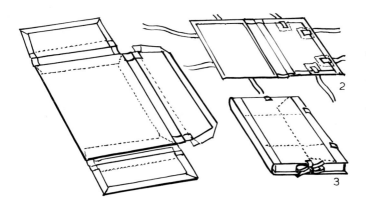

178 Portfolio
1 How made up
2 Cover made and tapes fitted
3 Completed portfolio

Papers to be contained in them may vary from imperial (22in × 30in) to royal (20in × 25in), imperial folio (22in × 15in), and so on. It is unwise to experiment with the larger sizes which demand experience in glueing large areas and working quickly. Having decided upon the paper size, cut a base of thin board about $\frac{1}{2}$in longer and $\frac{1}{4}$in wider and line it on one side with strong paper, turning over the edges to the back. Three flaps of thin board will be required about a quarter the width of the base, one of them equal to the length of the case and the other two to its width. These will require lined hinges of cloth totalling about 4in width and long enough to turn over the ends of the flaps. The cloth linings need be only about $2\frac{1}{2}$in wide and slightly shorter than the flaps. Paper stiffeners are needed for the cloth hinges and the spine of the cover. In assessing the width thought should be given to the total possible weight of the contents in relation to the strength of the materials. If this is overlooked, the cases may be unable to stand up to the intended use. An inch will allow for many sheets of paper and is suggested.

First the flaps are glued along the length to a width of $1\frac{1}{2}$in using a piece of waste card as a guard, and the cloth is placed to it and rubbed down. Paper stiffeners 1in wide, and as long as the flaps, are glued and placed on the cloth to within $\frac{1}{8}$in of the flap and also well rubbed down. The cloth turn-ins at the flap ends are glued and turned inwards, quite squarely, and rubbed down. Cloth linings are now added and should not extend to the full length. They must be firmly rubbed down, especially at the edge of the flap. The front flap is cut beyond the cloth at an angle of 45°; all others are left square. The flaps are sided with paper similar to that used on the baseboard, and the edges turned in. The inside paper linings should be $\frac{1}{8}$–$\frac{1}{4}$in shorter than the flap at all edges. Cut the free cloth at 45°, $1\frac{1}{4}$in from the edge of the card flap, to reduce the amount of cloth that would otherwise be there when the flaps are glued to the baseboard.

To do this place the piece of card previously used $1\frac{1}{4}$in from the inside of the flap, and use fairly strong hot glue quite liberally.

Lay the base board accurately over the glued portion of the cloth hinge (178–1) and rub down well with a folder. Turn over the base and flap and, if necessary, lightly hammer down the cloth on the back to make adhesion certain. Pressure will be needed while the glue dries; weights or even heavy books will serve if nothing more suitable is available.

The outer cover to be made like that of a book should slightly project beyond the base when the three flaps are turned in over it, except at the back edge where they are flush. The projection should not be more than $\frac{3}{16}$–$\frac{1}{4}$in. The paper stiffener at the spine should be wider than those of the flaps by an amount equal to the combined thickness of the base board and flaps.

If the cover is not to be in full cloth, a foredge strip is preferable to corners, providing greater strength at the front edge where ties will be added. There should be a minimum of $1\frac{1}{2}$in of cloth on the boards at the back and front edges. Fit the foredge strips before adding the spine cloth, finally lining the inside with cloth sufficiently wide to allow about $\frac{3}{4}$in overlap on to the boards and long enough to cover the turn-ins at head and tail. It must be worked firmly down on to the stiffener and tightly against the board edges at the hinges. A durable cover paper should be used for siding and one to match the base board and flaps to line the front board.

The number of ties required will depend upon the size of the case, it being usual to have two at the front edge and one at the head and the tail. Linen tape or webbing is suitable, but whatever is used must be able to stand up to continual tying and untying, for replacements are a nuisance. A chisel as wide as the tape is used to make slots about 1in from the edges of the boards, and these are cut at an inwards angle from the outside of each board. Those at the front edge should be made at each end at points equal to a quarter of the total length. The ties can be threaded through the board using either a very thin folder or the blunt end of a metal nail file. Glue the ends to the board and cover them with glued Kraft wrapping paper, hammering them down when dry to flatten them and to close the chisel slit in the board (178–2).

It remains only to glue the base board in position, and this is done by turning the flaps in tightly and liberally glueing the back. This is best done with a large glue brush using a dabbing movement to froth and aerate the glue, which makes for stronger adhesion. It must be quickly placed in position, and, with the flaps turned out, rubbed firmly down to the case with special attention to the edges. Speed is important as the glue soon coagulates.

The hammer may have to be used at the edges, but with care. Ideally, the back board, flaps thrown out, should be put into a press and left to dry under good pressure, but a clean bench, or even floor, space, with plenty of weights dispersed over the surface, particularly at the edges, will usually suffice.

Often the base board is dispensed with, but this reduces the life of the case considerably. The square ends of the head and tail flaps support the spine and front flap when closed, while the angled ends of this protect them from damage in use.

Pockets in Books

It is sometimes necessary to make allowance for the addition of extra material after a book has been bound. If there are likely to be many additions it is better to make a book box to match the original volume and letter it accordingly. Where a pocket must be incorporated in a binding, additional wide compensating guards must be sewn with the book to allow for the extra thickness. These should be similar in colour to the paper of the book and wide enough to permit the use of a straightedge when finally trimming to size. Between them and the book must be sewn the complete endpaper, less the paste-down sheet, and a strip of bookbinder's linen or cloth, whichever ties up the better with the endpapers. This must be wide enough to cover the stub of compensating guards and the book joint, plus a little to go on to the board.

After the book has been bound and the front endpaper put down, the compensating guards are cut, with knife and straightedge, to the required width, usually $\frac{1}{4}-\frac{3}{8}$in. To do this a metal plate is inserted *between* the linen or cloth strip and the guards to serve as a 'cut-against'. Using PVA adhesive, the strip can now be brought firmly over the guards and the book joint on to the board (179). It must be

179 Pockets in books—cutting and lining compensating guards 1 Stubs sewn with book awaiting trimming 2 Stubs trimmed and cloth lining brought over into the joint and on to the board

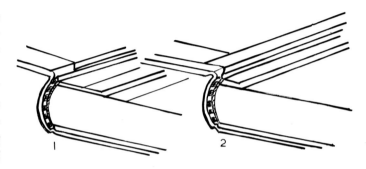

tightly in position and sticking thoroughly at every point. The use of PVA (it is essential with white linen) reduces 'stretch' in the strip and allows slightly more time to work the material than does hot glue.

The pocket is made in one piece from good-quality but thin

180 Simple one-piece pocket 1 Pattern for cutting board 2 Pocket made up, showing reverse side 3 Completed pocket

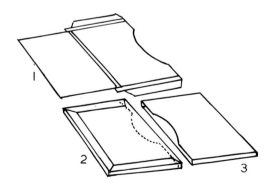

pasteboard, its finished thickness equalling that of the guard stub and its width that of the page area *less* the width of the stub (180).

Its sides are better reinforced with linen or cloth and its surface lined with paper matching the endpapers. The upper board should be shaped at the centre of the inner edge to permit removal of material, and the lining paper turned under there. The base board will require lining similarly at the edge to a point a little beyond that exposed by the cut-away portion of the upper one.

If the pocket is to be fairly wide at the edges, the front edge creates a problem since it interferes with the concave foredge of the book, causing a disfigurement. The alternatives are to build up the front edge of the pocket at an angle with strips of board, shaping them as required by cutting and filing with a rounded file, or with a strip of wood shaped with a carpenter's hollow moulding plane.

The ultimate refinement is to add sufficient blank leaves when binding the book, inserting a thin piece of pasteboard where they begin, to provide a cover for the pocket that is identical to the book size after the book has been cut. After the binding is completed the centres of the blank leaves may be cut away *en bloc* leaving only $\frac{3}{4}$–1in at the edges. The cut, inside edges are sealed with PVA and allowed to set under light pressure—not in the press—before cutting away to form the compensating guard stub. After cutting away the unwanted paper still left at the inside edge by continuing the cuts at head and tail, the inside edges are lined with paper that is turned over on to the upper and lower leaves of the block of paper. Cut at the inside edge, to the correct size, the piece of white card is now glued and placed with extreme accuracy over the cut edges of the blank paper thus forming the pocket.

After the linen or cloth joint has been completed and the paste-down fitted, the pocket can be glued down in position; check first to make certain that there is no break in the continuity of the edges. By this method the book edges are left completely intact, even if gilded, and the book form is in no way interfered with. The effect is incredibly good, but only when the work has been well done.

Books on Stilts

It sometimes happens that, to complete a set of volumes of a work, a shorter one is added and this must appear to be uniform in height to the others on the shelves. Even if the taller volumes are being bound at the same time it is quite inexcusable to cut them to the size of the smaller one. The answer is to set this volume 'on stilts'.

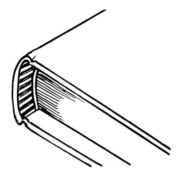

Until after the backing process, it is treated uniformly with the others except that the kettle-stitch at the tail cannot be at the same position. If the margins of the smaller book have been heavily reduced by cutting, it may be better to leave them without further trimming, unless the top or all edges have to be gilded.

Because of the difficulty of board adjustment, headbanding is best done before boards are attached. All headbands are uniform except that at the tail of the small volume, which must be sewn on to a vellum core wide enough to make the spine equal in height to the other volumes (181).

Boards are of uniform length, but the width of those for the smaller book allow for a normal square and are therefore narrower.

Back linings have to be carefully added so that they fit firmly and support the wide headband. In covering, the turn-ins at the tail of the smaller book must be sufficiently wide to cover the spine and boards beyond the paper of the book.

Trimming out of paste-downs will be as usual except at the tail of the small volume where none is necessary.

When tooling the spine, additional support may well be necessary at the tail, in which case a narrow piece of firm vellum cut to slightly less than the width of the spine and tapered a little for easier entry may be inserted into the hollow while tooling that part of the spine. The book must be opened to permit its entry.

Because the tail of the smaller book is some distance from the bottom edges of the boards, the use of a French joint binding is inadvisable, as it gives less support at the joint.

7

REPAIRS TO BOOKS

Cloth casings: cleaning covers and book edges—new endpapers—
plates and maps—recasing and reinforcing cover spines—
new spines—corners—Leather bindings: recasing—
'returned' cloth joints—corners—relacing boards
—rebacking—mounting original spines
—tight-back repairs

REPAIRS TO BOOKS

Cloth Casings

The refurbishing and repairing of cloth-bound books requires some knowledge of simple bookbinding operations and materials, while for major repairs equipment is necessary.

CLEANING COVERS

This requires caution, only a minority of bookbinding cloths being waterproof. To prevent penetration by adhesives most bookcloths are impregnated under pressure with a starch filler, usually soya bean flour; dyeing takes place afterwards, and the surface colour is not washable unless specially treated. With care it is possible to brighten a soiled cloth cover by lightly sponging it over with a very small amount of paste-water (diluted paste) which tends to make the soiled surface uniform rather than actually to clean it. The paste content helps to re-surface the cloth, and, should there be any broken threads at the board edges, will fix them if they are worked into their original positions. Care will be necessary where there is gold blocking for it is easily spoiled, or even removed, if worked on overmuch. Methylated or surgical spirit, benzine, or petroleum may be used to remove or lessen excessive soiling before the paste-water wash. After cleaning, the cloth cover may receive a thin coating of wax polish, best applied by 'aerosol', to protect it in future use.

Where the use of drastic methods is unwise, 'Backus' bookcloth restorer may be used. While it gives a pleasant finish to the cloth and to a small extent brightens the gold, its cleaning properties are only moderate. It has the advantage that it is safe in use, an important factor with heavily blocked Victorian cloth covers.

CLEANING BOOK EDGES

Soiled edges can be greatly improved by careful use of a soft pencil eraser (rubber), but the book must be held firmly under hand pressure during the operation. The rubber 'dust' may be shaken away if the book is securely held at the spine with the boards turned back. Gilt edges may be treated similarly, but if some soiling still persists, a modicum of saliva (not water), applied with a soft cloth stretched

over the finger, may help. The gold on the edges is but $\frac{1}{250\,000}$in
in thickness, and penetration by dampness can release it and the albumen glair holding it from the surfacing paste underneath, ruining
the gilt edge.

NEW ENDPAPERS

These are often needed, but will only neaten the book's appearance,
adding little, if any, additional strength to the joint. Moreover it is
not always a good thing to remove evidence of previous ownership,
which may be of interest to subsequent owners.

Endpapers of suitable paper are folded to a size rather larger than
the page area. The original fly-leaf is gently eased away from the
book by holding down the first leaf with the palm of the hand. This
leaf will probably be weakened at the back edge, and should at least
be tipped on to the next one for safety and additional strength where
the new endpaper will be affixed. Using a small bone folder against
a straightedge, the folded edge of the endpaper is turned up at
right-angles to form a ridge equal in height to the backing shoulder
of the book, which enables it to be placed accurately in position in
the joint. The correct size may then be marked by pressing down the
overlap of the endpaper at the book edges and cutting it away with
knife and straightedge. Done with care, this ensures complete
accuracy, and the endpaper can be tipped in position on the book.
When dry, it only remains to paste out the board paper, draw the
board over, checking that the new endpaper exactly covers the
old, and press the book between boards. Should a press not be
available one must be improvised (see p. 21).

Where endpapers are only split in the joint, a repair can be effected
by the use of a matching guard there. The fly-leaf is carefully removed and its broken joint edge lightly trimmed. A suitably strong
guard is cut the exact length of the page and wide enough to cover
$\frac{1}{4}$in on the board and all the joint, with sufficient to go down on to
the book proper for about $\frac{3}{16}$in with the grain running along the
length. By using PVA adhesive, the guard can be first mounted to
the board edge and, with the board held firmly in position, worked
over the joint by the use of finger and thumb on to the book. It
must be tightly worked into the joint, from which all unwanted
paper has been previously removed, and allowed to dry before
closing the cover. The trimmed fly-leaf can be returned to its

former position by tipping. This method reduces to a minimum the amount of guard left showing.

PLATES

To return a loose plate into a book is usually only a matter of care and neatness, provided the leaf from which it has become detached is secure. Any adhesive remaining on the back edge of the plate must be carefully removed, preferably by inserting the knife edge *under* it and prising it off rather than by trying to cut it away. It must be replaced by fresh adhesive (PVA or paste) fingered on, using a template, to a width rather in excess of $\frac{1}{8}$in. With edges of the plate absolutely level with those of the book at head and foredge, the back edge is gently pressed into the back of the book, using either a long, thin folder or paper-knife, or, failing these, a clean palette knife or even the back edge of a carving knife. Whatever is used, it must be quite clean and should have a long, straight and thin edge, so that the whole length of the plate can be positioned and pressed at one time. The book is closed and placed to dry under a light weight.

Because a plate that has only been tipped in position throws a strain on the 'host' leaf, this is often so much weakened that it is unwise to return the plate to it. Instead, a narrow guard should be used, first removing a narrow strip from the back edge of the plate which makes for free opening. The guard, tipped for $\frac{1}{8}$in plus to the back of the plate, is folded over to the face side and the turned-over portion is pasted (or PVA'd) on its upper side. With the plate accurately positioned, the guard is gently pressed into the back of the book, which is closed and allowed to dry under light pressure only. By the use of this method any strain is shared by the guard and the undamaged leaf. Points to remember are that plate and book edges (head and foredge) must be level; should the top edge be gilt it is wiser to let the plate lie minutely below the book edge. Should any adhesive get on to the plate or page and be allowed to dry while the book is closed, it could well result in both being badly damaged.

MAPS

The replacement of folded maps into a publisher's case binding is fraught with difficulty and seldom completely satisfactory, because usually no special arrangement has been made for their inclusion in the first place. If they have to be repaired along broken folds, it may be wiser, having allowed repair guards to dry with the map flat, to refold, if this is possible, away from print. If instead of using only one guard, a second is added on the reverse side, and each is affixed to the adjoining leaf, the strength of the hinge will be doubled and the strain on the book halved. A linen guard will be equally strong in itself but the whole weight will be thrown on to one of the adjacent leaves only.

RECASING

If a book is loose in its cloth case it is insufficient only to replace endpapers. If the original endpapers must be retained, and this is often difficult, the fly-leaf must first be eased away from the book and from the joint. It will now have to be lifted from the board for a distance of $\frac{1}{2}$in to $\frac{3}{4}$in to allow for fresh attachment there. Should the mull, any slips and back linings still be in good order (though this is unusual) they must be separated from the board. This can sometimes be done, after easing away at one end, by inserting a finger between them and the board and gently parting them. It can now be seen whether the back will need relining only or re-forming by being backed again. This is usually worth-while as, in conjunction with new mull and back linings, it will considerably lengthen the life of the book. Quite often when the original mull lining is removed much of the original glue on the spine comes away with it, and if this is so, re-glueing is simplified. If not, place the book in a bench press between waste boards with the back uppermost and prise off loose glue with an old blunt knife, taking care not to damage either sewing or book. If necessary, paste may be brushed on and allowed to soak into the glue (or back linings) which can then be removed using the back edge of a knife, and the spine sponged clean. While still damp the book is removed from the press and knocked level and square to the head and to the *foredge*, as edges will not be trimmed.

If endpapers are to be renewed, it is better to tip the first leaf of the book to the second, add a folded guard at the joint and stick the endpaper to this. This removes the immediate strain from the book and also strengthens the joint. Should the original sewing of the book be in good order but with no slips, new tapes can be sewn to the book without completely resewing it. The simplest method of doing this is to glue the back of the book, but only where the tapes will be, and stick them in position, leaving about an inch projecting on either side. When dry it is not too difficult to sew them to the book by sewing through the centre folds of some sections and round the tapes. It is not necessary to sew through all sections or even the majority of them, but at the beginning and end of the book the space left between resewn sections is lessened and the final two (and endpapers if thought desirable and if they are suitable) always sewn. It will be found easier to commence such sewing from the centre of the back, working upwards, reversing the book to complete the second half. It is emphasised that the method is suitable only where the original sewing is satisfactory, its real purpose being to provide new slips for attachment to the boards. The back of the book may now be glued up, and the book rounded and rebacked, first checking the width of the case at the spine. Where this permits, an Oxford hollow is recommended.

REINFORCING COVER SPINES

If the case is unbroken but weak at the hinges, and there is sufficient room in the spine, a cloth reinforcement may be added there. The cloth turn-ins are cut through at head and tail about $\frac{3}{4}$in from the spine and turned back. This permits the removal of the original 'loose hollow' from the cover, any parts of it remaining being gently glasspapered—but with care. The reinforcement, which may be of bookbinding cloth or linen, according to circumstances, is glued out and placed in position on the spine, being worked tightly against the board edges before being brought over on to the boards. It must be firmly rubbed down in position before glueing out and adding a new loose hollow. (If an Oxford hollow has been used, it will be quite light in thickness.) The original turn-ins, with the ends of the reinforcing material, are glued and turned back again to their original positions.

NEW CLOTH SPINES

Where the hinges have broken down, or if the original case is too small to take the book after rebacking, relining and reinforcing, the spine will have to be cut away and a new one inserted, the original backstrip being added afterwards. After cutting the turn-ins as previously described, the bookcloth is eased off the boards at the hinge; this is often easier if done before the original spine is cut away.

The cloth is turned back, care being taken not to crease it at the fold, any fibres that adhere to it are removed, and its edges are lightly trimmed with knife and straightedge with a small cutting board being placed underneath. Because of the enormous variety of bookcloths and colours, it may be difficult to find matching cloth for the new spine; it will generally be less obvious if a darker rather than a lighter shade of the same colour is used. The cloth is cut wide enough to go round the spine and on to the boards, its length allowing for turn-ins at head and tail; the warping threads should run along the length. The boards being placed accurately in position, the book is laid with the back towards the worker and slightly projecting beyond the bench edge to facilitate picking it up. A small weight is placed on the upper board and the cut edge of the cloth turned back—but not creased—so that the cloth of the new spine may be placed in position there. The spine cloth is glued out and its

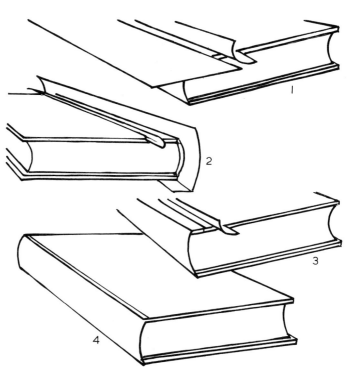

182 *Making a new cloth spine* 1 *New spine placed beneath original cloth* 2 *Book reversed, loose hollow positioned and cloth drawn over* 3 *New cloth spine fitted and ends turned in* 4 *Lifted side glued and returned to original position, with turn-ins replaced*

long edge placed on the upper board, under the original cloth (182–1), and rubbed down with the finger. With the weight removed, the book and boards are firmly held and the book turned sharply over so that the foredge is now facing the worker. This quick movement should prevent the glued cloth from sticking to the back of the book, and leave it lying on the bench. The new loose hollow is placed in position on the cloth, which is brought firmly over on to the back board (182–2), which has been held in position by the left hand. If the hand is extended along the length of the cloth it may be brought over the back uniformly, and this is important if the cover is to fit neatly. If a piece of cartridge paper is placed in such a position on the bench that the glued cloth rests on it when the book is turned over, it will assist when drawing the cloth over the spine uniformly and the material will be neither stretched nor strained at any point.

When the cloth has been rubbed down on to the back board, the book is removed from the cover and the new cloth is turned in at head and tail and well rubbed down (182–3). The loose cloth sides of the boards are separately turned back on to waste paper and glued, using little glue with a dabbing motion, and are rubbed into position with the fingers—the folder may be used afterwards, but through good-quality paper. The book is now fitted into the cover and the hinges are pressed home with a folder, which is also used to curve the spine of the case at head and tail by pressure from the inner side while the book is gently rolled from side to side while resting on its spine. It is placed between pressing boards and allowed to dry under a weight before pasting in.

CORNERS

Should the board have broken down at the corners but the cloth be still intact, they may be stiffened and reshaped by injecting a water-based adhesive such as cold glue with a no 1 (coarse) hypodermic syringe. The glue must be more dilute than when normally used, or the syringe may clog; it must in any case be thoroughly cleansed after use. Only sufficient glue is injected to allow the corner to be carefully moulded into shape first by the fingers followed by the use of a small folder. A superfluity of glue can discolour the bookcloth. If corners are so much damaged that this method is inadequate, it will be necessary to open them up by making cuts in the cloth turn-ins at a suitable point, turning them back, and lifting the cloth as far as necessary to effect repairs. These may require that the board be opened up and glue injected between the fibres before remoulding them. Should the board be very badly damaged and incomplete at the corner, the deficiency can be made good by the insertion during the glueing of a piece of thin millboard that has been heavily pared away at one edge. When dry, the surplus board may be cut away and any unevenness rectified with knife and glass-paper. Under such circumstances new cloth corners will probably have to be added and the original cloth cut away as necessary before glueing it back in position, but always, where possible, endeavouring to retain the original appearance.

After pasting the book into its cover and leaving it to dry, trim the edges of the old spine with knife and straightedge, cutting away only as much as is necessary to neaten it at the edges. If by any unlikely chance the turn-ins at head and tail are in good condition, they need not be trimmed but can be turned in over the new spine. The trimmed width should be such that it does not exceed that of the new spine. PVA adhesive is used for fixing the original spine, which, once in position, should be rubbed down through cartridge paper.

Leather Bindings

The most common harm to befall a leather binding is the dis-integration of the hinges, usually because the hemp slips holding the boards have broken down resulting in the complete detachment of the cover boards. Less frequently, with hollow-back bindings, the complete cover becomes detached from the book. In both cases the sewing is often in good condition. Sometimes, because of accident, or too-thin leather, hinges are broken at head and tail, or headcaps are damaged, often because they have projected above the board edges. The biggest problem occurs when the boards break away from tight-back bindings that have been tooled 'extra'.

RECASING

In most cases the problem is to re-attach the boards with the mini-mum effect upon the appearance of the binding. Unfortunately this is not always completely possible if a satisfactory and worth-while repair is to be effected.

Perhaps the simplest case is where book and cover have become separated and the problem is one of reattachment. If the book and binding are of the lighter kind this is possible by methods other than those normally used when 'forwarding', although they are seldom as strong.

The original back linings are removed as described on p. 43. When rebacking is necessary, and it is often desirable, it is now done.

described on p. 43

'RETURNED' CLOTH JOINTS

New cloth joints, known as 'returned cloth joints', are sewn at the front and back of the book over the original fly-leaves, unless new endpapers are contemplated, in which case the fly-leaves are removed. Strips of suitable cloth such as buckram, as long as the book height and 1–1½in wide, with the warping threads running along the length, are cleanly 'tipped' to the backing shoulder *face side downwards*. To do this accurately and effectively, each strip of cloth is turned up along one long edge to a width that equals the height of the backing shoulder. Holes going through the back of the book are made at the base of the backing shoulder (183–1), using a small awl or a large bookbinder's sewing needle set into a suitable holder such as an old penholder or the handle of a small paint brush—in these cases the metal ferrule must be covered by sticking strips of pared leather round it to prevent damage to the book. In use, the

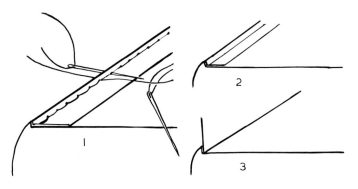

183 *Returned cloth joint*
1 *Cloth, face side down, tipped to backing shoulder and sewn to book*
2 *Cloth joint glued to backing shoulder*
3 *Cloth joint 'returned' on to itself and into the backing shoulder, concealing the sewing*

needle or awl will require frequent 'lubricating' by passing across the head or forehead. During the operation, the back of the book should be slightly twisted away from the worker which will prevent holes being made too deeply. A thin steel rule or other suitable guide may be held in position at the base of the backing shoulder to ensure the alignment of holes. These should not exceed

$\frac{1}{2}$in distance apart, and less with smaller books. Sewing is done with a thin linen thread (no 40 or 35) and may be either by the usual oversewing stitch or the saddle-stitch. With the latter, a needle is attached to both ends of the thread which is left in a central position at the first hole. From then onwards each needle is passed through every hole and tightened making a 'figure-of-eight' stitching. This confines the thread to the base of the backing shoulder and so tends to neaten the cloth joint. When the sewing is completed, the cloth strip is turned up against the backing shoulder (183–2) and turned back again on to itself quite level with the back (183–3); the inner part is now stuck firmly, using either hot glue or PVA. A protective sheet of paper should be lightly tipped to the reverse side of the cloth at the joint to protect the fly-leaf during subsequent operations.

This returned cloth joint can be used effectively in most forms of joint repairs, for it can be concealed by new endpapers and provides increased strength at the front and back of the book.

It is equally important that reinforced back linings be fitted, but with original covers the nature of the back linings will depend upon the amount of room available in the spine, for this must be adequate to allow the relined book back to fit comfortably. Original linings on the cover spine are carefully removed, and it is usually better to remove any false bands there, transferring them or replacements to the new Oxford hollow. These hollow linings have already been discussed (p. 153), but here the reinforcement should be as strong as circumstances permit. Finally the spine of the cover will be stuck to the Oxford hollow by pasting on the inside and lightly glueing the hollow. The binding is lightly tied round the hinges and the spine leather carefully worked upon with the folder, checking that it lies firmly at the bands and is set nicely at head and tail. Any heavy use of the folder should take place only through paper in order not to damage any gold tooling. When completely dry, the cloth joint may be put down under the lifted board paper and worked firmly into the joint. This is done with the cover boards turned back on to a suitable 'platform', using either PVA or hot, thin glue according to the type of cloth used in the joint. The joint is allowed to dry with the board open before the lifted board paper is returned to its original position, using either paste or PVA, and first using the finger to rub it down; the folder may be used afterwards, but gently and through strong paper. Waterproof sheets should be inserted when closing the book if adhesives have not completely dried out.

The lifting of board papers at the joint can be difficult. Much depends upon whether the boards were originally lined, in which case separation between the two papers can usually be effected by the careful use of a sharp, slim knife worked at an acute angle. Opening up must be done very gradually, keeping the point of the knife at a slightly downward angle and inserting it only a very short distance at each cut. Extra care is needed at points where slips have been laced to the board, for there is almost certain to be unevenness in the surface there.

If it is wished that the cloth joint be concealed, the fly-leaf must be removed and replaced by a blank sheet of suitable paper before affixing the cloth joint. When other work has been completed, it may be covered with a strip of paper that matches (or nearly so) the original endpapers and overlaps just sufficiently for it to be covered by the lifted board paper and the original fly-leaf, which is trimmed on its inside edge, pasted out and laid on to the added blank fly-leaf. The book is then pressed with waterproof sheets inserted at the ends.

The method depends entirely upon the strength given by the returned cloth joint and the reinforcement of the Oxford hollow now firmly stuck to the spine of the cover; under the best circumstances, this can be considerable.

CORNERS

What has been said with regard to repairing cloth corners applies in many respects to leather repairs. New leather corners or reinforcements must be neatly pared at the edges if they are not to appear bulky (184-1, 2, 3). On the other hand, little is gained if, for the sake of neatness, very thin leather is used. Because it is the life of the binding that is important rather than niceties in its appearance, fairly generously folded corners should be used that will support the probably already weakened board.

With large and thick book boards, should the corners be badly broken, they can be replaced (184-4) by cutting away the damaged part, using a wide, bevelled cut and fitting sound millboard (unless the boards are of wood) by first glueing the angled edges with an epoxy resin glue which gives much stronger adhesion than most others. In addition, the new corner can be pinned with fine beading pins or, in the case of thin boards, dressmakers' steel pins with the heads removed.

184 Corner repairs
1 Opening up the board
2 Pared millboard glued into the board
3 Cutting and filing to shape
4 Replacing a corner on thick board

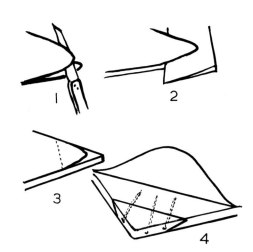

RE-LACING BOARDS

With heavier bindings on larger books it is necessary to add new attachments, slips of hemp cord or linen tape, to the book, and re-lace them into the boards. This can be done in several ways. With a tight-back binding to be rebacked and possibly re-lettered, after cleaning the back, additional cords may be sewn to the book by the side of original raised cords (185–2), or over existing recessed ones (185–3). In the first case sewing need only be round both cords—the old and the new—and not through the book sections. This is best done using an upholsterer's curved needle, using small pliers to pull needle and thread under the cords, the book being placed, back uppermost, in a bench press.

With recessed cords, sewing must be through some of the sections, the thread encircling the new cords, leaving them raised for tight-back covering. If a hollow back is required the cords may be replaced by tapes which can be laced to the boards as described under *Forwarding* (p. 135). With raised cords, an alternative to sewing new cords to the book is to sew linen threads round the cords some distance from the joint, leaving long enough ends for lacing to the boards (185–1). This is repeated a number of times, each succeeding stitch going round previous ones and tying them to the cords, until a point near to the joint is reached and the total number of threads is sufficient to effect a strong attachment to the boards when all are laced together at one point (see p. 134).

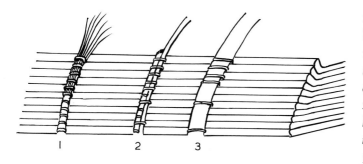

185 *Replacing broken slips* 1 *Adding linen threads to raised cord* 2 *Sewing new hemp cord beside the original cord* 3 *Sewing tape over recessed cord*

REBACKING

When rebacking a leather binding, the leather at the joint edge of each board is lifted for about an inch. What has been said regarding the lifting of board papers (p. 334) also applies to the lifting of leather at the hinge. Because they so often break away it is usually unwise to try to lift short lengths of turn-ins where the leather is old but to cut the cover leather through at the board edges when lifting it at the hinge. Should the turn-ins be tooled they will have to be lifted or even removed and returned later to their original positions. If the boards are to be re-laced to the book, sufficient room must be available for re-holing, should this be necessary. If tapes have been added, chisel cuts will have to be made; these may require even more room, and the leather must be lifted accordingly. For this the knife may be used as when lifting the board paper described previously. The leather is then cut cleanly with knife and straightedge, $\frac{3}{16}-\frac{1}{4}$in away from the joint edge of the board. To avoid the risky business of trying to pare old leather, a strip of board or leather equal in thickness to the original covering leather is stuck firmly to the exposed board, replacing the leather that has been cut away. This may be cut slightly larger than required and trimmed to size *in situ* later, after the boards have been re-laced and the slips moulded into the original kerfs.

If the back is to be hollow-lined, a reinforced Oxford hollow will add strength at the hinges. Because the board thickness at the joint has been slightly increased by the addition of the strip of board or leather there, it will offset any increased thickness caused by the hollow reinforcement. After lining the back, any false bands required are affixed to it.

The new spine is cut to a width that allows just sufficient leather on each board to fully underlap the raised leather. Any more than this will require lifting the board leather still further or re-cutting the new leather to the correct size and paring one long edge again. The length will, of course, allow for turn-ins at head and tail.

The spine leather is pasted, folded on to itself and allowed to soak. While this is taking place, the projecting ends of false bands are cut away at an angle that permits the boards to open freely without fouling them; the ends of the hollow-back linings are cut at the folds sufficiently to allow for the leather to be turned in comfortably there. With the book placed, back uppermost, in a bench press, the pasted leather is placed centrally over the back so that the overlap on each side is uniform. If the binding is to be tight-back, paste must be applied to the back at the head and tail in order that the turned-in leather will stick there. Using the palms of the hands, the leather on the spine is worked firmly down, accentuating the bands but without unduly stretching it. The overlapping leather at the sides is worked on to the boards, under the raised leather and firmly against the edge of the strip of board or leather that has been stuck there. At this stage the lifted leather on the boards is pasted and brought into position over the new leather, fitting neatly against the raised part of the board and level with its surface. If the side leather is old, great care is necessary and the fingers only should be used to work it nicely yet firmly down. Should this not be effective, paste on the surface may be used as a lubricant using a folder very carefully, but it should be cleaned away with a damp sponge as soon as possible or the leather will tend to darken there. Having checked that the leather is adhering firmly everywhere and the bands are nipped up, remove the book from the press, place it on waterproof sheets between pressing boards and under a weight, and allow it to settle or even dry out. This does not apply if the binding has a tight back when the leather of the new spine must be turned in at head and tail *before* paste on the spine dries on the back of the book. (This is described in Chapter 3, p. 175.)

With the hollow-backed binding, the turn-ins can be dampened and pasted and dealt with after the leather has dried. This method removes all fear of movement of leather on the boards and also simplifies the turning in of the spine leather.

MOUNTING ORIGINAL SPINES

Before the original spine can be mounted to the new one, it must be cleaned of all paper linings and, if necessary, its edges must be trimmed and pared. Every binder has his own preference for method, but perhaps one of the best is to undercut the leather with the edge-paring knife, with the face side of the leather uppermost. This requires considerable care as well as a sharp knife and cannot be done at speed for the fingers of the hand holding the leather spine must at all times provide pressure at the point at which the under-paring is taking place. Once again, previous experiment and practice are necessary. The original spine is well pasted, which will soften the leather, and while this is taking place the new spine can be glasspapered (but only where the old one will cover it) to roughen the surface slightly to make for better adhesion. The original spine is placed in position and gently patted and pressed with the hand until it settles to the shape of the back. Any rubbing with the folder must take place through strong paper stretched tightly across the spine. Should the bands offer any difficulty, they may be carefully 'nipped' into position through a strip of soft leather held firmly over them. If this is insufficient they may have to be tied down as with tight-back bindings (see p. 199). Any paste on the surface or at the edges of the original spine must be removed with a damp sponge. The spine can now be held very firmly in position while it is drying, by binding a surgical bandage tightly round the book. The bandage will adjust itself at all points, bands and edges, and will not mark the damp leather. It should be removed after a while to check that the returned spine is in position, that all-over adhesion is taking place, especially at the edges, and that paste has not exuded there to cause the bandage to stick. Provided the bandage is still clean and free from paste, it may be returned if thought necessary, but should be removed before there is any possibility of threads adhering permanently anywhere. The book must now be left to dry out, and this may take a whole day.

TIGHT-BACK REPAIRS

The disadvantage of tight-back binding is forcibly brought home when spine or hinge repairs are necessary, for to effect the best repair the spine leather, if it is to be retained, should be completely removed and this is seldom possible. While repairs to the head and tail can normally be achieved by inserting leather reinforcements, the replacement of broken hinges is invariably limited to strips of leather being fitted to the book boards and attached to the spine for seldom more than $\frac{1}{2}$in, which is about the distance that the original spine leather can be lifted at the hinges. For such work a special type of knife is preferable, and I have found that a short palette knife of good steel, the end cut away at a slight angle—in the opposite direction to an edge-paring knife—and ground with a wide bevel before being sharpened is a useful tool for the purpose.

The operation of lifting the spine leather is one that demands great care and control of the knife, being best achieved if the forearm is kept close to the body when working. The weakened fibres of old leather can be improved if it is given a dressing of British Museum Leather Dressing two or three days beforehand. If the leather at the bands resists lifting, it is better to cut it carefully close to the edge of the band, lifting only the leather in between. This will result in the new hinge leather showing at these points, but this is preferable from the point of view of final appearance.

For repairs at head and tail of the spine, after lifting the leather sufficiently there and on the boards the repair leather is cut very precisely to the necessary size and shape and the edges are pared with a wide bevel. The book can be placed in a bench press with the back uppermost and the boards outside, which will leave the hands free to manipulate boards and leather. The latter is pasted, as is the back of the book where the leather has been lifted. Fitting the new leather will be found easier by working it from the inside of the boards to the outside, that is, placing the turn-ins in position first. This is done by placing the leather, face downwards, on to the pasted part of the back of the book and on to the inside edge of the boards which can be lifted to facilitate this. The remainder is now brought over into position on the outside so that it underlaps the lifted leather of the spine and boards. The book is now removed from the press, the boards are closed on to it, and it is stood on end so that the repair leather can be moulded neatly on the spine and the boards, and in the joints. The lifted board leather can now be pasted and worked into position, the turn-ins readjusted, and the joint set.

To add new hinges, the required strips of leather are cut to an accurately assessed width and pared. The board leather will have been lifted at the hinge and the pasted leather is first fitted in position under it, leaving the exact amount required to be carefully worked under the lifted spine leather. Lifted spine and board leather can now be pasted and gently worked back into position with the fingers and the ball of the hand. If necessary they may be lightly rubbed down with a folder through strong paper. Any surplus paste at the edges is removed with a dampened sponge. Provided the leather is quite free of paste on the surface, the book may be bound round with a surgical bandage.

This sometimes long and tedious operation will preserve a treasured binding, provided the book is subsequently handled with care, but only posterity will know just how successful it has been.

Choice of leather for rebacking must depend upon availability and suitability, for although the repair would probably be stronger and so more durable, goatskin is not used on calf bindings. Some binders use 'fair' (undyed) calfskin and dye it to match the original leather when the work is completed. It is better to use a pre-dyed leather of a slightly lighter shade than the original and stain it to match it when the work is completed. Dyes may be water- or spirit-soluble, but although the latter tend to harden the surface slightly, if used in moderation and not left too long before using they generally seem more suitable.

After leather book repairs have been completed, the cover should receive an application of British Museum Leather Dressing, which is allowed to soak for two or even three days before polishing with a soft cloth.

8

MATERIALS

*Adhesives—boards—bookcloths, fibre felts and calicoes—leathers
and vellums—papers—gold leaf and stamping foils*

MATERIALS

Adhesives

Although glues have been in use for more than 3,000 years, it is only in the last 150 years that they have been made for, rather than by, the craftsmen using them. They are now so specialised that, commercially, their name is legion. Those in ordinary use may be loosely divided into eight or nine generic groups as follows.

Animal, which includes bookbinders' glue, Scotch and 'Pearl', also gelatine and fish glue.

Bitumen, which is not used generally in book production although it has been incorporated in boards for use in tropical regions to offset the ravages of termites.

Dextrine, which includes flour and starch paste and cellulose.

Emulsion, under which polyvinyl acetate, acrilic and latex are included.

Epoxy and polyester resins, which are of chemical structure, being 'set' solely by chemical action. The polyester variety usually employ a catalyst to improve resistance to water and heat but not necessarily to set them. Epoxy resin has tremendous strength and is dimensionally stable—neither contracting nor expanding upon setting. It is usually supplied in two parts which have to be mixed before use.

Rubber glues, which have a longer history, a sad one as far as it concerns bookbinding. Synthetic rubber is a different matter. Immediate contact occurs when two superficially dry surfaces are brought together, which demands absolute accuracy in the placing of the two parts to be joined.

Usually the solvent is water, but those known as *solvent glues* use acetone, amyl acetate, methyl, ethyl, etc. Such adhesives are usually made for specialised purposes. Synthetic resin is a term loosely applied to any glue that does not originate from natural sources, but for the layman it refers to glues in which a hardener, usually urea formaldehyde, is used. Their storage life is limited to about three months.

ANIMAL GLUE

Though in many binderies this has been completely superseded by PVA adhesive (because of its convenience and versatility), there are still many bookbinders who will not dispense with the glue-pot despite commercial coercion! The quick coagulation tends to limit expansion of the material being glued, and this is an important point in its favour. Another advantage, but only to posterity, is that glue is easier to remove from the surface of the paper than PVA when the book requires rebinding yet again. On the debit side, it requires controlled heating in a water-jacketed container, its 'gel' strength being considerably reduced by continuous overheating. By comparison with glues that can be used cold, it is messy in use, and 'brush-life' is comparatively short.

Normally, animal glues dry hard and brittle if used in excess, but flexibility can be imparted by an hygroscopic additive such as glycerine. While flexibility is of the utmost importance on the spine of the book, the boards are made firmer by the use of non-flexible glue, and so it is not unusual to have both available. Animal glues are now more usually sold in a prepared state ready for use and requiring heating only, and the glue is cleaner. For the amateur, small tins of prepared animal glue only require placing in a saucepan of hot water to liquefy it for use. It will be necessary to reheat the water from time to time.

Unprepared glue comes in either slab, powder or granulated form, the latter being known as 'Pearl'. Slabs must be broken into small pieces by placing them in hessian (sack cloth) and hammering on a hard surface such as concrete. Before use it should be put to soak overnight in enough water to just cover it. Powdered glue (sometimes sold as 'glue size') is *added* to cold water and allowed to soak for a while before heating in a glue-pot. Pearl glue can be soaked separately by adding cold water, or this may be done directly in the glue-pot. Because of evaporation, water will have to be added to the glue from time to time, when in use. If the water in the well of the glue-pot is used to thin the glue or to wash out the glue brush, it must be changed daily to prevent its boiling over and also becoming distinctly unpleasant and odorous. (Refer to *Glue-pots*, p. 24, and *Glue brushes*, p. 28).

POLYVINYL ACETATE EMULSION

Without doubt, polyvinyl acetate (PVA) is the most useful of the adhesives used in bookbinding today. The one objection that could be levelled at it is that its tenacity, which seems quite permanent, could imperil further rebinding of a book if this becomes necessary. It was first produced during World War II when experiments were made to produce resinous substitutes for animal glues. Vinyls are produced from the paraffin group of chemicals, while *poly* (polerma) refers to the joining together of them. The result is a hard film, and a 'plasticiser' is added to a water emulsion, during manufacture, to form a flexible adhesive. Complete drying-out is faster than with animal glue and it is especially effective for such fabrics as terylene, nylon and silk which do not adhere readily with paste or glue. The guarding of vellum is simplified by its use, while its water- and rot-resisting properties combined with its apparently indefinite flexibility make it unique. The fact that it is always ready for use at any required strength, by diluting with water (preferably distilled), normally at a ratio of 1:3, adds to its usefulness. At normal strength PVA adheres readily and without pressure, but because it is less affected by water than is paper, this tends to curl when PVA is used on one side only.

In use it is best stored in a wide-necked glass jar with a moulded screw cap, but it is important that all traces of PVA be wiped from the neck of the jar before returning the cap. Should this by mischance become stuck, immersion of the cap only in hot water will loosen it. Brushes, too, will dry out quite hard unless they are either well washed after use or left standing upright in water sufficient to cover the bristles only. It has been found that brushes hardened by PVA will soften if left (bristles only) in a fairly strong solution of certain domestic detergents.

As a sediment tends to form when PVA is left standing for some time, it should be well stirred with a wooden spatula or spoon before use. When using PVA a piece of rag is recommended for wiping fingers, as continual wiping on a work-coat or apron results in an accumulation which is extremely difficult to remove by normal washing methods. Except with cheap commercial cases, PVA has not replaced flour paste for use on leather, and it is extremely doubtful whether it ever will.

FLOUR PASTE

Adhesives made from starch—of which the sources are numerous—are known to have been used by the Egyptians for joining papyrus. Bookbinders have always used flour paste and will probably continue to do so, not only because it is satisfactory for paper work and for leather, but because it is both convenient and cheap. Before insecticides were introduced into it, it was an encouragement to book lice and similar enemies of books, but other problems were created, notably that of acidity, by the use of alum and other preservatives, and acids are paper's most deadly enemy.

For general purposes wheat flour (not self-raising) may be used as the basic ingredient for paste, but a whiter paste results from the use of corn (maize) or rice flour. The ratio of water to flour will vary according to the consistency required, and as bookbinders usually prefer a stiffer paste it can be about six to eight parts water to one of flour. It is made by first mixing the flour with a small amount of cold water to a creamy consistency, in an aluminium or enamelled saucepan, using a wooden spatula or spoon and making sure that no lumps remain. The remainder of the water is stirred in (some prefer to save time by heating this beforehand) and the whole brought gently to the boil, continually stirring the paste. It will begin to thicken before it actually boils, when the heat is reduced and stirring continued for a minute or so. When the paste cools to $120°F$ ($49°C$) an extremely small amount of thymol crystals (equal to about a hundredth part of the flour used) is well stirred into it. Surface skinning on cooling can be avoided by placing a piece of good-quality paper over it, and in direct contact, and adding just enough water to cover it. Other anti-mildew preservatives include Phenol, Formalin, and 'Shirlan', a trade name for Salicylanilide, which is considered to be the best by specialist chemists. Alum is best avoided not only because it introduces an element of acidity but because it tends to harden the paste when this dries out. No preservative is needed for flour paste that is to be used in two or three days, but as soon as souring occurs it must be thrown out because of the risk of acidity.

Once the amount of paste usually required has been determined, time is saved if glass containers are marked (a band of paper will serve) showing the amount of flour and water required. For example, a glass jar filled with 3oz wheat flour and marked, and a bottle containing 18oz water also marked, will make sufficient paste to comfortably fill a 2lb stoneware jam jar, which is a convenient amount for a small workshop. A few thymol crystals (representing about $\frac{1}{30}$oz) will need to be added. If a well-fitting plastic lid is available, and a hole, rather smaller than the handle of the paste-brush, is cut centrally in it with small radiating cuts made round it, the brush can remain in the pot when not in use, the jar being virtually airtight. During hot weather the paste can be kept in a domestic refrigerator overnight, but must not be allowed to freeze. The use of flour paste is limited, in the main, to paper, leather and vellum; it is not successful with bookcloths with the possible exception of linen buckram which, when softened, can be moulded for solid headcaps if needed.

COLD GLUES

These are almost invariably made commercially, although they probably originated from an admixture of flour paste and hot glue and in this form are still used by some bookbinders. One thing most of them seem to have in common is that they are not flexible when dry, like PVA.

In England, one particular brand made by Starch Products of Slough and marketed as Stadex 404 is very useful for a variety of purposes. At the right consistency it can be used for cloth case making and even for the covering of boxes and, because of its slower drying propensities, it allows more time for manipulation than does hot glue. It is pale fawn in colour, very smooth in texture.

There are numerous other proprietary brands, some having a gum base, not all suitable for bookbinding.

EPOXY RESIN GLUES

These have only special uses in bookbinding but are useful where great adhesive strength is necessary, such as in re-cornering book boards with millboard or wood. The assembling of book boxes is improved by them because of the great strength of the glue line.

POLYESTER RESINS

These have similar qualities. Industrially they are highly volatile, but the version sold in retail shops is much modified and easier to use.

Boards

'THAMES' BOARD

Book cover boards may be of wood, millboard, strawboard or (in

Britain) 'Thames' board, a proprietary brand used for packaging and bookbinding, especially for edition cased binding. It consists of bonded fibre, much of it waste material, pressed and rolled, during which process it is lined on both sides with Kraft paper under tension. Because of subsequent contraction of the paper linings the board is given greater rigidity as well as a firm, smooth surface.

STRAWBOARD

In Britain this is mostly imported from the Continent. It is one of the cheapest of boards, being made from cereal straws, and is soft and light in proportion to its thickness. It has little toughness and should be used only on light cloth casings and for the 'inners' of made-up boards. Thickness was originally denoted by the weight of a single board measuring 32in × 22in and varies from 4oz to 4lb. As with millboard, there are a number of different measures in use, despite 'industrial rationalisation'. They are:

Traditional	Caliper inch	Metric
8 oz	0·026	0·660mm
12 oz	0·040	1·016mm
16 oz	0·045	1·143mm
1½ lb	0·069	1·752mm
2 lb	0·090	2·286mm
2½ lb	0·116	2·946mm
3 lb	0·135	3·657mm

The 'steel wire gauge' (SWG) measurement, once used, appears to have been discarded. The size most commonly used by book-binders is 25in × 30in, but boards measuring 22in × 32in, 24in × 38in, and 30in × 40in are obtainable usually in ½cwt bundles.

MILLBOARDS

These were introduced in England about 1700, and then known as milled boards (as against 'paste boards' that bookbinders themselves made from waste material). Hand-made millboards which, in the second half of the nineteenth century, often comprised excellent fibre from waste sailcloth and rope, are no longer obtainable. The art died during World War II. Whereas three grades of machine-made millboard were previously available, BBM (best brown machine), BM (best machine), and GM (grey millboard), only this last seems to be made today. Although not comparable with handmade, the best machine-made millboard, if suitably prepared by the binder, will make book boards of a good standard.

As with strawboard, millboard has a variety of designations for thickness. The traditional form, believed to have been founded on the price of a standard number of boards of uniform size, is still in use today by some bookbinders. Caliper inch measurement has virtually replaced it, to be followed by a metric measurement. Even standard thicknesses are disappearing as manufacturers turn to metric measurement, but the following list, based on traditional measurements, forms a guide.

Traditional measure	Caliper inch	Metric (approx)	Metric (actual) millimetres
6d	0·036	1 mm	0·914
7d	0·048	1·2 mm	1·219
8d	0·064	1·6 mm	1·625
8dx	0·085	2·16mm	2·159
8dxx	0·116	2·9 mm	2·946
10d (or x)	0·144	3·6 mm	3·657
	(also 0·157)	4 mm	

Traditional millboard sizes were based on, and named after, paper sizes, being in each case an allowance beyond the paper measurement to provide for the 'square' of the book boards. Today there are machines that produce millboards measuring 104in × 124in, which are cut to 30in × 40in or 26in × 40in, although manufacturers will cut them to any given size from stock boards. To give complete economy, stock sizes are cut without regard to the directional grain, and, because of labour costs, sorting by grain direction does not always take place, the bundles being designated as being 'mixed grain'. Where bookbinders' stockists hold supplies of millboards, the most usual cut size is 'large' or 'medium' 24in × 19in, and most thicknesses can be obtained. Manufacturers no longer supply small quantities, and a minimum order may be 5cwt.

DIRECTIONAL GRAIN

All machine-made boards have a one-directional fibre grain which, unless running from head to tail on the book, can result in troublesome warping at the joint. The grain is easily detected by bending a board for an equal distance each way; there is a greater flexibility with the grain than against it. In addition, grain direction is usually marked on the outer board of every bundle by means of an arrow.

LEATHERBOARD

This term, now a misnomer, is still used to describe the modern, poorer version of the original, in which leather scraps were shredded and used with wood fibre. Because of the change of fibre it is also referred to as chipboard and is often tinted a brownish-red. Unglazed, it was known as imitation leatherboard. It is obtainable in various thicknesses, usually from 0·02in to 0·16in caliper. It is useful for filling-in purposes and for limp bindings.

MISCELLANEOUS BOARDS

Bristol board is correctly made from rag fibre. 'Pasted board' (sometimes used as a single word) indicates that the finished board has been laminated, using paste as the adhesive. 'Pulp boards' indicate a poorer fibre content. Of these boards, some are designated by a weight, as with paper, but the better ones (from 2 to 4 sheet) are sold by the hundred sheets. They are useful in many ways, especially for board fillings.

HARDBOARD AND FIBRE BOARD

These are a heavily pressed, more rigid and stronger type of board used mostly in the packaging and building trades, but they are useful for the making of larger book boxes. They are not generally suitable for book cover boards because of their tendency to crack rather than bend.

WOODEN BOARDS

The use of wooden boards is usually restricted to the rebinding of large, heavy books, generally of an antiquarian nature. They are attractive when used with tawed pigskin for quarter-leather bindings, the leather recessed into the board. Oak is invariably used and must be well-seasoned by natural processes, and not kiln-dried. It should always be treated against possible ravages by the rapacious woodworm.

Bookcloths, Fibre Felts and Calicoes

BOOKCLOTHS

If the untreated fabrics used for embroidered bindings of the Tudor and Stuart periods, and experiments carried out by individual binders towards the end of the eighteenth century, be excepted, books were not bound in cloth until 1825 when Archibald Leighton introduced 'dyed glazed calico'. Today, the wheel of 'progress' has turned, if not full circle, then almost so, for while cloth is still used on the better class of book, 'fibre felt' is used for much edition binding.

Bookcloth has to be specially prepared to prevent adhesives percolating through it to the face side. Usually dyed cotton cloth is impregnated with a starch filling, passing through a 'starch mangle' until it is completely filled, when it is 'calendered' and the finishing materials are fused with the fabric base. This requires pressure of from 20 to 50 tons and heat of from 300°F to 400°F (113·4°C–141·2°C). Other bookcloths are tissue-lined instead, either to preserve their natural texture or because the weave is too 'open' for filling; canvas comes into this category. Neither of these methods will result in water- or grease-proof surfaces for which the material must be impregnated by synthetic resins or re-surfaced with a suitable finish.

The strength of bookcloth depends upon the closeness of the weave and the nature of the fibre of the thread used. To some extent it can be checked—especially with starch-filled cloths—if the cloth is crumpled by rapidly rubbing it backwards and forwards at one corner when held between the finger and thumb of each hand. This will cause any filling to fall out and the true nature of the cloth can be assessed.

The actual quality of the bookcloth can be easily disguised by the filling, and the American Library Association has set a standard of a total of 110 threads (warp and weft) per square inch for library cloths. At the other end of the scale, buckram may be made of cotton and linen, linen only, or even double warp linen which is the strongest of all. Its initial cost is high by comparison with other cloths, but, at its best, buckram may well outlast medium-quality leather. It is suitable for most cloth bindings except on small, light books. Its one disadvantage is that, unless prepared by the binder, the surface is susceptible to dampness. Law buckram is especially strong and usually has a slightly textured appearance.

In between these extremes there are a considerable number of variations, manufacturers giving each its own name. Art canvas is an exception, the name always indicating a coarsely woven, strong material, tissue-lined. Having a fairly open texture, it is not as receptive to finishing as cloths with smooth surfaces, but its strength is undeniable. Not to be confused with traditional buckram is *Art Buckram* in the 'Sundour' range of bookcloths. This is a much lighter grade, unlined and having a filling applied to the back only; if creased or folded, the adhesive will penetrate to the face side. Within its limitations this cloth has much to commend it, for it looks well with its slightly textured appearance and is very reasonable in price by comparison with traditional buckram. 'Sundour' bookcloths, originally produced by the Morton Sundour Company, have a delightful textured surface and are 'filled' at the back only. They are fast to light and washable, and there is a comprehensive range of colours and qualities. Like Art Buckram, they do not take gold tooling or stamping as well as smooth-surfaced cloths but are extremely pleasant in appearance.

When first introduced, bookcloths were not readily acceptable and in consequence were given a variety of embossed grains, from fern and floral effects to leather grains and geometric patterns. Today it is still possible to have most bookcloth grained, but its use has diminished almost to the point of extinction. However, many librarians realise that a book bound in a grained cloth is more securely held in the hand than one in a smooth, shiny cloth and so suffers fewer accidents.

ART VELLUMS

These, now less used than previously, are very smooth cloths with a textured pattern printed upon a white base cloth. They were much used for siding quarter- and half-bindings and it does not seem impossible that their popularity may return one day.

Bookcloths usually have a 'directional grain', like paper and board, because the warping threads that extend along the length of the roll are usually required to be stronger, as they are under tension during weaving. Most bookcloths can therefore be torn in a straight line along the length of the material, but not across the warping threads, the width, though this does not apply to the tougher, stronger cloths such as buckram and art canvas. This characteristic tends to result in greater expansion of the cloth across the width than along its length when dampened by the adhesive in making up cases. The possibility of covers warping at the hinge is reduced if the warp threads of the cloth run from head to tail of the book cover. (The English language has two meanings to 'warp', and here both are in use!)

On the other hand, the result of this is that weaker threads form the hinge of the book, and it has been proved that, provided any warping of the boards at the hinge is controlled, warping threads running *across* the hinge make for greater strength there. Where large numbers of identically sized cases are being made in the same cloth, economics take a hand and the cloth is usually cut in the way that causes the least wastage, without other considerations.

When cutting cloth for half- or quarter-bindings, the warp should always run from head to tail of the book; cut the other way, weft threads, which are not always straight in the woven cloth, may be cut through and cause fraying.

LEATHERCLOTH

This was the original waterproof cloth first made at the turn of the century, one of the best known being 'Rexine', with a surface consisting of several coatings of nitro-cellulose. The base cloth, known as 'greycloth', varies in composition and weave according to the grade of leathercloth. Polyvinyl chloride (PVC) has now replaced nitrocellulose, the continuous sheet meeting the pre-heated base cloth under heat and pressure. Embossing is done with engraved steel rollers and almost invariably imitates leathers. In combination with the special vinyl (V) stamping foil the PVC can now be tooled or stamped at a heat insufficient to cause it to melt.

FIBRE FELTS

It is debatable whether these should be classed with bookcloths or paper, as they are not woven and much more closely resemble paper—albeit of an extremely good quality. As they are used far more frequently for the making of publishers' cases than for other purposes they are dealt with here.

'Linson', the original name given to the material by Watsons of Linfrew, persists as a generic term; but there are a number of different brands, 'Glindura' by Arborfield Products, 'Coverdale' by Winterbottom's (now 'English Sewing') and 'Elephant Hide' which is marketed by the Red Bridge Book Cloth Co. This last can be obtained with 'quiet' contemporary designs and of a thickness that makes it extremely good for endpapers. With lighter grades, this also applies to other brands. The tensile and bursting strengths of the best of fibre felts are quite remarkable, but in actual use as book covers they tend to tear at the head of the hinge.

CALICOES AND MULLS

Calico is a generic term applied to woven cotton cloths that are heavier than muslin but lighter than canvas. Other materials such as cambrics and jaconettes are calicoes of a kind, variations being made by the quality of the raw cotton used originally, the fineness of the threads and the closeness of the weave. According to their suitability they are used in bookbinding for repairing or reinforcing guards and for map mounting; they are sized and calendered for such purposes. Special 'flexible' calico is made for use with unsewn binding and will expand in one direction so that backing may take place *after* it has been attached to the spine. Linen is used when greater strength is required and its thickness is no hindrance.

Mull is a coarse muslin or scrim, sized, and with an open weave to allow penetration of glue when used as a spine lining. It is made in various strengths and also with additional reinforcements woven into it by using stronger warping threads set closer together at intervals. 'Taped' mull has similar reinforcements set even closer together in groups and about $\frac{3}{8}$in wide and spaced wider apart, so that they give the effect of sewing tapes on the book.

BOOKBINDING HOLLANDS

Hollands, originally used for window blinds, are medium-weight linens or cottons, plain-woven, stiffened and glazed in finishing to close the texture of the cloth. If made of linen they will wear well, and are usually reasonably priced. White hollands fill the gap between cotton calicoes and true linens and are useful where a stronger material is needed for map mounting or reinforcements. Generally hollands take paste or PVA better than hot glue.

Lengths and widths of these materials vary but range from 36–54in wide by 38–40yd or 50–100yd lengths to a roll. 'Splitting' for smaller quantities is charged extra by the yard, but the larger manufacturers discourage the selling of smaller quantities than a roll and in some cases refuse it. It is fairly usual with most retail distributors to supply bookcloth by the yard, but an extra charge is made for the service.

Leathers

'Nothing better than good leather has been found for covering and protecting books', wrote Douglas Cockerell many years ago, and, despite all scientific progress since then, few informed bibliophiles would dispute this today.

Leather has unique properties that cannot be produced artificially; it has strength, flexibility, and natural fibre that is blended by growth in a manner that no machine can emulate. Add to this its innate surface beauty, and it is difficult to see how it can be surpassed. But its preparation depends upon man, his knowledge, ability, and integrity; for in the production of good-quality leather tanning is all-important.

Vegetable tannage produces leathers which have good substance and are well filled, having less 'stretch'. Vegetable tanning materials are roughly divided into two groups, Pyrogallol and Catechol, the former being more suitable for bookbinding leathers. They include sumach leaves, chestnut wood, oak galls, wood and bark, and similar natural materials. Sumach is considered to be the most suitable for bookbinding leathers. Mineral tannage is, from the binder's viewpoint, restricted to the alum and chrome processes. Alum dressing, used by the Babylonians and the early Chinese, and in Britain in the ninth century, was, and still is, known as 'tawing'. Alum, which is a compound of aluminium sulphate and potassium sulphate, is mixed with common salt, and the skins are soaked in a strong solution of the two. Tawed leather is quite white and easily stretches. It is still regarded as the longest-lasting of all binding leathers, if vellum be excluded.

Chrome tanning, a nineteenth-century discovery, is a much quicker method, and chrome leathers are much more stable to acids and water than vegetable-tanned leathers. They do not, however, always take tooling well, their water-resistant properties demand different and stronger adhesives than paste or even glue, and their resilience makes the moulding of headcaps and corners extremely difficult.

The fibre strength of a skin is not uniform, being firmest in the region of the back and shoulders, while the flanks will be soft and 'stretchy'. At the neck the leather may be so harsh that it is unsuitable for binding, let alone tooling, which can be near-impossible. To expect a skin of leather to be flawless on the surface is unjustifiable optimism, and in a world given to artifice it is not surprising that methods of concealing flaws are a regular feature of leather production, 'surface colouring' with a pigment being used to cover defects or to give a uniform colour and surface to satisfy an uninformed public. The enormous use of plastic materials with their monotonous uniformity may result in a greater appreciation of the natural beauty and individuality of leather. To retain its natural character, aniline dyes are used, but they will not conceal inevitable blemishes; in some cases they may even tend to emphasise them. Natural growth produces variations in the surface appearance of leathers, and most skins can be known by the individual 'grain' of the animal. With goatskins, there are variations according to the size of the animal and its life conditions. Sheepskin, because of the looseness of its fibre, can be, and often is, artificially grained to represent almost any animal skin in a way that successfully deceives the uninformed but does not prolong the shorter life of the leather.

THE PIRA TEST

This test was the result of investigations made in 1933 for the British Leather Manufacturers' Association by R. Faraday Innes and its findings were published in conjunction with the Printing Industry Research Association. It established that leather decay by sulphuric action took place when a protective agent known as 'natural water-soluble non-tans' was washed away during tanning. By the simple means of rubbing the leather over with a 7 per cent aqueous solution of potassium lactate the original protection was returned. Leathers so treated can be obtained and are stamped 'Guaranteed to resist the PIRA Test'. As it is inevitable that during binding leather will be sponged with water, many binders now give a final sponging with potassium lactate to offset loss of protection.

Where deterioration has already taken place it cannot be cured but the leather can be improved by the application of British Museum Leather Dressing.

Beginning with the leathers which are best suited to bookbinding, the following details are given.

GOATSKIN

Outside bookbinding circles, goatskin is more often referred to as 'morocco'—an ambiguous term, as it means different things in different trades. The finest bookbinding goatskin has the cosmopolitan title of 'French Cape Levant Morocco' which should indicate that it is the large goat of the Cape of Good Hope, that it has the bold 'Levant' grain (so-called because it originated there), and that it has been dressed by the French, who have always been considered the best dressers of bookbinding leathers. Real morocco has a much smaller grain and is sumach-tanned by the 'bottle' method, where the skin is sewn up, filled with a strong infusion of sumach, sealed, and floated for about twenty-four hours in a sumach bath. Such skins carry the sewing marks round their outside edges. Well-tanned goatskin is strong and flexible, and its surface is hard-wearing.

The term 'Crushed Morocco' refers to the Levant-grained goatskin that is polished by machine or by hand and afterwards crushed by plating; it has a very attractive, if sophisticated, appearance. Nigerian goatskin, commonly referred to as Niger, is softer than morocco but has good wearing qualities and, if aniline dyed, has a very pleasant appearance. It is popular with the British craft bookbinder. Goatskins vary considerably in size, the smallest Nigers being only about 4sq ft while the Cape Goat can be as large as 12sq ft.

CALF

Calfskin comes from an animal no older than six weeks, and the immaturity of the fibres reduces its durability. Its smooth surface, especially when hand-polished, makes very elegant bindings which had great popularity in earlier days. The fact that calf has fewer blemishes and skins are fairly large (8–10sq ft) is an added attraction from the bookbinder's viewpoint. The bad reputation earned by bad tanning and overmuch paring, combined with the damaging effect of sulphur fumes from gas lighting at the turn of the century, still attaches to it. The use of acids to produce the then popular 'tree', 'marbled' and 'sprinkled' calf all contributed to its poor reputation for wear.

PIGSKIN

This is a very durable leather if used at its full thickness; its surface is firm and takes frictional wear better than almost any other leather. It is characterised by the open hair follicles, set in triangular formation and going right through to the flesh side where they can be readily seen. Because the follicles are so 'open', any thinning of the leather reduces its strength disproportionately, so that it is more suitable for large and heavy books. When 'tawed' it is one of the longest-lasting leathers used in bookbinding. Skin sizes vary from about 8sq ft to as much as 16 sq ft.

SHEEPSKIN

This has a large, open texture and is very flexible, but the fibres are fine, and tensile strength is only moderate. There is considerable variation in the strength of sheepskin according to the terrain on which it has been bred; for instance, the hardy mountain sheep of Wales and Scotland have a much tighter fibre than the well-fed sheep bred on the plains. Sheepskin offers little resistance to surface friction and soon becomes shabby if subjected to hard wear.

Basil is the name given to sheepskin that has been 'rolled' to give a plain and firmer surface; it is usually bark-tanned. Commercially its use has been largely confined to the bindings of the cheaper account books. When dressed less firmly it is known as 'calf basil' and is used to imitate genuine calf.

Roan is the name given to sheepskin that has been artificially grained to represent morocco. It is softer than basil and is used for cheap work when true morocco would be uneconomic. Sheepskin can be artificially grained to represent almost any leather, but, in the main, these products are used more in the leather goods industry than in bookbinding. The sizes of skins vary, but average $6\frac{1}{2}$–8sq ft.

Sheepskin splits easily, the outer side being made into skivers which, although they have the beauty of the grain, have ridiculously poor wearing qualities. The 'inner' or flesh side is made up into 'chamois' leather for cleaning purposes.

SEALSKIN

Once thought to be stronger than goatskin, sealskin is seldom used today for bookbinding. Its strength is more uniform throughout the skin than any other and it is very durable; this is due to the natural grease remaining in the skin after tanning, which prevents penetration of dyes, and this in due course causes it to revert to a brown shade—usually on the exposed spines only!

VELLUMS

Because vellum is not 'tanned' in the accepted sense it is not strictly classed as leather. As its name suggests, it is derived from the same source as veal—calfskins, which, after long exposure in lime are scraped and rubbed down with pumice-stone. It is extremely hard-wearing but much less flexible than leather and is badly affected by both dampness and heat. 'Vellumised' goatskins have a similar appearance but are often beautifully grained, which makes them very acceptable for book covers. Because of the reaction to damp and dry atmospheres, vellum must always be strictly controlled by the bookbinder, and this is dealt with in Chapter 3 (p. 205).

PARCHMENT

Nowadays, the term 'parchment' refers to sheepskin that has been dressed in the same way as vellum. Being sheepskin, it is not as strong as vellum and is, perhaps, more suitable for the inside of the book than its cover; it is used for this purpose by calligraphers.

FORIL

'Vellumised' split sheepskin is known as Foril and is naturally very much thinner than parchment, while its strength is only comparable with skiver. It is difficult to recommend it for anything, except, possibly, siding small quarter-bindings.

Leather is priced by the square foot, which includes all irregular edges; holes in the skin are not included in the measurement and allowance for them is made only in the quality grading of the skin.

Usually there are three grades which are known as 'firsts', 'seconds' and 'thirds', in which account of flaws and blemishes are taken.

For fine bindings, only the first grade is acceptable; the second grade may permit the cutting out of an area large enough, and free from bad flaws, for a full binding; but the remainder of the skin is generally suitable only for half- and quarter-bindings. It is rare that a full binding can be cut from a third-grade skin. Leather thickness is uniform on each skin, but can vary from 0·1in, which is normal, to 0·08in and 0·06in should these be required for lighter work, but any reduction in thickness is reflected in the leather strength.

The area, in square feet, is normally marked on the flesh side, larger figures representing square feet and smaller numerals 1, 2, and 3 denoting quarter, half and three-quarters of a square foot.

Prices vary so rapidly that it is unwise to suggest them; but the fact is always with us that to obtain the best quality the highest price must usually be paid.

Paper

As with boards and bookcloth, the quality of paper is dependent upon the fibre used in its manufacture. This is almost invariably vegetable, although papers incorporating man-made fibre are now made. Cellulose from flax and cotton produce the best-quality paper; in machine-made paper their use is restricted by cost, but in hand-made paper they are essential. Esparto, a long, rough grass with fine soft fibres, is much used in Britain because of its bulking qualities. There are two types of wood pulp, chemical and mechanical, vastly different in quality as the fibre in one is broken down by the use of chemicals, while the other is ground by machine, and, although more quickly produced, has short fibres and is suitable only for the cheaper grades of paper such as newsprint. With the chemical process the timber is cut at an angle into widths of $\frac{3}{4}$–1in, disintegrated in a 'hammer mill' or other form of disintegrator, and finally broken down by either the bisulphate or the alkaline process.

Other constituents of paper can be china clay, chalk, sizes such as resin, and dyes. Size is added to paper to make it resistant to dampness, and may be of resin or gelatine. Resin is used when paper is 'engine-sized', and the size is added to the pulp, but it adds little, if any, strength to the paper. Gelatine is used when paper is 'tub-sized', sizing taking place after the paper has been made. It adds considerably to the paper strength and its use is mainly restricted to hand-made papers, although writing paper is sometimes treated in this way to give a better writing surface.

PAPER SIZES

Over the 500 years during which paper has been made in Europe, there has grown up an incredible variety of paper sizes, most of which are the result of the original restrictions imposed by the size of the mould used. With machine production, these sizes were multiplied because the paper could be made in double and quadruple sizes. At last, in Europe, by the use of the 'Din' (Deutsche Industrie Normen—the German equivalent of the British Standards Institution) system, established before World War II, basic paper sizes have been reduced to three standard sheet sizes, designated A, B and C. These may be sub-divided, A being used for printing and writing papers, B for posters, and C for envelopes. The system is analysed on p. 374.

PAPER SUBSTANCE

In Britain this has always been expressed in pounds per ream of 500 or 480 sheets, so that paper of the same weight was given different designations according to the size of the basic sheet. By the use of the grammes per square metre (GSM or GM^2) method, the weight is that of the basic one-square-metre sheet, no matter what size a particular sheet happens to be.

HAND-MADE PAPER

Outside the art world, the cost of making paper by hand limits its use to high-class book work, but in England it is still produced in good variety.

The raw material for the making of hand-made paper is always rags, which are usually cotton, linen or hemp, the grade used depending upon the type of paper being made. Because the 'stuff' (pulp) is shaken in the mould with a slightly circular motion, the fibres are intertwined more or less uniformly in all directions, and this eliminates the directional grain which is a constant feature of machine-made paper. The frame which fits round the mould is known as the 'deckle', and fibres flowing under it give a rough, uneven edge to the paper known as a deckled edge. As this edge is sometimes simulated with machine-made paper, an uneven edge does not necessarily indicate a hand-made paper.

Three different surfaces occur with hand-made paper, 'not', meaning not hot pressed, 'rough', which is not finished, and 'hot pressed', which has a smooth, plated finish. It is also classified into three quality groups, 'good', which means just what it says, 'retree' (XX) not quite up to the standard of 'good', and 'outsides' (XXX), defective paper, with edges sometimes slightly torn. 'Retree' is often priced at 10 per cent less than 'good', and 'outsides' at 40 per cent less. When ordering from the makers it is necessary to state both the surface *and* the quality required. Reams of hand-made paper are always of 480 sheets, but are usually priced by the quire.

MOULD-MADE PAPERS

'Mould-made' papers, made in cylinder machines using good-quality 'stuff' (pulp), could be described as a manufactured imitation of hand-made. They very successfully bridge the gap between hand- and machine-made papers in both quality and price. As with hand-made papers, they are 480 sheets to a ream, but are priced and sold by the quire.

MACHINE-MADE PAPERS

All machine-made paper has directional grain and this is clearly marked on the outside of the package. Whether the grain is 'long' (running along the length of the sheet) or 'short' (across the width) is very important in bookwork. If the sheet is to be folded folio or octavo, the grain should run parallel to its width, while quarto and sextodecimo (16mo) folds require the grain to run along the length of the sheet. The position is reversed when basic sizes are doubled, eg 'double crown', but remains the same with quadrupled size stock. This and the variations in book sizes constitute a problem for the smaller bookbinder, who must either hold a stock of paper of varied sizes and grain direction or face much wastage.

TYPES OF PAPER

Each bookbinder has his own ideas regarding his paper stock, but the following is a generalised list of types used in bookbinding.

Cartridge Machine-made drawing paper, the cheaper grades being engine-sized with resin and composed of wood-pulp fibre. Better grades are tub-sized with gelatine and may consist of rag and chemical wood mixture. As with other papers, cartridge paper can be obtained off-white, lightly tinted, or pure white, but this latter is usually too harsh in colour for bookwork. Cartridge paper is most usually sold in 'double crown' (20in × 30in) size while its counterpart in hand-made quality is normally 'imperial' (22in × 30in). The most suitable weights with double crown are 45lb and 60lb.

Bank (or bond) These may be either hand- or machine-made, the former having pure rag fibre only, the latter, rag and esparto. Because they are primarily writing papers, they are tub-sized. 'Large post' (16$\frac{1}{2}$in × 21in) is the size almost invariably used, especially for machine-made. Three weights are generally required, 11lb for average work and 7$\frac{1}{4}$lb and 15lb for the lighter or heavier. In Britain, up to 15lb large post is termed 'bank' and above that, 'bond'; in America 'bond' is used for all weights.

Tissue Formerly known as Japanese tissue, but now conveniently boxed as lens tissue, is used, in the main, for repairs over print, and must be of good quality.

Newsprint Made entirely from mechanical wood pulp and the cheapest of all papers. It is used by bookbinders for 'packing' books with compensating guards, in order to give them a uniform thickness so that they can be bound by normal processes.

Coloured papers Coloured papers, such as cover paper, are available in an almost endless variety of colours and textures and are made from all classes of fibre from good to poor. With bookbinding, the cheaper types should be shunned because of the poor quality of the fibre and the probability that the colours will fade. For endpapers their thickness and fibre must permit adequate flexibility in the joint.

Cobb's end The original name given to a thin, coloured paper invented by Thomas Cobb at the end of the eighteenth century and still in use today. Its colours are nearly always of subdued tones and it has the advantage of being relatively inexpensive.

Ingres paper (pronounced 'Arngr') A superfine laid paper of French and Italian origin named after the nineteenth-century artist, Jean Auguste Ingres. It has a smooth, matt surface with very slightly textured appearance and is obtainable in a comprehensive range of extremely pleasant shades. It has the appearance of a mould-made paper and is relatively inexpensive. Its subdued colours make it popular with craft bookbinders for endpapers. It is also known as 'charcoal paper'.

Decorative papers The foremost in this class is 'marbled' (or marble) paper, which, in differing styles, has been in use in Britain since the early seventeenth century. Traditional designs are numerous and have such names as 'Dutch', 'Stormont', 'Gloster', 'Antique Spot', 'Shell' and 'Italian', nearly all of which have lost favour for letter-press binding, although some modern versions are seen occasionally. The only traditional designs produced today seem to be 'Spanish' and 'German Marble' still used on some stationery binding.

The main English 'marbles' today are those made by Messrs Douglas Cockerell and Son, the quality of which almost defies the use of superlatives. The use of water-based colours as against the traditional oil colours gives Cockerell marbles a cleaner, fresher appearance, while the varied styles and soft colourings make their production an oasis in a usually inartistic desert. They are entirely hand-made, using hand-made and Kraft paper, and so, by comparison with commercially produced 'Spanish' on poor paper, are rather expensive. Other productions are available but are seldom of the same high standard. It is quite possible for the binder to emulate his predecessors and make marbled papers for his own use, but to achieve good results, the work is so specialised and time-consuming as to be uneconomic.

Paste-coloured papers For those who have both the time and the inclination to produce decorative papers, the age-old method of paste-colour and combing is very simple. It consists of mixing colour (powdered poster colours serve admirably) with a thin, smooth starch paste, brushing it over the surface of suitable paper and making patterns by redistributing it, using metal combs (as used by decorators for imitating wood grains) or combs cut from fibre or tough card. Variations can be introduced by the use of everyday objects as 'stamps'. Fountain-pen caps will produce circles; indeed, the possibilities for inventive minds are endless. Calligraphic designs are possible with small, thin, flat pieces of wood. By far the simplest method is to paste two pieces of paper with the colour, place them face to face, and rub lightly before separating them again by pulling from one corner. The effects that are possible can be quite acceptable. Because of the materials used, paste-colour papers tend to become sticky on the face side when adhesives are used on the back. If a modicum of white wax polish is lightly rubbed over the face side when this is quite dry, it will not only prevent movement of the paste-colour but will also make for a more durable surface. Old-time marblers used to grind a small quantity of soap in with their colours to assist in the polishing of the finished surface, and this could help with poster colours.

The artist-craftsman will wish to use his ability to design and produce special papers for individual bindings, using a medium known to him. In this field, lino-blocks and wood-cuts are very effective.

Printed pattern papers   These are available in variety and are used effectively in edition binding. It is a personal opinion that few designs can be used repetitively without eventually becoming stale and monotonous in a way that is not shared by good marbled papers, traditional or modern.

Kraft paper   The word 'Kraft' means strength and this is the *sine qua non* of this type of wrapping paper as used in bookbinding, since its main use is for back linings. It is made from sulphate pulp in large sizes such as double imperial (30in × 44in) and in this size should be from 80lb to 140lb per ream. This latter weight is that of stout Rope Kraft, which is very good for use on medium to large books. For smaller or lighter volumes something lighter is better for the making of Oxford hollows, for while the lining supports the back it must still remain flexible.

Whatever type of paper is used in bookbinding, consideration must be given to its main purpose. In addition to tying up with the colour scheme of the binding, endpapers must be flexible and strong if they are to be satisfactory, especially in the book joint. The size and weight of the book, in addition to the sort of use to which it may be subjected, must be considered at all times. The surface of cheap papers, especially cover paper, will seldom stand up to abrasive wear if used on the outside of book covers. Actual thickness is not a real criterion; the nature of the 'furnish' that goes into the making of the paper is of greater importance.

PAPER SIZES

Traditional Paper Sizes

	Inches	Folio (*fo*)	Quarto (*4to*)	Octavo (*8vo*)
Foolscap	$13\frac{1}{2} \times 17$	$13\frac{1}{2} \times 8\frac{1}{2}$	$8\frac{1}{2} \times 6\frac{3}{4}$	$6\frac{3}{4} \times 4\frac{1}{4}$
Pinched post	$14\frac{1}{2} \times 18\frac{1}{2}$	$14\frac{1}{2} \times 9\frac{1}{4}$	$9\frac{1}{4} \times 7\frac{1}{4}$	$7\frac{1}{4} \times 4\frac{5}{8}$
Crown	15×20	15×10	$10 \times 7\frac{1}{2}$	$7\frac{1}{2} \times 5$
Post	$15\frac{1}{4} \times 19$	$15\frac{1}{4} \times 9\frac{1}{2}$	$9\frac{1}{2} \times 7\frac{5}{8}$	$7\frac{5}{8} \times 4\frac{3}{4}$
Large post	$16\frac{1}{2} \times 21$	$16\frac{1}{2} \times 10\frac{1}{2}$	$10\frac{1}{2} \times 8\frac{1}{4}$	$8\frac{1}{4} \times 5\frac{1}{4}$
Demy	$17\frac{1}{2} \times 22\frac{1}{2}$	$17\frac{1}{2} \times 11\frac{1}{4}$	$11\frac{1}{4} \times 8\frac{3}{4}$	$8\frac{3}{4} \times 5\frac{5}{8}$
Medium	18×23	$18 \times 11\frac{1}{2}$	$11\frac{1}{2} \times 9$	$9 \times 5\frac{3}{4}$
Royal	20×25	$20 \times 12\frac{1}{2}$	$12\frac{1}{2} \times 10$	$10 \times 6\frac{1}{4}$
Imperial	22×30	22×15	15×11	$11 \times 7\frac{1}{2}$

Double size sheets are the length by *twice* the width of the single sheet.

Quadruple size sheets are *twice* the length by *twice* the width.

The application of the metric system in the United Kingdom has meant the adoption of the ISO paper sizes. Under this system paper sizes are divided into three series, A, B and C, the first (A) being allocated to printing and writing papers. An important feature of the system is that whenever a sheet is folded or cut into half along the long side, the proportions remain constant.

The basic sheet, AO, is equal to one square metre, measures 841mm by 1189mm and is fairly close to quad demy in size (35in × 45in). Folded in half it becomes A1, 594mm × 841mm ($23\frac{3}{8}$in × $33\frac{1}{8}$in approximately). Subsequent folds are shown below.

There are two sizes above the basic AO, designated 2A and 4A, each being twice the size of the preceding one.

ISO paper sizes, 'A' series

	mm	in (approx)
2A	1189 × 1682	$46\frac{13}{16}$ × $66\frac{3}{16}$
AO	841 × 1189	$33\frac{1}{8}$ × $46\frac{13}{16}$
A1	594 × 841	$23\frac{3}{8}$ × $33\frac{1}{8}$
A2	420 × 594	$16\frac{1}{2}$ × $23\frac{3}{8}$
A3	297 × 420	$11\frac{11}{16}$ × $16\frac{1}{2}$
A4	210 × 297	$8\frac{1}{4}$ × $11\frac{11}{16}$
A5	148 × 210	$5\frac{13}{16}$ × $8\frac{1}{4}$

As they stand, these sizes are considered unsuitable for books and are not used in practice. Instead, traditional book sizes have been reduced in number and a new quadruple size introduced, based on multiples of 24mm which, being divisible by 8 and 4, eliminates fractions of millimetres in subsequent folded sizes.

The new sizes, known as metric sizes, are as follows:

		Quad size
Metric crown octavo (8vo)	186 × 123mm	768 × 1008mm
Metric large octavo (8vo)	198 × 129mm	816 × 1056mm
Metric demy octavo (8vo)	216 × 138mm	888 × 1128mm
Metric royal octavo (8vo)	234 × 156mm	960 × 1272mm
A5	210 × 148mm	RAO 860 × 1220mm

These are trimmed sizes, allowing for a 3mm trim on each edge.

Gold Leaf and Stamping Foils

GOLD LEAF

The art of gold beating appears to be dying out in Great Britain, and much of the beaten gold used is imported from the Continent, mainly Italy. It is still packed in books of twenty-five leaves, each $3\frac{1}{4}$in square. For bookbinding, loose gold leaf is used as against 'transfer', which is mounted on to thin tissue and is used by sign-writers and others. 'Illuminator's' and 'Fine' in single or double thickness are available. Variations in shade are today reduced normally to white, red, and middle green, made by incorporating other metals such as silver and copper. Silver and platinum in leaf form are also available, as is 'Palladium' which is a nickel product and much less costly.

Beaten gold leaf is extremely thin—about $\frac{1}{250,000}$in—and the booklets of rouged tissue in which it is supplied should always be kept flat. As gold leaf ages it tends to become brittle and is then unusable. If a cut piece of potato is placed in the box, before it reaches this state, it will provide sufficient humidity to delay the drying-out process.

STAMPING FOILS

These consist of atomised metals such as gold and aluminium on polyester film. Pigment colours, matt and gloss, are also available in a large variety. Genuine gold foil is priced by 1in width on 95ft spools and is obtainable in a number of shades from deep gold to lemon. Generally speaking, the natural shade and finish is most suitable for traditional bookbinding purposes, but the alternative shades are useful for special purposes.

Made primarily for use with blocking machines, foils are being increasingly used by the general bookbinder. Pigment foils in about twenty different shades can be obtained in widths of 1in to 30in and in rolls from 200ft to 1,000ft long. While most have a paper carrier, gloss pigments are usually on polyester film.

GLAIR

The traditional gold size used by bookbinders is made from the albumen contained in the white of eggs. That for edge gilding is very much weaker, the white of one egg being sufficient to make a cupful of glair. The egg white is whisked, using either a domestic whisk or what was known as a 'devil'—a short length of $\frac{1}{2}$in wooden rod near the end of which are fitted (by drilling) two short lengths of $\frac{1}{8}$in rod at right-angles to each other and projecting about $\frac{1}{2}$in or so from the main rod. This is inserted into the egg white and revolved backwards and forwards between the palms of the hands. After whisking, a cupful of water is added and mixed with it; it is left to stand for twenty-four hours before being strained through fine muslin.

Finishing glair is used at different strengths by different binders, and is mixed with vinegar, not water. Some prefer only a few drops of vinegar added to the albumen and others an amount equal to half of it. A one-third mixture suits the author's purpose. Whisking takes place as before, and the glair stands for twenty-four hours before being strained. The big disadvantage of egg albumen is its abominable odour after it has putrefied, which, however, in no way affects its efficacy. A minute amount of phenol ($\frac{1}{200}$th part) added to the water when making will help to preserve the glair. Albumen crystals solve the storage problems but not odorous ones! The crystals are mixed, one part albumen to four parts water or vinegar, left to soak overnight, stirred, and allowed to settle before straining. Glair should be stored in a wide-necked bottle with a screw cap— preferably moulded—but should glair get on the screw portion of the bottle, the cap will stick firmly and partial immersion in hot water will be necessary to loosen it.

'BS Glair' is one of a number of shellac-based glairs marketed today. They are preferred by many binders for their convenience inasmuch as they do not putrefy and can be tooled (using a very much cooler tool than is usual) the next day if necessary.

GLOSSARY

A selective list of bookbinding terms used in Britain and the United States (the latter marked 'US'). It is not an exhaustive list, and the index should be consulted for references in the text.

Absorbent cotton (US)   cotton wool.

Accordion pleat (US)   concertina guard or fold.

American bookboard (US)   'Thames' board or similar.

Antique tooling (US)   blind tooling on moistened leather.

Arming press   a small blocking press used for stamping heraldic arms on book covers.

Backbone (or *'shelf back'*) (US)   the cover spine.

Backsaw (or *moulding saw*) (US)   tenon saw.

Beating   the operation of hammering flat the expanded portion of (usually) hand-printed sheets; it was superseded by the use of the rolling machine. With today's mechanical printing accuracy, it is no longer needed.

Bench shears (US)   millboard shears.

Binder's board (US)   millboard.

Blank binding (US)   account book binding.

Bolt   the folds of a book section.

Bookmarkers (US)   ribbon registers.

Book-plate   an engraved, often heraldic, label pasted into a book to indicate ownership. It may provide proof of the book's provenance and should usually be replaced in the book after rebinding. Also referred to as 'Ex libris'.

Book trimmer (US)   book guillotine.

Cancels   replacement leaves for serious errors in the originals which are removed.

Card (US)   Bristol board.

Catch stitch (US)   tying-down stitch used when sewing. A kettle-stitch.

Catchword   usually in older books. The first word of the following page, printed at the base of the text for check purposes when making up the book.

Cloth boards (US)   brass-edged pressing boards.

Collate   to check a book, page by page, for completeness. It is used haphazardly to refer to checking the sequence of sections in a book.

Conjugate leaves   pairs of leaves joined at the fold.

Crash (US) or *Super*   mull.

Die (US)   blocking brass.

Embossing press (US)   blocking press.

Endsheets (US)   single-fold endpapers.

'Extra' binding   trade term denoting best quality work; the superlative is 'super extra'!

Fence (US)   paper or card used to ensure uniform edge pasting. Synonymous with pasting template.

Flexible cover (US)   a limp binding made with very thin card.

Fly-leaf   correctly, blank sheets following the free front endpaper, but also used to refer to this.

Folding stick (US)   long wooden or bone folder used in folding sheets.

Foredge   the front edge of a book (pronounced 'forrej').

Foxing   brownish spots caused by accumulation of iron salts due to chemical action resulting from excess humidity.

'Frattoir' (US)   a wooden scrape used for cleaning paste off the backs of books when 'setting' them.

Gilt all round (US) or *full gilt*   all edges gilt.

Grooving (boards) (US)   cutting kerfs to recess hemp slips when lacing boards.

Ground glue (US)   animal glue.

Head and Tail   the top and bottom of a book (when stood upright).

Hidden corners (US)   French corners.

Hubs (US)   raised bands on account books.

Insert   additional matter being added to a book.

Inset   a special printer's imposition such as duodecimo (12mo) in which a portion of the sheet must be cut away, folded separately, and inserted into the folded remainder.

Jogged (US)   knocked up level to an edge.

Joints   bookbinders' term for the groove made in backing, and so refers to the *inside* of the hinge in the bound book. It is logical to refer to the *outside* of the joint as the *hinge*, the covering material there acting as the hinge on which the board turns.

Medium grade book paper (US)   cartridge paper.

Moulding saw (US) or *Backsaw*   tenon saw.

Newsboard (US)   chipboard.

Nicking (*boards*) (US)   back cornering.

Preliminaries ('*prelims*')   all printed matter preceding the actual text of the book.

Proof (or *witness*)   leaf edges left uncut as evidence that book edges have not been unduly cut.

Protection sheet (US)   waste sheet (endpapers).

Recto   the front side of a leaf—the right-hand page of a book when open. The reverse side is a *verso*.

Register   1 In folding paper; when the print on one side of a leaf is exactly over that on the other.

2 A book marker of ribbon bound into the book.

Right-angle gauge (US)   carpenter's square.

Saddleback (US)   a soft-back single-section binding as opposed to a stiffened or hard back.

Semé   in finishing, the almost indiscriminate placing of dots or other small tools in one area. (French, literally 'sown'.)

Sheet   the full-size sheet before being folded.

Shoes (US)   metal protectors placed on the bottom edges of heavy books. 'Roller' shoes have tiny rollers to facilitate returning a book to its place on the shelves.

Signature   a letter or figure printed at the bottom of the first page of a section, indicating its correct position in the book. Sometimes replaced by *Collating marks*, small black marks printed on the fold of the outer leaves and placed in such a position that they form 'steps' after the book has been gathered. Tradesmen sometimes refer to a section as a signature.

Signature mark (US)   collating mark.

Slips   the ends of tapes or hemp cords that are attached to the cover boards.

Smooth gilt (US)   solid gilt.

Spine   the back of a book that is visible when it is on the shelf. In the antiquarian book trade it is sometimes referred to as the 'backstrip'.

Square   the projection of the cover boards beyond the book proper.

Square knot (US)   reef knot.

Stamping (US)   blocking.

Super (US)   mull.

Tampon (US)   inking pad.

Tampon, cotton (US) a small ball of cotton wool covered with thin cotton cloth for laying-on gold leaf.

Trimmed edges referring to book edges that have had only projecting edges of leaves cut away (as opposed to 'cut' which indicates a solid edge).

Trimming (US) cutting book edges.

Utility knife (US) shoemaker's knife as used by bookbinders in Britain.

Verso the reverse of *recto*.

Yawning (*bookboards*) (US) bookboards with an outward warp.

SOURCES OF SUPPLY

As with most other crafts that have been mechanised for mass production, bookbinding supplies have tended to become 'rationalised' which, in effect, means that only users of large quantities of materials are catered for by the manufacturers. This leaves the craftsman in the position of having to locate retailers who will supply smaller quantities. Unfortunately, many bookbinding requirements are specialised which results in fewer retailers of them. There are still firms who supply smaller quantities but costs are inevitably higher. A few of these firms cater, in the main, for schools and colleges, and for this reason issue useful catalogues for which a charge is sometimes made.

In Britain, the two main suppliers of bookbinding materials in small quantities, and equipment for the amateur rather than the professional are: Russell Bookcrafts, Hitchin, Hertfordshire, and Dryad Handicrafts, Northgates, Leicester.

Messrs J. Hewit and Sons, 97 St John Street, London, EC1, and 125 High Street, Edinburgh, who are also leather tanners, provide a good service to both the craftsman bookbinder and the tradesman. They will supply most normal equipment (not miniature) and materials.

Suppliers of more specialised requirements are listed below, but reference to a current directory, such as Kelly's Directory of Merchants and Manufacturers, at a local public library may provide information about suppliers in the reader's area. An enquiry is advisable before ordering or visiting such firms. The absolute amateur may be well advised to obtain introductions to local trade bookbinders who, if competition is not feared, may oblige with small quantities from their own stocks. Very occasionally, an association of craftsmen, even bookbinders only (as in the Bournemouth and East Dorset area where the Wessex Guild of Bookbinders flourishes), may exist and membership is possible. With such associations, bulk buying is a distinct possibility. Where such facilities exist they are usually available only to members who must be *bone fide* craftsmen.

The following classified list has been arranged by subject and is not completely comprehensive; some firms may no longer be in business and this should be checked.

To prevent excessive repetition, no addresses are given in the classified list; these will be found in the alphabetical list of suppliers which follows.

Classified List of Suppliers of Materials

Adhesives, animal glues Adams, Arebol-Edwardsons, Associated Adhesives, Cox, Croda Polymers, Hewit, Starch Products

Adhesives, general Arebol-Edwardsons, Associated Adhesives, Ballanger Rawlings, Clam-Brunner, Croda-Polymers, North British Adhesives, Williams Adhesives, Wilson Adhesives

Adhesives, pastes French, Hewitt, London Adhesives, Sichel Adhesives

Adhesives, Polyvinyl Acetate Arebol-Edwardsons, Croda-Polymers, Hewit, National Adhesives (Spynflex), Taylor

Blocking brasses Bowers and Freeman, Briggs Engraving Co., Mackrell

Blocking foils, see *Foils*

Boards, art Slater and Leigh

Boards, backing, cutting and pressing Dryad, Hewit, Russell

Boards, mill- Jackson's, Machin and Kingsley, Thames Board Mills, Thompson's, Western Board Mills

Boards, straw- Adamson, Machin and Kingsley, Thames Strawboard Co, Wood, H. B.

Bookcloths Bentley Smith, Darbel, Dryad, Hewit, Holt, Ratchford, Red Bridge, Russell, Taylor, Winterbottom

Brushes, glue and paste Dryad, Hewit, Russell, Taylor

Calicoes Hewit, Holt, Ratchford

Chemicals British Drug Houses, ICI (Nobel Division)

Colours, edge Ballanger Rawlings, Dane

Colours, marbling Dane

Cords, hemp Barbour Threads, Hewit, Pymore Mills

'Durofix' cutting sticks Ballanger Rawlings

Equipment, general Bain Hogg, Harrild and Partners, Hewit, Hicks

Fibre felts Grange Fibre Co, Red Bridge, Winterbottom

Finishing stoves Hewit, Russell (Cockerell pattern)

Finishing tools Cockerell (asbestos handles), Mackrell, Midland Engraving Co, Whiley, Winter

Foils, blocking American Roll Leaf, Goulding, Peerless Gold Leaf, Whiley

Folders, bone   Dryad (small), Hewit, Joyce, Russell, Taylor
Gold leaf beaters   Lawton and Fenner, Sale, Whiley
Guillotine cutting sticks   Ballanger Rawlings ('Durofix')
Headbands, tape   Hewit, Taylor
Hemp   see *Cords*
Knives, paring   Buck and Ryan, Dryad, Hewit, Russell, Tyzack
Leathers   Band, Garner, Hewit, Heyneman and Miller, Russell
Millboards   see *Boards, mill-*
Mull   Hewit, Ratchford, Red Bridge, Taylor, Winterbottom
Needles   British Needles, Dryad, Hewit, James, Morrall, Russell
Paper, coloured (including cover)   Dryad, Keay, Lepard and Smith
Paper, general   Baker, Dryad, Grosvenor Chater, Hale Paper Co,
   Ironmongers, Russell, Spicer-Cowan
Paper, hand- and mould-made   Barcham Green, Falkiner, Lawrence,
   'Paperchase', Reckner
Paper, kraft   Kent Kraft Mills, Spicer-Cowan
Paper, marbled   Cockerell, Compton Marbles, 'Paperchase'
Paper, tissue (repair)   Barcham Green, Burt, Evans Adlard
Parchment   see *Vellum*
Tape and webbing   Dryad, Hewit, Russell, Rykneld Mills
Thread, linen sewing   Barbour Threads, Dryad, Hewit, Knox,
   Russell, Taylor
Tools, general   Dryad, Hewit, Russell
Type, Bookbinders'   Hewit, Mackrell, Winter
Typeholders   Hewit, Mackrell
Vellum   Band, Cowley, Elzas and Zonen, Hewit

Alphabetical List of Suppliers

Adams, Alfred, and Co., Reliance Works, West Bromwich, Staffs
Adamson and Co., Cumberland Street, Hull
American Roll Leaf Co. Ltd, 30 Canal Street, Manchester
Arebol-Edwardsons Ltd, Marsh Lane, Ware, Herts
Associated Adhesives Ltd, Knights Road, Silvertown, London E16
Backus, Edgar, 144–6 Cank Street, Leicester
Bain Hogg and Co. Ltd, Cambridge Works, 2a Lansdowne
   Gardens, London SW8
Baker, Charles, and Sons, Ltd, Service House, Woodside Road,
   Eastleigh, Hants

Ballanger Rawlings Ltd, Rembrandt House, Whippendell Road, Watford, Herts

Band, H., and Co., Brent Way, High Street, Brentford, Middx

Barbour Threads Ltd, Hilden House, Frogmore, London SW8; also at Birmingham, Bristol, Glasgow, Manchester, Northampton, and Norwich (see local directories)

Barcham Green, J., Hayle Mill, Maidstone, Kent

Bentley Smith and Co Ltd (Courtaulds), Bengal Mill, Upper Helena Street, Manchester 10

Bowers and Freeman, 15 Saffron Road, South Winston, Leicester

Briggs Engraving Co Ltd, 196–8 Alder Road, Parkstone, Poole, Dorset

British Drug Houses, BDH Laboratory, Chemical Division, Poole, Dorset

British Needles, Victoria Street, Redditch

Buck and Ryan, 101 Tottenham Court Road, London W1

Burt and Co, 38 Farringdon Street, London EC4

Clam-Brunner Ltd, Maxwell Road, Boreham Wood, Herts

Cockerell, Douglas, and Son, Riversdale, Grantchester, Cambridge

Compton Marbles, Compton Press, Compton Chamberlayne, near Salisbury, Wilts

Cowley, William, Parchment Works, Newport Pagnell, Bucks

Cox, J. B., Ltd, Corgie Mills, Edinburgh 11

Croda Polymers, 153 New Bedford Road, Luton, Beds

Dane and Co Ltd, 1 Sugar House Lane, London E 15

Darbel, Ltd, 87 Long Lane, Aldersgate Street, London EC 1

Dryad Handicrafts, Northgates, Leicester

Elzas and Zonen Ltd, Celbridge, Eire

Evans Adlard and Co Ltd, Postlip Mills, Winchcombe, Glos

Falkiner Fine Papers, 302 Lillie Road, London SW 6

French, J. W., and Co Ltd, Frenlite House, Lots Road, London SW 11

Garner, James, and Sons, The Grange, Bermondsey, London SE 1

Goulding, V., and Co Ltd, 650–2, High Road, London N 12; also at 28 South Street, Redditch, Worcs

Grange Fibre Co Ltd, 20–6 Wellesley Road, Croydon, Surrey

Grosvenor Chater Ltd, 68 Cannon Street, London EC 4

Hale Paper Co Ltd, 92 Fleet Street, London EC 4

Harrild and Partners Ltd, 58 Redchurch Street, London E 2

Hewit and Sons, 97 St John Street, London EC 1

Heyneman and Miller Ltd, 50 Weston Street, London SE 1

Hicks, Russell, 15 Appold Street, London EC 2

Holt, A., and Sons, 115 Whitecross Street, London EC 1

Imperial Chemical Industries (Nobel Division), Stevenston, Ayrshire, Scotland

Ironmongers Ltd, Glenville Hall, Oldfield Road, Bristol 8

Jackson's Millboard and Fibre Co Ltd, Bourne End, Bucks

James, John, and Sons, Studley, Warwicks

Joyce and Co Ltd, Clerkenwell Road, London EC 2

Keay and Co, Church Street, Birmingham

Kent Kraft Mills Ltd, Northfleet, Gravesend, Kent

Knox, W. and J., Ltd, Kilburnie, Scotland

Lawrence, T. N., and Son, 2 Bleeding Heart Yard, Greville Street, London EC 1

Lawton and Fenner Ltd, 15 Grimshaw Street, Liverpool, Lancs

Lepard and Smith, Earlham Street, London WC 2

London Adhesives Co Ltd, Arlington Works, Maxwell Road, Boreham Wood, Herts

Machin and Kingsley, 61 Charterhouse Street, London EC 1; also at 25 High Street, Keynsham, Bristol BS 18

Mackrell, T., and Co, Industrial Estate West, Colchester Road, Witham, Essex; also at 9 Russell Chambers, Bury Place, London WC 1

Midland Engraving Co Ltd, Wollaston, Wellingborough, Northants

Morrall, Abel, Clive Works, Edward Street, Redditch, Worcs

National Adhesives and Resins Ltd, Galvin Road, Slough, Bucks

New Die Ltd, Industrial Estate, West Colchester Road, Witham, Essex

North British Adhesives Ltd, Dunedin Street, Edinburgh, Scotland

'Paperchase', 216 Tottenham Court Road, London W 1

Peebles, R., and Co, 3 St Edmund's Lane, London EC 3

Peerless Gold Leaf Co Ltd, Fairfield Works, Fairfield Road, Bow, London E 3

Pymore Mills and Co Ltd, Bridport, Dorset

Ratchford, F. J., Ltd, Kennedy Way, Green Lane, Stockport, SK4 2JX

Reckner, and Co, 68 Newington Causeway, London SE 1

Red Bridge Bookcloth Co Ltd, Ainsworth, Bolton, Lancs

Russell Bookcrafts, Hitchin, Herts

Rykneld Mills, Bridge Street, Derby

Sale, E. and W., 71 Vyse Street, Hockley, Birmingham 18

Scott, Bader, and Co, Wollaston, Wellingborough, Northants

Sichel Adhesives Ltd, 6 Friars Lane, Richmond, Surrey

Slater and Leigh, Lower Mills, Bollington, Macclesfield, Cheshire

Spicer-Cowan Ltd, 19 New Bridge Street, London EC 4

'Spynflex', see under National Adhesives and Resins, Ltd

Starch Products Ltd, Stadex Works, Green Road, Langley, Slough, Bucks

Taylor, G. E., Ltd, Wapping Wharf, Cumberland Road, Bristol 1

Thames Board Mills, United Africa House, Blackfriars Road, London SE 1

Thames Strawboard Company, Barrington House, Gresham Street, London EC 2

Thompson's Board Mills, Little Salkeld, Langworthy, Penrith, Cumberland

Tyzack, S., 341 Old Street, London EC 1

Walker, R., and Co, North Street, Wigston, Leicester

Western Board Mills Ltd, Treforest Industrial Estate, Pontypridd, Glam

Whiley, Geo. M., Victoria Road, Ruislip, Middx

Williams Adhesives, 179–80 Gresham Road Trading Estate, Slough, Bucks

Wilson Adhesives, Brook Street Works, Hazel Grove, Stockport, Cumberland

Winter and Co Ltd, 12 Charterhouse Buildings, London EC 1

Winterbottom Products (English Calico Ltd), Victoria Mills, Weaste, Salford 8, Manchester 6; also at Argyle House, 29–31 Euston Road, London NW 1

Wood, Henry B., Ltd, 1–3 Thompson House, Withy Grove, Manchester M 4

BIBLIOGRAPHY

Clements, Jeff. *Bookbinding* (1963)

Cockerell, Douglas. *Bookbinding and the care of books* (1st ed 1901, and later editions)

——. *Some notes on bookbinding* (1929)

Cockerell, Sydney. *The Repairing of books* (1958)

Corderoy, John. *Bookbinding for beginners* (London and New York, 1967)

Diehl, Edith. *Bookbinding: its background and technique*, 2 vols (New York, 1946)

Harrison, Thomas. *The Bookbinding craft and industry* (nd)

Horton, Carolyn. *Cleaning and preserving bindings and related materials* (Chicago, 1969)

Langwell, W. H. *The Conservation of books and documents* (1957)

Lewis, A. W. *Basic bookbinding* (1952)

Mansfield, Edgar. *Modern design in bookbinding* (1966)

Mason, John. *Letterpress bookbinding* (1946)

Matthews, William. *Bookbinding* (1929)

Middleton, Bernard C. *The restoration of leather bookbindings* (Chicago, 1972)

Philip, Alex J. *The business of bookbinding* (Gravesend, 1935)

Plenderleith, H. J. *The conservation of antiquities and works of art* (1956, 2nd ed 1971)

——. *The preservation of leather bookbindings* (1946, 2nd ed 1967)

Robinson, Ivor. *Introducing bookbinding* (London and New York, 1968)

Smith, Philip. *A New direction for bookbinding* (London and New York, 1974)

Town, Laurence. *Bookbinding by hand* (1951)

Vaughan, Alex J. *Modern bookbinding* (1946, re-issued 1960)

Zaehnsdorf, Joseph W. *The art of bookbinding* (1890, latest ed 1967)

History

Baltimore Museum of Art. *History of bookbinding AD 525–1950* (Baltimore, 1951). Has many illustrations.

Bodleian Library. *Gold-tooled bindings* (Oxford, 1951). Illustrated.

Brassington, W. Salt. *A history of the art of bookbinding* (1894)

Harthan, John. *Bookbindings* (in the Victoria and Albert Museum) (1950)

Horne, Herbert P. *The binding of books . . . history of gold-tooled books* (1894)

Leighton, Douglas *Modern bookbinding* (J. M. Dent memorial lecture) (1935)

Middleton, Bernard C. *A history of English craft bookbinding technique* (London and New York, 1963)

Prideaux, Sarah T. *An historical sketch of bookbinding* (1893)

Also recommended

Struwe, Carl. *Formen des mikrosmos* (Munich, 1955). This is not about bookbinding, but the 96 micro-photographs can stimulate fresh design ideas.

Weisse, Franz. *Der Handvergolder im tageswerken und kunstschaffen* (Stuttgart, nd (c 1960)). Contains 230 photographs devoted to gold-tooling.

ACKNOWLEDGEMENTS

The author extends his sincere thanks to:

Miss M. A. Brett for abundant help with the revision of the text.

Frank Turland for much co-operation, especially with photography.

Eric Manton for printing aid and advice.

Allan White for considerable photographic assistance.

Brian Robinson who made the improvised equipment for glueing the backs of unsewn bindings and also gave assistance with sources of supply.

John Harthan, Keeper of the Library, Victoria and Albert Museum, London.

His very good friends, Edgar Mansfield, Ivor Robinson and Bernard Middleton, especially Edgar Mansfield who not only loaned photographs but also allowed quotations from his book to be used.

Philip Smith for the loan of, and permission to use, photographs.

Members of Designer Bookbinders (especially its Honorary Secretary, Elizabeth Greenhill) who loaned bindings or photographs.

Alan G. Thomas for permission to reproduce the coloured photograph of Paul Bonet's 'Irradiant' binding which was specially commissioned by him.

Miss A. Cutler of Bournemouth who typed the manuscript.

Those others who, probably unaware, have helped in one way or another, if only by much-needed encouragement.

INDEX

Page references in italic indicate black and white illustrations; those in bold indicate colour plates